HOMEMADE
FOOD FOR THOUGHT

by
PEGGY GOODRICH

FRONTIER PRINTERS, INC.
STILLWATER, OKLAHOMA

Homemade Food For Thought

ISBN 0-9668261-0-8
Printed in United States of America

Dedication

This book is lovingly dedicated to my grandparents, parents, brothers and sisters, teachers, and special people who helped shape my life: and to my husband, Jim, and family and two granddaughters who have given my life that special dimension and purpose.

Peggy Goodrich

Table of Contents

Acknowledgments

I will be forever grateful to my grandparents, parents, siblings, teachers, and friends for taking the time and energy to answer my endless questions of what, who, and WHY.

I appreciate Jim's patience with me and his help in supplying just the right word I am seeking to express how I feel. I value his judgement and suggestions about recipes to use.

My life would not be complete without Jamie and Shelby, our granddaughters, who listen to my "vast store of wisdom" and give me fresh ideas and great hope for the future.

I could not have produced this book without my sister, Marianne, who proofed every page and gave helpful suggestions along the way. She could have written this same book, as we think alike and enjoy the same memories.

I am indebted to my weekly readers who have been so kind and faithful and encouraged me to "get it together" in a book of some kind, instead of clippings in drawers and taped on cabinet doors.

I thank the "Enid News & Eagle" for allowing me to contribute to their paper. I also thank them for permission to reproduce those articles in this book.

These recipes are not original with me. Many are gleaned from boxes and pages of Grandma's and Mama's "receipts". Many have been shared by readers, friends, family and acquaintances. I thank them all.

Nor are the ideas original with me. They came from many sources, and have shaped MY basic philosophy of life.

Introduction

Welcome to my world. I was reared in the country in Pawnee County, Oklahoma, during the Great Depression and World War II era. I was educated the first eight years in a one room schools. My grandparents settled in Indian Territory before Oklahoma Statehood. We, like everyone else, were poor but we had no idea we were because it was fun growing up in a large family with such devoted parents.

The chapters of this book are articles published in the "Enid (Oklahoma) News & Eagle" over the years. The dates and times jump around a bit and may not be in age sequence. I repeat myself from time to time, but isn't that the way we "think about it"?

You may find a few errors in this manuscript. They are there for a reason. Some people are always looking for others' mistakes and I try to provide something for everybody.

I had taken a writing course from the Western writer, Johnny Quarles, and he encouraged me and challenged me to write. His positive reinforcement gave me the confidence to put on paper some of my memories and recipes. I owe him a debt of gratitude.

Some of the articles I have written sound almost like my mother or grandmother talking, so I share with them any credit of success. I feel so fortunate to have a background of sturdy pioneer stock that molded my being.

I hope you enjoy reading as much as I enjoy writing about my family and friends and reflections and food.

Peggy Goodrich

Chapter 1 — Childhood Pastimes

What was your favorite childhood toy, game, or pastime? Think about it!

I was moving some stuff recently and found Margaret, my rag doll lovingly made from a flour sack during the depression. Her yarn hair is molting. She has the limber neck. But she smiled when she saw me and her eyes were as bright as ever. We talked about old times and the fun we had together, before I carefully folded her in a towel and placed her back in the box. She will come to visit again at Christmas because I invited her to sit under our tree.

Mother saved all of our old toys. But, of course, we didn't have gobs and gobs of toys and games and we took care of the ones we did have. I still have my Lincoln Logs in the original box, and my blocks, and my two dolls, Margaret and Janet.

I have my doll house and all the furniture. That house takes an entire shelf of the hall closet and I could use the space for something else but when I mentioned putting that old doll house in a garage sale, the granddaughters wouldn't hear of it. It brings back memories for them too and they like those old attachments to early childhood. Both girls have spent many happy hours with that house.

I have a box of junk. You know, marbles, jacks, a top, string and wonderful things like that. We made lots of kites but they hardly survived a good windy day, much less a generation.

All our dolls got new dresses at Christmas, to match our own dresses. We sewed lots of doll clothes. We played paper dolls but none survived.

I have a doll quilt made for me by my grandma who died when I was four years old. A walk through any antique shop reminds us of our toys of yesterday. Recently I saw an old doll buggy like mine. All I have left is one wheel. Why I have saved it all these years is a mystery. I guess it just reminds me of a lighter, easier time...a bygone era.

There is something about looking back to our childhood that almost makes us wish we were kids again. It was a calmer, easier time. We played house and made tons of mud pies. We climbed trees. We kicked rocks. We watched the grass grow. We drew pictures in the soft flour-like dirt. We went wading when it rained and made "Loblollies" in the mud puddles.

We played in the hay barn when it was cold and when it rained. We played hide and seek in the barns and grain bins. We stayed outside to play on summer evenings until it was real dark. We blew soap bubbles through a spool that thread came on. We fished, and rode horses, and caught tadpoles in small streams.

At school we played Hide and Seek, Red Rover, Blind Man's Bluff, Annie Over, Kick the Can, King of the Hill, Hop Scotch, Jacks, Jump Rope (with hot pepper). We played stick hockey, roll the hoop, and London Bridge.

We made scooters of old roller skates, stilts, and soap box vehicles. We made tire swings and rope swings with swing boards cut from a 1" X 6".

We made elm whistles. They lasted only one evening before they dried out and wouldn't blow any more, but they sure made great music for a little while. (Parents might disagree with that statement.)

Peanut butter and syrup mixed together piled high on bread was a favorite food when we were kids. We could survive for days on this simple fare. Another favorite was Peanut Butter Cookies, that were so simple even kids could make them.

Peanut Butter Cookies

1/2 C. soft shortening
1/2 C. peanut butter
1/2 C. sugar
1/2 C. brown sugar
1 egg
1 1/3 C. flour
1/2 t. baking powder
3/4 t. soda
1/4 t. salt

Mix shortening, peanut butter, sugars, and egg together. Sift dry ingredients and stir into egg/peanut butter mixture. Chill. Roll into balls the size of large walnuts. Place on baking sheet. Flatten with fork dipped in sugar, crisscross. Bake 10 to 12 minutes in 375 degree oven. This makes about 3 dozen cookies.

Close your eyes and think back 30, 40, 50, 60 years to your childhood. We wouldn't want to go back there except in our memories...but what happy memories. Think about it!

Chapter 2 — Gossip

Do you gossip? Think about it!

When you speak of someone, ask yourself:

Is it true?

Is it kind?

Is it embellished?

Is it personal?

Is it sensational or juicy?

Is it rumor or opinion?

Is it catty or chatty?

Will it harm their reputation in any way?

Is it spiteful or mean?

Does it follow the Golden Rule policy?

Would you wish it said about you?

I am reminded of a simple, yet graphic story of the extent of gossip. Take a feather pillow. Step outside on a windy day and rip open one end of the pillow ticking. Empty the contents. Now, go back and gather up all those feathers and restuff the pillow and sew it up again. It is as impossible to gather all those feathers as it is to retract something harmful or unkind that has been said about someone.

Being "two-faced" is almost like being against someone, except the person thinks you are his friend and then you betray him and discuss him behind his back. This back-biting can, and usually does eventually destroy a friendship. If you have something to say about a person, it is better to say it right to their face, than it is to talk about them behind their back. Usually someone will accept criticism given in a loving way if they know it is said with no malice. It is when we are all sweetness and love to a person and then turn to talk bad about them when they are not there that it is damaging to a relationship. Betrayal always seems to find its way back to the originator.

Friends are so great, that it is better that we accept everyone's differences and learn to love them the way they are, than to try to change them by talking about them. There is so much good in the world it is a shame to not talk about that and see that.

Equally as bad as talking behind someone's back is whispering in front of them. It is degrading and demeaning, beside being rude. If it is worth saying, it can be said aloud.

Crowd out any ill feelings for others and make room for only good feelings. Think ahead of the consequences that will follow the telling of gossip or unkind things. Do we really want their reputation tarnished or splintered or smashed? Even if we don't care for someone much (and this CAN happen) do we want their name dragged through the mud? If a name is dragged through the dirt (whether it is true or not) some of that dirt will stick...and some of that dirt may stay on us. We need to keep our tongues still unless we have something good to say about someone.

A recipe with a good reputation that only good things are said about is Marinated Salad. It can be made ahead of time and is pretty to serve. We let it take the place of all veggies and another salad. Just add a casserole or meat dish and the meal is prepared.

Marinated Salad

2 C. cauliflowerettes (raw)
2 C. broccoli (broken into bite sized pieces)
1 can ripe black olives (pitted and drained)
1 C. raw carrots, sliced thin
1/2 C. onion, chopped large
2 C. salad tomatoes (drained well) or use fresh if available
1/2 C. chopped green peppers
one cucumber, peeled, sliced, and seeded

Cover with Italian Dressing. Marinate several hours or overnight until ready to serve. Omit any of the veggies you don't like or add others that you do like.

Let the words of our mouths and our thoughts be kind and acceptable. Someone's life depends on it. Think about it!

Chapter 3 — Collecting

Are you a collector? Think about it!

You ARE a collector or at least off to a great start if you have at least three of something...anything. Sometimes even one of something begins a yen for more.

I have a collection of ironstone that started with Grandma's old plain white heavy platter that was always at our Thanksgiving and Christmas tables, and many times in between too. It was always laden with turkey, a roast, or fried chicken or fresh fish. No matter what was served on it, it was something delicious and I looked forward to the meal. When she died, and then Mother died, and the things were divided, my sister got that lovely platter. I was glad that she got it because she loved it too, and I have been in a position to be able to buy my own through the years, where perhaps she might not have been so able to. She lives on a farm and doesn't have the free time to look in antique shops like I have been able to over the years. She has been busy with family and farm chores whereas I have a ready-made family.

Anyway, back to the ironstone: Now I have a great collection and we look every chance we get to add to that collection. Most of it is just plain white, which I like best, but I have a few pieces of tea-leaf too. If you know of a piece for sale, give me a call and I will drop everything to check it out. Every piece has a story to tell, whether real or imaginary.

At our house, we also collect bells, alabaster eggs, belt buckles (especially Marine), fossils, old books and classics, old children's books (or should I say children's old books...or maybe I was right the first time), tatting shuttles and old tatting patterns, every special valentine, birthday card, or Mother's Day card I have ever received, pictures, letters, the list goes on. I am sure that Della, who helps me clean house twice a month, wishes I would not be such a pack rat but I just love to keep old things. I got a lovely clock for my birthday with the inscription on it, "Grandmas are just antique little girls" and most of those antique little girls, like me, collect something from their younger past.

There is a collector for everything under the sun. Everything from match book covers to car parts to old magazines. They will go anywhere to any lengths to find what they are looking for and eventually they will find it because someone else is collecting the same interesting thing.

A person can go as extravagant or as "cheap" as the pocketbook allows. Antique cars cost a fortune. On the other hand, remember the lady on the Johnny Carson Show that collected odd shaped potato chips. I saw that collection and it was unusual and interesting and she had devoted her life to collecting those irregular shapes and preserving them. Some people collect menus from restaurants or napkins from those same restaurants. Leaves is another inexpensive collection, or rocks, or many things from nature. It just depends on what you wish to spend and what your interests are. The sky is the limit.

I have many of my grandma's old cook books and many of Mother's also. I just love to read those old recipes which call for a "gill" of something or a half an egg shell full of something. Many of those recipes are "by guess and by gosh," as they would say. Many don't even tell how to put the ingredients together. One was just supposed to KNOW. And the oven temperature was seldom mentioned. It would depend on whether you were burning green wood or dry wood, and many other factors of those old ranges and fireplaces. People were not so choosy back then so ate what was put before them and were glad to get it, so if the recipe was imperfect it really didn't matter all that much. I have recipes for head cheese, white wash for fences, soap, salves, hominy, Scottish haggis with tatties and neeps, and then some edible things like: Raisin Biscuits

2 Cups flour
4 teaspoons baking powder
1 teaspoon cinnamon
1/2 teaspoon salt
1/4 Cup sugar
5 tablespoons butter
about 1 cup milk
1/2 Cup raisins

Mix dry ingredients. Cut in butter. Stir in milk until dough is manageable. Stir in raisins. Pat out on floured board to about 3/4 inch thickness. Cut with floured cutter. Place fairly close together on baking sheet. Bake in 425 degree oven about 12 minutes. Glaze with vanilla glaze: 2/3 Cup powdered sugar, 1 tablespoon warm water, and 1/4 teaspoon vanilla, beaten together until smooth.

Look around you. There is something you collect. Happy Hunting! Think about it!

Chapter 4 — Frivolous

Are you frivolous or frugal? Think about it!

Back during and following the depression and with World War II, everyone was frugal. We did it for the war effort, as our patriotic duty. Everyone had victory gardens and saved oil, tires, sugar, meat, shoes, and other things because they were rationed to us.

Many products came from an earlier era of saving...things like making soap from old grease, quilts from scraps of fabric, soup from left-over vegetables and meat. Jams, jellies, and butters were made from the imperfect fruits. It seemed that we never wasted anything or threw anything away that had any good left in it. I remember my great-aunts saying not to throw an old coat away because it had lots of warmth left in it. It was a way of life...a way of thinking frugally, all the time.

Being economical was not at all the same as being cheap, nor stingy. We shared everything we had. If we outgrew anything or had no need for it any more, it was passed on to someone who could use it. If anything, those years taught us to be sharing and generous with what we were fortunate to have.

John D. Rockefeller, Jr. said that he believed that thrift is essential to well-ordered living and that economy is a prime requisite of a sound financial structure, whether in government, business, or personal affairs. Some things seem like a bargain until hidden costs are added. Then it seems extravagant and it is hard to find the money to pay the "bills".

Being frivolous with time seems just as bad as wasting money. What is the old saying..."Do not waste time, for that is the stuff of which life is made". This may be a misquote and I cannot recall where or when I first heard it but I believe it is true. Life is too precious to waste in self-indulgent lapses of time.

Recycling things like plastic, paper, glass, and "junk" is not a new concept. Ben Franklin, in "Poor Richard's Almanac" recommended it with his phrases of "A penny saved is a penny earned". "Waste not. Want not". "Don't be penny-wise and pound foolish". The ultimate recycling method is garage sales. One man's trash is another man's treasure. And it is fun too!

That earlier era did produce a lot of "pack-rats". We saved things that we might use sometime. It became a habit to save buttons, string, ribbons, and things like that. You just never know when you might need some of that wonderful stuff. I can still produce a bit'o ribbon or fabric or scrap of nothing for crafts if anyone needs them...if I can find it.

During World War II a favorite supper was this "Beef 'N Bean Bake". We served it with slaw and an easy dessert or fruit.

Beef 'N Bean Bake

1 pound hamburger
1 medium onion, chopped
1 can (16 oz.) pork and beans (or use Ranch Style beans)
1 can (16 oz.) tomatoes
1 t. salt
1 T. brown sugar (optional)
3 strips bacon

Brown hamburger and onion. Add salt, beans, tomatoes, and brown sugar. Pour into casserole. Lay bacon strips across top and bake one hour at 350 degrees. Do not cover.

It is a challenge to watch your pennies. Watch those pennies and the dollars will take care of themselves. Live within your means. It is not how much we make, but how much we spend that makes one frugal or frivolous. We would not want to return to the depression/World War II era, but it would be wise if we would put into practice those saving ways we learned back then. Think about it!

Chapter 5 — Favorite Foods

Do you have a favorite food? Think about it!

Most people have different favorite foods at different times. Take for instance, in the summer it might be ice cream made in an old crank ice cream freezer. You know the kind that we used to sit on while it was cranked. I have always wondered why we did that. Any ideas? Anyway, back to food...In the winter we would prefer something steaming and warm like banana pudding, or hot apple pie.

It seems that some of us live to eat instead of eating to live. Food is such an important part of our lives and the desire for food is affected by many circumstances. In the spring one just naturally gets hungry for green onions and beans and cornbread. In June, our appetite turns to fresh green beans and new potatoes. In the fall our thoughts turn to pumpkin pie and baked squash, and winter brings on hunger pangs for hot apple cider or hot chocolate. Chili, popcorn, fudge, turkey and dressing, potato salad, cob corn, apple dumplings, and many other things have a special time attached to it.

Recipes remind us of special people or places. Who has not eaten a fresh loaf of hot bread with apple butter and thought of their grandmas, or aunts. And who can resist thoughts of "Smores" at camp, or popcorn and malt balls in the movies. Remember too those wonderful hot lunches at schools, with the perfect cinnamon rolls and great stews. At least in my small country school we had great lunches prepared by great cooks who volunteered to do it for us. Everyone donated to the lunches from the bounty of their harvests.

There are favorite foods we cook for certain people, and we are hungry for certain things in different areas. Why else would you be hungry for fried chicken in the country, along with all the fixings of real mashed potatoes and gravy. In the mountains we are always hungry, but especially for sour cream biscuits that raise so high, and bacon and eggs. Coffee smells so good there, right before going out into the mountain air. On the road traveling to anywhere there is a special hunger. In fact it begins when we pull out of the drive. Although we do not eat in our car, we sure do take frequent stops for nourishment, and we always take plenty of supplies along, in case we get caught in a snow bank. Don't ball games make you hungry for hot dogs with mustard and soda pop? Or hamburgers with onions?

Another thing that can bring on hunger is T.V. at night.. Those ads for ice cream concoctions and other goodies sure make the juices flow. Or reading magazines can make you want to get right up and hop to the kitchen to cook up something that looks so good, even if one has just finished eating a short time earlier.

Just plain old talking about food can bring on hunger. People who love food seem like happy people to me. They aren't grouchy all the time. They enjoy entertaining and cooking and eating and talking.

When the jonquils bloom and the strawberry plants begin to peep their leaves from under the mulch to get ready to blossom and bear, we begin to get hungry for strawberry pie. It is a favorite of ours, yet it is relatively easy. I hope you enjoy it.

Strawberry Pie

1 small box Strawberry Jello
Pour the dry Jello in cup and fill rest of the way with sugar
1 C. water
6 T. corn starch
1/4 t. salt
1 t. vanilla
1 t. red food coloring
2 C. strawberries (sliced)
9" baked pie crust

Mix all the ingredients (except pie shell and strawberries) and cook until thickened (about 5 minutes). Cool. Stir in strawberries. Pour in cooked pie shell. Chill. Serve topped with whipped cream or Cool Whip.

Walk into a house sometime with a beef roast cooking or hot bread in the oven and you will have instant saliva attacks. Cultivate those people who cook like this, even if you don't. Food is a blessing in many ways. Everything is a favorite to someone. Think about your favorites and remember good times. Savor the moments. Think about it.

Chapter 6 — Role Models

Who is your role model? Think about it!

Usually we look to someone, good or bad, as an example for our lives. We want to pattern our lives after theirs. It is like an American dream to be like someone who is famous. Perhaps that person is in the movies, a sports figure, a political figure, a school official, a church officer, or our parents. It is a sad thing that sometimes these idols disappoint us with their conduct. Those heroes may turn out to be just humans after all with flaws. It seems that more and more those we tend to look up to have morals and actions and habits and attitudes that are a disappointment. Then we are crushed and have to look to someone else. There is corruption in every walk of life. None are exempt. Maybe this has always been so and only with the availability of T.V., radio, and newspapers that keep us so informed, we are aware of happenings now where years ago we were not so well enlightened.

Another thing to consider is that someone may be looking up to you as an example. Does someone stand in awe of you? If someone does, why does he/she? Is it because you are a top-notch executive with lots of money? Or is it because of your social standing? Or is it because of your strong moral fiber? I would hazard a guess it is because of your honor and your good reputation. You may not even know that you are looked to as an example or a hero.

There are so many heroes in all our lives: People who were heroic in the wars. People who were our teachers when we were in school. Everyone knows of someone who is an example of courage, decency, and kindness. Have you ever told them what you admire about them and how they have influenced your life and what they have meant to you over the years?

Does your hero motivate and inspire you to be the best you can be? Are you that kind of inspiration to someone else? It surely makes us look inward, knowing that someone might be watching our every move and action and attitude.

Wasn't it Clarke who wrote: "I saw him once...he stood a moment there: He spoke one word, which laid his spirit bare: He grasped my hand, then passed beyond my ken; But what I was, I shall not be again." Our daily lives are made up of an intricate network of associations. Some personalities touch ours so lightly that we are scarcely aware of the contact. Others affect us so vitally that the channel of our lives is changed forever. If we are going to have a mentor it should be someone with the same moral values that we want. It should be someone who truly is a hero. They should be someone who deserves a following.

Serve this salad/dessert at a luncheon and you will be a hero to your guests. It is easy and can be made the day before serving.

Jubilee Salad/Dessert

1 pkg. cherry Jello
1 C. hot water
1 can sweetened condensed milk
1 (21 oz.) can cherry pie filling
1 (20 oz.) can crushed pineapple (drained)
1 (13 1/2 oz.) container Cool Whip
1/2 C. chopped pecans

Dissolve Jello in hot water and cool to room temperature. Drain pine-apple. Stir pineapple into milk and pie filling. Fold into Jello, then fold into whipped topping and nuts. Pur into 13" x 9" Pyrex dish. Chill thoroughly. Cut into squares to serve. If using as a dessert (as we do) top with dollop of Cool Whip. If using as a salad (as I have) serve on lettuce leaf. You will love it.

Keep your words and your actions sweet. You don't know who is watching or when they are watching. Think about it!

Chapter 7 — Saturdays

Do you remember Saturdays in the City? Think about it.

We lived in the country and worked or went to school all week. But on Saturdays, after the chores were done, we went to town to do our "trading", as we called it...not shopping. We took the separated cream and eggs to town to be sold for cash. Then we went by the grocery store and bought our necessary staples and specialities. Sometimes we went late and stayed into the evening. The stores stayed open as long as there were any people buying or even looking.

People would sit in their cars around the "square" and watch the people go by. Their neighbors would stop and talk and catch up on their visiting and who was doing what.

There were wonderful stores to see. Who can forget the old "racket" stores, that were the five and dime stores, that sold everything. You could browse for hours and never see all the terrific things for sale. And the candy stores were beyond your wildest dreams. All the candy cost only one cent each and you could pick and choose to your heart's content. They even had rings in those penny candy choices, and those rings would last almost until you got home before they would break. But what finery until they did break.

The mercantile was also interesting. It was full of every kind of fabric, shoes, accessories, ready-to-wear, etc. The thing I remember about this store was the little cylinder that the money was placed in. Then the clerk pulled a handle and the little cylinder traveled up a wire to the cashier on the balcony. She would make change and send the cylinder back to the clerk. Then the clerk would give you your change and a hand written sales slip with a description of what you had purchased. I was always spellbound with this handy contraption.

It was an adventure to go to town on Saturdays. It made all the waiting and working worthwhile. We kids did not go every Saturday. Sometimes the folks went alone and left us at home in the care of our older sister. That was great fun too because she would let us bake cookies or make fudge or something wonderful. Funny, the folks never caught on to what we did while they were gone. I was surprised that Mother never missed all that sugar or cocoa or other ingredients, nor noticed the dirty utensils or could smell the aroma that lingered. Here is a recipe that we used those ingredients on: Peanut Butter Fudge

2 1/2 C. sugar
1/4 C. cocoa
1 C. milk
1 T. light corn syrup
1/2 C. butter (or margarine), divided
1 C. chopped peanuts
1/2 C. peanut butter
2 t. vanilla

Combine first four ingredients in a heavy kettle with lid (like a Dutch oven). Cook over medium heat, stirring constantly, until sugar dissolves. Add 2 T. butter, stir until butter melts. Cover and boil mixture 3 minutes. Remove cover, and continue to cook, without stirring, until mixture reaches soft ball stage (234 degrees). Remove from heat, and without stirring, add remaining ingredients. Cool ten minutes. Beat mixture until blended, and pour immediately into a buttered 9" square pan. Cool and cut fudge into 1 1/2" squares. Yield 3 dozen.

Those Saturdays were special. Whether we went to town or stayed at home didn't matter much. What was important was that it was a weekend...a Saturday, a let-your-hair-down day of relaxation. Aren't they still much that same way no matter where we are or what we do. Think about it!

Chapter 8 — Family Gatherings

Don't you enjoy family gatherings? Think about it!

This time of year many families have their annual reunion. Cards go out, a place is secured, and recipes are dug out of the file box. Picture albums are dusted off. The kids are briefed on their ancestors.

I remember when I was a kid, two elderly great aunts came every summer from Missouri. We had a ball with them. It was certainly an occasion for a family gathering. They visited my grandparents and stayed with them. They laughed a lot, joked a lot, talked a lot. Even the kids were included in everything. I don't recall that the 'old folks' kept to themselves to visit. It seemed like I was always right in the big middle of things. What fun we had. Those aunties are gone now, as many of our ancestors are, but what memories we have. One of the joys of getting together is to remember those deceased family members and get acquainted with new members of the family by marriage or by birth. We talk of our heritage and family ties.

Speaking of talk...we do a lot of that. Sometimes we sing and pour over picture albums or family history, but mostly we just talk and talk and talk...with siblings, cousins, aunts, and uncles. Seems like one never catches up on their visiting.

We tell the same stories over and over and over and over. They are good stories. If the kids complain that they have heard them before, we just remind them that they buy records or C.D.'s and play them repeatedly. Those stories are our records of yesteryear.

Another fun thing is taking pictures. It is difficult, and almost impossible, to get everyone still and together at the same time. And there is always one clown in the bunch, so every year we have a "V" sign over a favorite auntie or cousin. It seems to add to the fun the next year when we view those pictures.

Of course, there is usually the picture of a last time we saw a particular relative. Then it is sad. Who knows who will be next!

Family reunions take a certain amount of organization. We usually convene at Pawnee, where most of the members still live. We have it at a park, or this year, in an air-conditioned building. Everyone brings in food...too much food. But it is all good. We never assign a particular dish to bring. We figure if there are six potato salads that show up, they all are different and they all taste great.

It doesn't have to be a big family reunion to enjoy family. It is always fun when a sister drops in or a niece or my dad, or a granddaughter with friends, or our daughter and son-in-law. It is always a special occasion...and an excuse to sit and talk and cook up something for them.

Occasionally when we have a get-together, we just bring finger foods...you know, sandwiches, cookies, pickles, deviled eggs...whatever doesn't need a spoon or fork to eat. That way, we use paper plates and throw them away, and have no dishes to do. On these occasions, cream puffs are great...a little messy but they are delicious.

Cream Puffs

Heat to boiling point in saucepan:
1 C. water
1/2 C. butter
Stir in:
1 C. flour
Stir constantly until mixture leaves the pan and forms into a ball. Remove from heat and cool.
Beat in, one at a time:
4 eggs

Beat until smooth. Drop by spoon onto ungreased baking sheet about three inches apart. Bake until dry, about 50 minutes at 400°. Allow to cool slowly. Cut off tops with sharp knife. Scoop out any fragments of soft dough. Fill with sweetened whipped cream or rich custard sauce. Replace tops. Dust with powdered sugar. This makes about eight large cream puffs.

People without family ties miss SO MUCH. In our families are our past heritage and the hope of the future. Think about it!

Chapter 9 — Summertime

Do you remember the good ole summertime? Think about it!

As I remember it, we did most of our work in the early morning, gathering corn or garden produce early to prepare for canning. Of course, canning always took place during the hottest part of the summer. We worked outside in the breeze, where there was shade. We took a break during the heat of the day and resumed our work when it cooled off in the evenings.

For air conditioning, we used the front porch to catch a breeze, moving around the house to find shade on the porch, or under a tree.

When it was terribly warm, and we couldn't even feel a breeze through the open windows, we slept out on the porch or out in the yard. We were completely safe with never a fear of anyone coming around our house. Jim remembers that they sprinkled water on the sheets outside to have a coolness. He also remembers hanging a damp towel up to the window. I don't remember this, it seemed like it was always sticky in the country, and we didn't need any more moisture in the air.

Remember the summer haircuts? They were so short they lasted all summer. When school was out you got your summer haircut and a pair of high-topped tennis shoes. By the end of summer those shoes stunk so bad they had to be left outside on the porch. Girls braided their hair or pulled it back into a pony tail. Beauty was secondary to comfort.

In church or funeral homes, we used hand fans made of cardboard to fan ourselves. They always had advertising on them...Rexall Drug, etc.

We wore clothes then to protect us from the sun. Even boys and men always wore shirts. They didn't (and don't) get any hotter than ladies do, and ladies wear clothes at all times. Women wore sunbonnets and men wore straw hats to protect themselves from the hot rays. I don't remember anyone wearing sunglasses.

When work was done we cooled off in the pond or horse tank. Or we waded in the creeks in between hoeing rows of corn. That was very refreshing.

We delivered water to the men working in the fields, especially harvest or hay fields. The jugs were covered with burlap sacks, and soaked in water, to keep the water cool. "Pop" was a treat saved for the 4th of July. We drank water to refresh us otherwise.

I don't remember that we were so hot all the time. It was hot everywhere. We didn't have a cool place to be and then go out in the heat. Therefore, there was not the contrast and one didn't notice it so much. Summer was supposed to be a "scorcher". We just accepted it that way.

We'd listen to the radio through the open windows while we sat outside trying to "catch a breeze". Movies finally advertised "20 degrees cooler inside". I think it must have been from a water cooler though. When water coolers came into being, many people had them but it seemed it only added to the stickiness of Oklahoma humidity. Fans were wonderful (when we finally got electricity) as they really stirred the air. What a luxury!

We looked forward to having ice and making ice cream. This is a recipe that hardly anyone would make now days. It has all those eggs, and raw ones to boot! But in the old days it was a treat. I still make it occasionally just for old times. Remembering...

Ice Cream

6 eggs, beaten
2 C. sugar
1 t. lemon extract
3 T. vanilla
2 C. cream (or two cans evaporated milk)
milk to fill freezer to within three inches of top of container.

Use plenty of ice cream salt with ice. Freeze until crank is real hard to turn, or freeze in electric freezer for about 20 minutes. Some people pack it to "ripen" it, but I like it real soft. Why make it if it is to be the consistency of purchased ice cream?

Now spoon up a dish of this ice cream and sit a spell with me on the porch in the evening shade and talk about the weather and world affairs.

Some things haven't changed all that much. Think about it!

Chapter 10 — Gardens

How does your garden grow? Think about it!

Remember when we all had gardens? In fact, we lived out of those gardens. We ate all that we wanted when the vegetables were fresh, and then we canned everything. What we could not keep up with by canning, we gave to neighbors or the church or to anyone who could use it. Nothing was wasted. We worked too hard to get those gardens going. Seeds were expensive or we saved them from the year before, carefully selected from best stock.

During World War II, everyone had a Victory Garden. Even little kids had a plot that they tilled and ate the food produced by their little hands. It sure made us appreciate the work that went into producing fresh garden stuff.

Our very survival depended on those gardens. We lived off those gardens, canning quarts and quarts of carrots, green beans, peas, tomatoes, and corn. It was hot when we snapped green beans, or scraped that corn off the cob, but it sure did taste good in the winter. We were mighty glad we worked so diligently in the summer.

I can still taste how delicious that first mess of green beans was, along with that first gathering of wild greens, before the spinach came on. The green onions were just delicious. So were the little red radishes. But so was every bit of the vegetables we planted. I just loved the taste of those vegetables, and still do. There is nothing that compares with fresh tomatoes, or fresh snapped peas, or green beans and new potatoes, or wilted lettuce, or even wild onions with scrambled eggs.

I am attempting to recapture that appetite for fresh tomatoes. I have three pots of tomatoes I am growing. I look at them every day. I have done everything anyone has suggested I do. They are potted in 5 gallon plastic buckets. I planted them in special soil. I mulched them with alfalfa hay. I planted marigolds on either side of them. I have caged them. The other evening I called my dad. He was busy cutting wires in 4 inch lengths. I asked what on earth for and he said it was to put at the base stem of his tomatoes. He says that keeps the cut worms from squeezing them off at the ground. I didn't have any wire but I used long nails. I hope that will help.

I think positively because I already have dug out the old recipes of Grandma's for catsup, tomato preserves, and chili sauce. I plan to freeze every one we don't eat fresh. They will be great in stews this winter. I planted a few here and there in our flowers but they are not doing as well as those in the buckets. I will keep you posted. In the meantime, if you have a suggestion about growing tomatoes, let me know. I am learning and want a good crop. I have hovered over those plants like an old setting hen over her eggs. I hope something hatches!

One of the best things from the garden is the salad that is made simply by chopping onions, cucumbers, and tomatoes, and adding salt and pepper to taste. I can eat this for every meal. It is wonderful and goes with everything.

Some people like wilted lettuce but most of it is just greasy and over-rated to my way of thinking. It seems a waste of good time to harvest buckets of lettuce and clean it and pick it over and then wilt it down to one little bowl of salad. Some of it is good, but I would just as soon have plain lettuce with salad dressing. Or this one:

Fresh Spinach Salad

1 pound fresh spinach
1 large head lettuce
1/2 pound mushrooms
1/2 pound bacon, cooked and crumbled
1 bunch green onions, chopped
Add any other vegetables you like (radishes, tomatoes, etc.)

Wash and drain greens until dry. Tear into bite-sized pieces. In a large bowl mix all other ingredients. Toss with your favorite dressing. (Mayonnaise and catsup of equal parts makes a good dressing.) Decorate with sliced hard-boiled eggs if desired.

If you just cannot cultivate a garden, then do your best to cultivate friends who do garden. Think about it!

Chapter 11 — Senses

Do you take your sight for granted? Think about it! Or your hearing? Or your sense of smell? Or taste? Or your feeling?

Only after blindness and surgery to see, did I really appreciate my sight. Never, ever again will I fail to see a sunrise, a sky, a tree or flower. Everything is beautiful and a treasured creation. All it takes is "floaters" or "sparkles" to bring me back to the realization of the blessing of sight. I am somewhat like a country girl in New York City, I just can't believe all the things there are to see. Oh, sure, I can now see dust on things and fingerprints on windows but they really are insignificant when one is looking only for beauty.

I am sure the hearing impaired also miss a great deal of lovely things to hear. Like "I love you", or "supper is ready", or important messages like that. They also miss the quiet sounds of children's voices or symphony music or everyday sounds of planes overhead or wind howling to tell of winter weather. They miss words of love, hope, and courage.

People with decreased sense of smell miss a lot in the way of tasting. Think back to when you have had a bad cold and could not tell onion from apple or smell even the strongest fragrances. They miss the cooking aromas of the holidays, the fragrances of flowers, the sweet smell of a baby.

Touch is an important sense. Scarred children or those with injuries to the nerve endings miss so much in touching. They miss the feel of the velvet of a rose petal, the fur of their dog, the touch of a loved one. 'Reach out and touch someone' has a completely different meaning to that person.

Helen Keller was once asked what she considered a worse misfortune than being blind. She replied: "To have eyes that see not". It would seem to me that could be taken a step or two further: to have ears and not hear, or a voice and not use it to encourage others, or taste and not enjoy good food, or have feeling and not share them or use them to touch something interesting. Every sense should be appreciated and used fully. They add so much pure joy to life and living.

A simple meat loaf evokes the senses of smell, sight, taste, and satisfaction. We like it even better the second day in sandwiches.

Meat Loaf

About 2 pounds of lean hamburger
2 eggs, beaten a little
1 small can tomato sauce
about 1 T. Lowry Seasoned Salt
1/2 C. chopped onion
1/4 C. chopped green pepper
1/2 C. oatmeal

Mix all together thoroughly. Shape into loaf, place in pan, score on top. Cover with thin layer of catsup if desired (I don't usually but your family may like it better this way). Bake at 350 degrees about one hour or until brown.

There comes to mind the beautiful words of Edna St. Vincent Millay:
"O World, I cannot hold thee close enough!
Thy winds, thy wide gray skies!
Thy mists, that roll and rise!
Thy woods, this autumn day, that ache and sag
And all but cry with color! That gaunt crag
To crush! To lift the lean of that black bluff!
World, world, I cannot get thee close enough!"
Sometimes it seems we just cannot hear enough or see enough, or feel enough of the world's beauty. May we never take our sight, or our hearing, or our senses of touch or smell, or taste for granted. These are all gifts...think about it!

Chapter 12 — Beautiful Things

What do you think is beautiful? Think about it!

Have you ever noticed how a dandelion with a quarter inch stem can become like a dozen long stemmed roses when that little yellow flower is delivered by a tiny child to a grandma?

Old wrinkled hands can be beautiful when you consider the hours of labors they have put in to scrub on a wash board or pick cotton or sew doll clothes or a million things it takes to raise a family. There is beauty in a wrinkled face that has seen better days (and years)...wrinkles that are caused by smiling or laughing. Those hands express more beauty than a perfectly manicured hand that does nothing for anyone. And a face that has time lines is like poetry...expressing feeling.

Look at the beauty in nature...an aspen tree when it turns yellow in the mountains. The mountains themselves. These flat lands with the fields of wheat, or pasture with cattle grazing. The snows of winter are like Christmas cards. The rains of summer are beautiful and make the world look like it has had a fresh bath. Spring is a burst of beauty when everything begins to bring forth leaves and flowers. Autumn,...ah, Autumn...it is the most gorgeous time of year. I guess we just appreciate all that beauty after so much heat. Every season has its beauty and every animal, bird, or fish has a beauty to behold.

There is nothing quite so beautiful or meaningful as HOME. When my husband came home from World War II, wounded, and arrived in San Francisco, he said there was nothing quite so beautiful as the Golden Gate Bridge. I have seen it and it is nice, but it holds special meaning and beauty for him because it meant HOME.

I was waiting in a doctor's reception area one day and met a lady who had had cancer of the jaw. Much of her jaw had been removed as well as her lower teeth and ridge, for her own health's sake. But this lady was one of the most beautiful people I have ever met. She was neat, clean, attired beautifully, and most of all she had an inner beauty that is rarely seen. She was with her little grandson, and I am sure all he saw was the love in her expressive eyes. I feel certain that he never noticed her "difference" and saw only the beauty that radiated from within. My life will never be the same since I saw her and visited with her. She truly touched my life, and I am sure she is an asset to her neighborhood, her family, her church, and to all those around her. She was such a beautiful person.

Art is beautiful, but here again, art can be a crayon drawing on the refrigerator door. It doesn't have to be the Mona Lisa to be appreciated. The May basket my granddaughter made me from pink construction paper was a centerpiece at a supper we had recently. I thought it was beautiful because across the handle it said "I love you, Grandma". That is art in its finest form!

Music is soothing, or can be, whether it is classical symphony music or a rendition of "Twinkle, Twinkle, Little Star". It depends on the performer and the listener.

I see beauty in rocks, especially fossils. I have a nice collection of them and I am always picking up another one, I find them in the most unlikely places. They are fun to collect and reflect a time that is even older than I am...ha!

June is wild blackberry time. For every blackberry we pick out in the pasture, we get at least one chigger. I love the berries. I hate the chiggers. But just forget about the chiggers...enjoy the pie or cobbler made from those great berries. My sister made blackberry cobbler the first time my husband met my family. He was hooked. He was hoping I cooked like my sister. Blackberry cobbler, or pie is a special favorite of his.

Blackberry Pie

Combine 4 Cups prepared wild blackberries, 3 T. Minute Tapioca, 3/4 C. sugar, 1/4 t. salt, 1 T. melted butter. Let stand 15 minutes. Use as a filling for a 9" two crust pie. Bake at 400 degrees about 50 minutes until brown on top. Perforate top of pie crust before baking and better put a cookie sheet under it too, because it is sure to boil over and make a mess in your oven.

Beauty is in the eyes of the beholder. Whether it is to see a blackberry pie, or hear a child's song, or see the gift of love expressed in a tiny forget-me-not in the spring. A thing of beauty is a joy forever. Think about it!

Chapter 13 — Kids

Aren't kids great? Think about it!

When I was young(er), we celebrated Mother's Day, Father's Day, AND Children's Day, which fell sometime in June. Our folks made a big deal out of that special day and made us feel real honored. Do they even celebrate it now? If people do, it is not with any fanfare. Too bad because it is a wonderful time for children.

There are so many things we can learn from being around kids. Things like enthusiasm, their music, about movies, computers, VCR's and how they work. Just being around them and their happy, energetic friends is a pleasure.

I had a great childhood. We worked hard on the farm, but we played hard too. Everything was done by teamwork with my sisters and brothers. Life was enjoyable. Because of that I don't have to live out my ambitions and dreams in my child and my grandchildren. Because of a special lady, I have those grandchildren and a child to enjoy and bring me great happiness.

It is just fun to hear kids giggle, and sing, and watch them at play. When both granddaughters were tiny I would hold them and think that they could not get any more precious nor perfect than they were right then. But I was wrong...every age is perfect...from the time they are just little pink bundles to the terrific two's, to kindergarten, to elementary age, to junior high era, to high school, and then up, up, and away...We train them to fly the nest and be competent adults but it is hard to see them leave us. We need to protect them, letting them be kids while they are young. They are too soon old with adult responsibilities.

Kids are a reward. They make life worth living. Looking at one's grandchildren gives faith in a new generation. We know the world will be a better place because of them and what they stand for. It is too bad that sometimes all we hear about are the bad kids and problem kids. Thank goodness newspapers now accent the kids that are on honor rolls and excel in sports and do meaningful things for society. I am not too sure that some of these bad kids are due in part to our own fault as adults. We allow them to be misfits in society. We do no service to kids when we stick up for them when we know they are clearly wrong or to blame for something. This is part of the problem teachers have. The parents defend their child whether he is right or wrong. Boy, when I was a kid, my parents didn't even ask what I had done...they KNEW the teacher was right and I was in trouble twice, once at school and again when I got home. Therefore, I never tried anything twice. I knew better!

Deeply disturbed by the prevalence of juvenile delinquency in his community, a certain writer was moved to present the situation in these stinging sentences:

"Our youth now love luxury. They have bad manners, contempt for authority, disrespect for older people. Children nowadays are tyrants. They no longer rise when their elders enter the room. They contradict their parents, chatter before company, gobble their food, and tyrannize their teachers."

The writer? Socrates. The time: The 5th century before Christ.

I like to believe that there have always been and always will be great kids. Don't let one "bad" one spoil the whole bushel.

My kids know that I love to make chicken and noodles the old fashioned way. But the other evening Shelby√as over and wanted Grandma's noodles. I concocted noodles using things from the pantry and they tasted pretty good. We ate them, anyway, and named them Cock-A-Doodle Noodles. Here is the quick recipe.

1 1/2 C. dry noodles, cooked in salted water
1 can (16 oz.) white chicken
1 can cream of chicken soup
1 can (16 oz.) chicken broth
1/2 t. poultry seasoning
salt to taste

Cook noodles until tender. Drain. Add all other ingredients. Heat over low heat until hot, but not boiling. Serve over mashed potatoes. Chopped onion may be cooked and added if desired.

Try it...you'll like it. We did, and we do.

Young people are terrific. Even as we get older, kids keep us young at heart. They are our greatest natural resource. The future of our universe is in their hads. Think about it!

Chapter 14 — Losers and Winners

Are you a good loser and/or winner? Think about it!

We've been to about a zillion basketball games with our two granddaughters and have enjoyed every one...well almost. What a joy it is for me to keep a score for my own record. I am sure every grandma feels the same way about keeping score for her "own". Since their first games at the "Y", I have kept a tally of their hits, misses, and assists along with total scores.

In every ball game someone has to lose and someone has to win. That means one side is elated, while the other side is deflated.

Sometimes a team will just be absolutely positive they will win, and are surprised at the outcome. I have always told our granddaughters that if we KNEW who was going to win, there would be no point in playing the game. Teams have good days and bad days, times when they can do nothing wrong and times when nothing they do seems to go right.

Another thing I have stressed to our granddaughters is that we come to see them play ball...win or lose. We just love watching them on the court. We love them just as much when they lose, as we do when they win. Sometimes we might show more love when they do lose because they seem to need more affection then than when they are celebrating a victory.

When I come home from nearly every game, I can hardly talk. I get quite excited and I urge the kids on, even when they don't have a chance in a million they will win. I still get worked up.

I am always pleased when the winning team doesn't lord it over the losers and make them feel worse than they already do. This is true sportsmanship. It is hard to be a good winner like it is difficult to be the loser. But when the game is over and the girls (or boys too in their games) walk by and say "good game" or "you played well", etc., they are showing just how kind and considerate they can be. These expressions of friendship cannot help but spill over into their daily lives.

Life is a lot like a ball game. There are winners and losers. Some get raises. Some stay in place. Some are achievers. Some are satisfied at things the way they have always been. Some play to win, while others don't seem to care. They have no competitive spirit.

It seems to me that the real test of character is how one reacts to new circumstances, or new attitudes, or winning or losing. Some come out on top no matter what the outcome. They seem to rise above a situation and look forward to the next "game" or challenge. This builds character into the fiber of our being. This must be how we arrive at the conclusion that it matters not whether we win or lose, it is how we play the game. We need to be a good winner as well as a good loser and neither get the "big head" or give up. There is always the next game or challenge to look forward to. It is always better to strive to win and be beaten than to yield without effort. Just keep on keeping on!

If your family likes chocolate, you will always be a winner when you make these brownies. They are the greatest!

Best Brownies

1/2 Cup butter or margarine
1 Cup sugar
2 eggs
1 teaspoon vanilla
2/3 Cup flour
2 squares bitter chocolate (melted)
2/3 Cup chopped pecans

Cream butter and add sugar. Stir and add eggs and vanilla. Mix until smooth. Stir in flour, melted chocolate and nuts.

Pour in 8 inch pan, lined with wax paper. Bake 25 minutes in a 325 degree oven. Be watchful not to over bake. To have "under done" is part of the delicious secret.

Whether you have lost the game or won the game, shake it off and look forward to the next event. Life does not stand still. Think about it!

Chapter 15 — Harvest

Isn't there something special about the bounty of harvest? Think about it!

In Oklahoma we almost take the bounty of harvest for granted. We can enjoy the beauty of the waving fields. We can enjoy the work of harvesting the grain. We all benefit when there is a good crop and yield. It does affect everyone in the community. To lose a wheat crop whether to hail or too much rain or bugs is like losing a year's worth of pay checks. There is no income when the crop fails. Almost always there is some kind of harvest. I have never seen that an entire county was wiped out because of weather conditions. Although it can do drastic things to an area and certainly can affect an entire family.

When I was young, we used to play in the newly thrashed wheat. Back then, we cut the wheat, then shocked it and cured it, and waited for the thrasher to come when it was our turn. The thrashing crew went from farm to farm and everyone helped everyone else. My main job was carrying water to those who were on the wagons taking the bundles to the thrashing machine. And the best part of the thrashing at our farm was the food. We had gobs and gobs of it, and all of it was hot and fresh and homemade. We cooked for all the farmers who came to help us...sometimes as many as forty or fifty, but it was fun to cook for those men because they were hungry and really enjoyed whatever was cooked.

Now, combining is over almost before one starts. For most farmers it takes no more than a week if the weather holds out and there isn't too much dew in the mornings. And there isn't a breakdown of machinery. Times have changed, but the bounty of the harvest remains about the same. Now binder twine and thrashing machines are only a thing of the past and of festivals of history to demonstrate to the younger set how we did things in the "olden days".

Making bread is now a snap with the new bread machines. Now there is no excuse for not serving fresh bread. But I don't own a bread-machine. I prefer making it the old fashioned way. There is something therapeutic about kneading bread and forming it into rolls or loaves. And there is something rewarding when it comes from the hot oven. I feel like the "Little Red Hen". I want to do it myself. So I do. Here is a simple recipe that is non-fail that anyone can do. The trick is not to get the lukewarm water too warm. Use it no hotter than baby formula. Test it on your wrist if necessary to make sure it is not too warm. Then proceed.

Simply Delicious Bread

1 Cup lukewarm water
1 package active dry yeast
3 tablespoons sugar
2 teaspoons salt
3 Cups flour

Combine warm water, yeast and sugar in small bowl. Set aside and let it dissolve at least 5 minutes. Combine salt and flour in a large bowl. Stir yeast and water mixture until smooth with a fork. Then stir it into flour/salt mixture. Dump onto floured board and knead until smooth (this can take as long as five minutes). Place in well greased bowl and turn dough so it is coated on the top side. Cover with a tea towel and place in draft free place to rise. When double in bulk (about 1 1/2 hours) mix down. Let rise again. Then make it into about twelve rolls or one large loaf (9 x 5 x 3 inch pan). Let rise again. Cook in 350 degree oven about 30 minutes for a loaf or less if it is made into rolls. Now don't say you can't make bread...You just did!

From field to table there is something very special about wheat, What a blessing! Think about it!

Chapter 16 — Stress

Are you stressed out? Think about it!

Some stress is good. Look at the differences in a race horse and an old plow horse. If we cannot cope with our daily stress and we cannot control it, then it may be time to reassess our situation. Might it be time to change a job? Or our way of living? We might even need to try counseling if it is severe and life debilitating. Could it be anger that causes stress? Or disorganization and poor planning? Financial worries? Health problems? Family problems? Or could it be relationships at work or home or others we are in contact with, and not the actual work or activity that causes stress? Or insecurity or lack of self esteem or self worth? Or lack of sleep? Or eating improperly? Or an accumulation of various things?

Prioritize the things you need to do and want to do. Do the most important things first. Don't panic if you don't get everything completed. It only adds stress to try to accomplish too much. We are not all Super-Mom or Super-Dad, or Super-Anything.

To help ease a stressful situation get away for awhile. Shop, or go to a movie, or pack a picnic and go to the park. Visit a museum. Go to the library and check out a book and stay there and enjoy the peace and quiet. Visit a neighbor or a sick friend. Browse in an antique shop and remember old times when things were slower and calmer. Go to a ball game.

Take a "Day-cation". Do something...anything, with your kids or grandkids. Slide down the slide. Play on the swings. Laugh.

Read, read, read...a favorite book, old love letters, or a magazine. If you can't find something interesting to read, then write something...a poem or a letter.

Crochet, knit, tat, or quilt. Paint or sketch a picture. Whittle. Do a decorating project in your house.

As a last resort, bathe the dog or arrange pictures in the album, or sharpen all your pencils, or have a cup of tea and just sit a spell. The main thing is to do something entirely different than what you have done all day. Take a few minutes for yourself. You deserve it! Reflect on your day and see if you can think of a way to make tomorrow better. Don't dwell on it, just evaluate it. Look forward.

Here is a stress free dessert recipe for "Smoosh". That is what our youngest granddaughter called it when she was tiny. Consequently, we still call it "Smoosh". Isn't it funny how names stick? It is also called Pink Fluff.

1 16 oz. can cherry pie filling
1 12 oz. can crushed pineapple (drained)
1 can sweetened condensed milk
1 med. carton Cool Whip

Mix cherries, pineapple and milk thoroughly. Fold in Cool Whip. Chill. It is that simple. I also add pecans, sliced bananas, drained peaches, or other fruits at various times. Pour into your prettiest crystal bowl. Chill until ready to serve.

We are all special in some way. We all have days that just don't go right and are stressful. Things do get better with time. Count your blessings. Be thankful for all the good in your life. Don't let one bad apple spoil the whole bushel. For every stressful thing in the world there are at least forty relaxing things. Let those positives be your driving force. Remember the race horse. Think about it!

Chapter 17 — Names

Do you like your name? Think about it!

I was not named after anybody. It was just a name my parents liked. I asked Daddy once why they named me Peggy June, since I was not born in June nor after anyone. He said, "Well, we couldn't very well name you November." Guess that makes sense! I like the name Margaret, but am glad I was named Peggy, so people call me by my real name and not a nickname.

Jim's name is James. His old Scottish Grandpa called him Jamie all the time. His father called him Jimmy. We can always tell how long our friends have known Jim by what they call him. His school buddies call him Jimmy. All his old Marine buddies call him Jim. Nearly all of those special friends have nicknames. I asked them what they called Jim, and they said, "Just Jim, the peacemaker". What a compliment!

I have always loved the names of our granddaughters, Jamie Ann, after James Andrew, and Shelby Lorraine, after her other grandmother. Those names have a special ring to them. Jamie thought Shelby was named after their car, which is a Shelby. She said one day she was glad they didn't name her Mustang, after their other car. Names used to have to mean something special, but now babies are named just because the parents or grandparents like the sound of a special name or because they are named in honor of someone very special.

Of course, the sweetest name known to mankind is the name Grandma. I love the sound of it and what it means.

More important than what we are called is how we guard our good names and keep a good reputation. Some family names when said just reflect honest, upright citizens, who are loved by everyone. Those families worked at making their name well respected. They have upheld what is right and true and honest. The respect didn't just happen. One must guard what they do and with whom they do things and where they go to uphold a revered name. A bad reputation is difficult, if not impossible, to change once it has been established. Don't let peer pressure tarnish good character.

Our heritage reflects some odd names. Scottish cookies are called biscuits, which are nothing at all like the usual biscuits I make. But for the sake of our ancestors I'll share a biscuit (cookie) recipe that is light and good when served with afternoon tea. The original recipe calls for caraway seeds, but I don't put them in the cookies. If you want to, add 1 teaspoon caraway seeds.

Brodie Biscuits (Sugar Cookies)

1 3/4 Cup flour
1/2 teaspoon baking powder
1/2 Cup sugar
1/2 Cup butter
1 egg, beaten
1/2 teaspoon grated lemon rind
1 tablespoon lemon juice

Sift flour, baking powder, and sugar into bowl. Cut in butter until mixture is like course meal. Add egg, lemon rind, and lemon juice (and that caraway seed if you wish). Mixture will be stiff. Turn out onto floured board. Roll thin and cut with 2 inch cookie cutter. Prick top with fork. Bake at 375 degrees about 7 to 10 minutes until slightly brown. This makes about 5 dozen great cookies.

Your name is highly important, because whatever it is, just seeing it or hearing that name will conjure up a certain impression. Think about it!

Chapter 18 — Help or Hindrance

Are you a help or a hindrance? Think about it!

Are you part of the problem or part of the solution? We have all known of people who got in the way. They mean to be helpful but don't know how, and without realizing it are contributing to the problem at hand. These people require a little extra patience, and tolerance, and guidance. I am not referring to little kids who are always wanting to HELP in the kitchen or when you are painting or with other messy jobs. They are in the way, in a sense, but they are fun to have around and that is how they learn. We all learn that way. They are a help and not a hindrance.

I love having help in the kitchen, but it is frustrating when the help "hides" my favorite spoon or skillet. Putting things away in another person's house can be a disaster unless one knows where things go. You know how much "help" it is for someone to file something and put it in the wrong place. It takes twice as long to find it...if you ever do. But appreciate the trying to help. It counts for something. I'd rather have the help even if later I have to hunt.

Positive people become stepping stones to positive actions. A person's creative power may be a help or a hindrance. The novelists and playwrights who produce vulgar, degrading books and plays have resigned their powers of creativity for the sake of the money. Musicians who degrade their high calling by writing cheap, noxious music are destroying that talent. What a waste!

The beauty of work depends upon the way we meet it, whether we arm ourselves each morning to attack it as an enemy, or whether we open our eyes with the sunrise and welcome it as an approaching friend who will keep us delightful company all day, and who will make us feel at evening that the day has been well worth its fatigue. The way we are challenged by our work is a help or a hindrance...attitude is everything! It is the stumbling block or stepping stone.

I remember an old poem I learned as a child, but had to call my sister long distance for the entire poem. She knew it so recited it to me. It says so much about how things are: help or hindrance, stumbling block or stepping stone... written by R.L. Sharpe.

"Isn't it strange that princes and kings
And clowns that caper in sawdust rings
And common people like you and me
Are builders for eternity?
Each is given a bag of tools,
A shapeless mass, a book of rules
And each must make...e'er life is flown
A stumbling block or a stepping stone."

Some recipes can be a stumbling block if you are trying to lose weight or stay on a sugar-free or low-fat diet. We have to always be on guard. This pie is rich so it will serve at least eight people.

Peanut Butter Pie

one prepared graham cracker crust
8 oz. softened cream cheese
1 Cup peanut butter (creamy or crunchy)
3/4 Cup sugar
8 oz. Cool Whip

Mix cream cheese, peanut butter and sugar together and beat until well blended and fluffy. Fold into Cool Whip. Spoon into graham cracker crust. Sprinkle with chopped peanuts. Chill until ready to serve.

By changing your attitude one can change a stumbling block into a stepping stone, a hindrance into a help, a negative into a positive. It is one's own choice. Think about it!

Chapter 19 — Organization

Are you organized? Think about it!

Some people get everything done. Others get nothing done. Yet all have the same 24 hours in every day. Some just use time wisely. Others procrastinate and are always running late. Some have too many irons in the fire and should learn to say "No" or get organized, as they are constantly running in circles and are habitually late. The solution is plain...plan ahead. Make lists of everything, menus, groceries, things to do daily, monthly, weekly, yearly. Check off each job as it is done. It gives one such a feeling of accomplishment to get things done.

Think ahead of birthdays and Christmas and other holidays. Leave nothing to the last minute to allow time for unexpected setbacks.

I was lucky to attend a one-room school with one teacher for eight grades. One of the things that impressed me most about that wonderful teacher was the way she organized the day. She had to organize with planning all the subjects for all the grades day after day after day. She also planned things differently for the slower students or those with a particular problem in a subject. Yet her entire day ran with ease.

She arrived early before any of the kids came. She built a fire in the winter and had the school house all cozy when we arrived frozen to the bone. She was on the playground during recess and at noon, so she couldn't do her planning then. And on rainy or snowy days we stayed inside and she always had organized games for us to play during recess and noon.

She graded all our papers and wrote most of the tests on the blackboard, which took considerable time.

That teacher must have loved teaching or she would never have given so much of her time to the education of her pupils. She could have written the book on organization and getting the most from the allotted time she had. She made it look so easy. She made every minute count. She was teacher, referee, janitor, building engineer, organizer and friend. She had it all.

She set a great example for her students by her planning and structuring...and her caring.

A recipe that takes some planning and organization is Lasagna, but is well worth the effort. Make the sauce the night before and cook it slowly in the crock pot. The noodles, sauce, and cheeses go together quickly the evening it is to be served. Serve it with French bread and a simple salad. For dessert have ice cream with caramel sauce. A feast.

Lasagna

1 box Lasagna noodles (about 12)
2 large packages mozzarella cheese (grated)
1 large package mixed cheeses or Romano cheese (grated)
1 pound American cheese (grated)

Sauce

1 1/2 Lb. extra lean ground hamburger
1 (16 oz) tomatoes
2 (16 oz) tomato sauce
6 fresh green onions chopped (or one large onion chopped)
1 t. oregano
1 t. Italian seasoning
1 t. garlic salt
1/2 t. salt
1/2 t. pepper

Cook hamburger, add onion and cook until clear. Add all other sauce ingredients and cook in crock pot or simmer in pot for several hours.

Cook noodles by package instructions in rapidly boiling salted water until almost tender. Drain well.

Layer sauce, noodles and cheeses in large Lasagna pan, alternating layers until all ingredients are used, ending with sprinkled cheese on top. Bake in 350 degree oven until cheese is melted and bubbly. Let set 5 minutes before serving.

When dinner is over and you are sitting there stuffed, plan tomorrow. Make a check list. Once you get organized you will stay organized and life will run more smoothly for you and those around you. Think about it!

Chapter 20 — Creativity

Are you creative? Think about it!

Of course you are creative. We all are, in our own way. Look at small children. Play music and they will dance and love it. Give them paints or crayons and they make a picture for you. It may need some explanation but it is their creation. It looks right to them. Our creations are the same way, if they look right to the creator, they are right. The secret ingredient in art is that everyone is different. If two people cook from the same recipe, or use the same pattern, the finished product will be a tad different because of the creators being different. The different personalities show through their work.

Creativity is the sum total of our culture and heritage and training and imagination. "Art", says Ruskin, "is that in which the hand, the head, and the heart of man go together". Wouldn't you agree?

Have you seen the beautiful crosses made of three small nails and copper wire? Now, THAT is art. It is seeing something beautiful in the ordinary and creating something of their imagination.

Art and creativity go beyond coloring within the lines, paint by number, or copying someone else doing something. However, these activities will give you a "feel" for doing something and your own imagination can take over from there. It is not necessary to have an abundance of talent to be creative.

Creativity must not be stifled. Here are some reasons that we fear creating: making mistakes, being criticized, disturbing traditions, or fear of being an individual. Had it ever occurred to you that you might just be the envy of your crowd to be creative and an individual? Most really great artists were not like their peers.

An active imagination is crucial to the mental health of adults as well as children. We tend to think that as grown-ups we must leave those fantasies behind but without them we would never grow or push ourselves. Imagination lets us try new roles or test new ideas and concepts. Imagination and creativity help us master negative emotions and events. It relieves boredom or an unpleasant experience. You may think that you lack creative expression but you don't.

Here is a creative recipe...easy and good.

Caramel Apple Cake

2 C. flour
1/4 t. salt
1 t. soda
1 t. cinnamon
3/4 C. oil
1 1/2 C. sugar
3 eggs
1 t. vanilla
2 tart apples, peeled, cored, and cut into 1/2" chunks (about 3 C.)
1 C. chopped pecans

Caramel Glaze

1/2 C. butter (or margarine)
1 C. brown sugar
1/4 C. milk

In large bowl mix oil, sugar, eggs and vanilla until well blended. Sift dry ingredients and add to sugar/egg mixture. Stir in apples and nuts. Pour batter into greased 13" X 9" pan. Bake at 350 degrees for 50 to 55 minutes. Remove from oven.

For sauce: place ingredients in sauce pan over medium heat. Bring to full boil. Boil one minute. Pour over hot cake. Let cake stand 15 minutes before cutting. Serve with whipped cream.

If you feel you are not making or creating anything...that you are just a machine for menial chores, get busy and do something creative. Whether you sew, decorate, garden, paint, write, do needle work, perform musically, cook, or WHATEVER, do it! Try doing something you have always hankered to do. Try it on your own or go to the Vo-Tech school or elsewhere and pick up a creative art. You might be a late bloomer but you might as well start to live. Think about it!

Chapter 21 — In Step

Are you out of step with the times? Think about it!

Do you project an old-fashioned image? Are you just old fashioned? Do you accept new ideas? Bear in mind, all new ideas are not necessarily better. Change doesn't always mean progress. It is good to incorporate our old standards and practices with new, fresh ways of doing things.

What ever happened to the old way of a hand shake being as good as a signed note, or a signed bond? Now sometimes even a signed note doesn't guarantee payment. Too bad!

And our morals have gone downhill. Some of the things on T.V. are not worth watching. Yet the tube is left going all the time so some of the stuff is absorbed by osmosis. It is sad that there are such words on T.V. I would hope this is just for the shock effect and that people really don't talk that way in real life. I cannot imagine what would have happened to me if I would have said some of the words that even men did not say when I was younger. I would have had my mouth washed out with soap for sure...and maybe another lesson teacher used too.

Remember when we used to take food in to neighbors who were ill or saddened by a loss in the family. Is it old hat? Food was also a way to say "I love you", with a batch of cookies for the kids or a grandparent. When I was a kid I felt like Little Red Ridinghood. I was always taking food some place for someone. And I loved doing it. It was a way of sharing. Now, we just go to the store and pick up something to deliver. It may help the person delivered to, but does it help the person who delivers?

Speaking of soap...what has happened to old time cleanliness? We were all poor during the depression and later too, but we were always scrubbed clean. Our clothes may have been patched but they were as clean as lye soap and the wash board could make them. We never went anywhere without cleaning up and did not go cruddy, no matter how tattered we were. I have trouble understanding what the message is when people are dirty about themselves. My mother used to say, as I am sure your mothers said too, "Soap is cheap". There is clean dirt...like working in the field or garden. There is also dirty dirt...an accumulation of grime and body odor over a period of time. I AM old fashioned about being clean.

Another thing that has almost gone by the wayside is the art of visiting. People get together now and feel that they have to DO something to have a good time. What is wrong with friends getting together to visit and talk about what has been happening? No money is involved to have a good time. Try going to the park to swing, or feed the ducks, or take a walk, or gather around the piano, or read poetry. There are a million things one can do that are just fun and require no funds.

When I think old fashioned food, I think of Oatmeal cookies. These are so simple. Need no chilling or any special treatment. Just stir, drop, and bake...and eat.

Old Oatmeal Cookies

2 C. rolled oats
1 C. packed brown sugar
1/2 C. sugar
1 C. flour
1/4 t. salt
1 t. baking soda
1/4 C. hot water
1/2 C. shortening, melted, and cooled
1 t. vanilla

In mixing bowl, combine oats, sugars, flour, and salt. Combine soda and hot water: stir into oats mixture along with the shortening and vanilla. Roll into balls the size of walnuts. Place on cookie sheets. Bake at 350 degrees for about ten minutes or until golden brown. Remove from the oven but allow to stand about 2 or 3 minutes before removing from cookie sheet. This makes about 3 dozen wonderful, memorable cookies. Enjoy.

In step or out of step, march to your own drummer. You gotta be yourself, and not be influenced by what is "in". Think about it!

Chapter 22 — Dreaming

Are you a dreamer and a schemer? Think about it!

I have a magnet on my refrigerator that a friend gave me. It says, "Sometimes I sits and thinks and sometimes I just sits". And that is the way I do. It is okay to just sit and dream occasionally and let the mind rest and go blank. Sometimes that brings spurts of planning and rejuvenation.

Even to imagine you are an Olympic participant, or pretend to be Erma Bombeck, or Magic Johnson, or Jay Leno, or Johnny Quarels is okay, but luckily we are still ourselves when our dreaming is over. It was a pleasant visionary for awhile. This dreaming is different than the imaginary tea parties we all have had with our children and grandchildren. It is more like a situation we dream of attaining and pretend we can accomplish that certain feat.

A certain amount of dreaming is healthy and fun. It raises us from a sometimes dull, routine situation to an imaginary higher level of enjoyment. We may need to see a picture of achievement in our mind to really accomplish it in reality. Basketball players standing on the foul line, project the picture of making a basket before the ball leaves their hands. Golfers do much the same thing, picturing where the swing is going to take the ball.

During a period of dreaming and inspiration, fresh ideas can be born. Lots of books have been outlined, necessary inventions are created for a particular need. Inspirations to write letters or get in touch with friends or relatives can come from this quiet time, this melancholy moment. It is good to count your blessings and enumerate your accomplishments.

We dream of a clean house and perfect meals and neat closets. But in reality, that isn't always the case. It might be easier to go back to dreaming than try to bring everything up to our expectations.

Scheming goes a step beyond dreaming. Scheming involves the planning and designing of our visualizations. It is the working blueprint of the thing we wish accomplished.

Last but not least comes the work. I don't even like to talk about doing all the things that need to be done just before the heat of summer sets in. Things like clean the garage, clear the flower beds, put away winter clothes, put other winter things away and drag out the water hoses and garden tools. It almost makes me tired just to think about it...so back to dreaming, a more pleasant way to pass time!

Here is a recipe that is a dream to eat and a dream to prepare. A friend of ours made it the first time for us when we had guests coming. She said it was easier to make than to tell someone how to make it. She was right. It was the hit of the party. Since that time I have made it many times. It is perfect for the summer months. It is soothing and delicious.

Sis's Sunshine Pie

One can sweetened condensed milk
One small can frozen lemonade (thawed)
One small can crushed pineapple (drained)
Small carton Cool Whip

Mix milk, pineapple, and lemonade together until smooth. Fold in Cool Whip. Pour into baked 9" pie crust. Chill. I have used prepared graham cracker crusts and it is almost as good as baked pie crust.

Dreaming brings a tranquility akin to a delicious midday nap. It just feels good to let your mind rest or think about what could be or once was. Dream on...think about it!

Chapter 23 — Sentimentality

Are you sentimental? Think about it!

Do you have a special song as a couple that reminds you of old times? Or a school song? Or an old hymn? Or a patriotic song that moves you?

Do you keep old love letters? Or old valentines? Or birthday cards from years past? Do you have letters from friends and family that brought happy messages or sad ones that you still keep? Jim still has the letter that was in his pocket when he was shot through the chest in Iwo Jima. The hole is clearly visible in it where the bullet went through. We also have the letter telling of his grandfather's death that we have kept all these years. Mama had letters written during the Civil War that she still had bound in a ribbon. I keep EVERY card that the granddaughters and family have given me over the years. I cried when I first read them and I still can cry easily over them. And none of them are sad...It is just that I am sentimental and love things like that.

I keep everything. . . old toys, old books, old travel folders that remind us of a special vacation. I keep every drawing that family has given me, some of them framed, some just lovingly put away in drawers.

I guess I came by it naturally as my mother was also a "saver". She was sentimental too. She wrote wonderful little notes in the margins of her books...notes I treasure and that give insight to what she was feeling or thinking. We both went by the philosophy that one just never knows when one might need something, so we cannot discard it as long as there is feeling or good left in it.

We have drawers full of family pictures and pictures of friends. Each one spurs a memory. . . and can bring a tear of joy or sadness.

I have always wondered how people who move around all the time can throw away perfectly good stuff and start all over. They discard old family treasures and keepsakes that I would have a difficult time getting rid of. What will they have when they get old to remind them of their youth and to remember the good times they had?

I am moved by patriotic songs or speeches, or when I see military films on T.V. I am so thankful I live in America with its many blessings and opportunities. Seeing Old Glory brings a lump to my throat and a tear to my eye, every time I see it, whether it is at a ball game, a parade, or just on a flag pole. I am reminded of the sacrifices made to keep that flag waving.

I am moved by the Grand Canyon, or mountains, or a ripening wheat field, which reminds me of the bounty of harvest. See what I mean, everything is sentimental to me. It is because I have had such a rich and blessed life through no action on my part. . . it has all been handed to me, whether it is deserved or not. . .and I am grateful for it all.

When I was a kid, my grandma used to pick the seedling peaches and make pickled peaches. They were wonderfully good. She died when I was four so I have few but fond memories of the things we had together. She made me a doll quilt which I still have. I also have her recipe for pickled peaches but no seedling peaches so I improvise and make them with canned peaches that sort of remind me of the ones I used to love so much. Here is an adjusted recipe for those pickled peaches:

Drain the juice of two (2 1/2 size) cans of peaches. Add:
1 1/2 C. brown sugar
1 C. vinegar
2 sticks cinnamon
2 t. whole cloves

Boil liquid from peaches, sugar, spices, and vinegar for five minutes. Add peaches and simmer (don't boil hard) for five minutes. Cool and put in jars. Keep chilled until ready to eat. I guess one could can these and seal the jars but with this small amount I never do. We will eat them within a week or so, so they are fine refrigerated. I hope these stir memories for you too.

No day is lost if you make a memory. Enjoy everything about life. Memories are made of this! Think about it!

Chapter 24 — Courtesy

Are you courteous? Think about it!

When we were little kids we were taught to say the magic words, "Thank you, and Please". We were reminded many, many times, any time we were given something or asked for something. We were probably even taught that little poem that went something like, "Of all the nicest words are these, thank you and if you please." It was drilled into our heads that to be courteous we must say those words often.

Then we grew up, and somewhere along the way, some of us forgot those magic words. Maybe it is because our parents aren't right with us to remind us, but some now demand instead of ask, and completely forget to acknowledge something done for them.

A simple "Good morning", or a greeting of some kind is essential to good manners. It must be more than being ignored or a grunt. The same goes when someone leaves, some kind of dismissal is in order. . . at least a nod.

There are books and many newspaper columns written about manners. There is a vast difference in protocol, etiquette, and simple manners. Protocol is the code for strict adherence. Etiquette is the conduct of good breeding of social observation. Manners is mostly just plain thoughtfulness.

It is difficult to cover all the areas that are affected by simple good manners and courtesy. It is simply (and not so simply) a reflection of being treated like you would like to be treated. Being courteous is a genuine, thoughtful, respectful, consideration of others' feelings.

I can give you a prime example of true courtesy and good manners. We had gone to a track meet and as usual the Oklahoma rains had done their thing and the ground was mud up to your ankles. We were interested in the event that was at the far side of the field, so we could not see from the bleachers. We had to walk several rods through mud that could ruin your shoes. Our son-in-law walked it first to pick a high ground so that we wouldn't slip in the mud or get too muddy. He came back and showed us clearly the path to take. No one could write that thoughtfulness into a book. It just came from the heart and from being kind and considerate. We appreciated it. He was clearly thinking of our feelings first. He did the considerate thing. That's the Golden Rule.

Our parents also told us that "Pretty is, as pretty does." No matter how fine we dressed and were gussied up, we had to act pretty to look the part. This also applies to people who have not so pretty faces but are radiant from the inside out. Those are the most beautiful people and the ones we want to know and remember. If we think of other people's feelings first, then courtesy is automatic.

You don't have to serve high tea to extend courtesies to your friends. If you really want to please them serve Praline Coffee Cake.

Cake Part

1/2 Cup shortening
1 Cup sour cream
1/2 Cup brown sugar
1 teaspoon vanilla
3 eggs
2 Cups flour
1 teaspoon baking powder
1 teaspoon soda
1 teaspoon salt
Mix all together and set aside.

Praline Part

1 1/2 Cup raisins, chopped (I use golden raisins) optional
1 Cup brown sugar
1/3 Cup butter
2 teaspoons cinnamon
3/4 Cup chopped pecans

Mix all together. Alternate layers of cake batter and praline mixture, beginning with cake and ending with praline mixture in a loaf or tube pan. Bake at 350 degrees for one hour. Yield: about 8 servings.

Courtesy costs nothing, yet buys much. Think about it!

Chapter 25 — Songs

Do you have a song in your heart? Think about it!

Most couples have a song that is known as "our song." It is difficult to narrow it down but our song could be "It Had to Be You", or "It's a Wonderful World", or maybe "String of Pearls", yet nothing says it all for us like "The Marines Hymn". We, like most others, can remember a special song connected with special times.

When Jamie was one year old, she was in the hospital and so very ill. To calm her, I'd put the railing of her crib down and lay my head down on her mattress and sing over and over to her the same song, "Sing a Song of Sixpence". I sang that same song one hundred gillion times and it worked, as she would go to sleep and rest. It also formed a kind of bond between us at that special time. She probably doesn't even remember the incident but I'll bet she sure remembers that song.

I can still remember the silly songs my daddy sang to me when I was little. He still probably sings them to his grandchildren, and great-grandchildren. Those songs live forever. . .at least in our memories.

I love to sing. I am not a good singer, but my sisters and I used to sing a lot. We sang at church, Rotary meetings, reunions, school assemblies, etc. Mostly just for the joy of singing. I don't remember that we ever got paid but we enjoyed doing it just because. When we worked, we sang. When we played, we sang. When we get together now we sing, if we ever get caught up on our visiting.

There is no music quite so sweet as a bird in spring. If we have any appreciation of music it enables our intellect and emotions to respond to its message and it does affect our lives.

Music affects emotion. Emotion affects thought. Thought affects action. Action affects conduct. Conduct affects character. Therefore music affects our character. What we cannot say, we often can express by music, because we can feel it.

Listen for music in the rain, or the wind. Listen for the soundless symphonies that flow from a landscape. Listen for music in the surf. It is there but you have to stop and listen to hear it.

I've had to learn to appreciate the music from a bagpipe. It is the music of my heritage and Jim's too. When I first heard it, I thought it was so much screeching. But now when I hear it, it seems to take me back to another time and it is beautiful indeed. It has a soothing effect.

Nothing makes one as melancholy as the old school song. It stirs so many happy memories of our youth. We jump to our feet, and begin to sing whenever we hear it, and whether we sing well or not, we fit right into the harmony of it.

Maybe I am showing my age, but as much beautiful music as there is in the world today, it seems a pity that so much of the newer music does not even have a hummable tune, nor words that one can understand. Of course, we had sensible songs like "Mares Eat Oats, and Does Eat Oats." Now THERE was a classic! Have things changed all that much?

When you have to go to a covered dish dinner or otherwise "sing for your supper", here is what to take: Mean Bean Casserole

2 cans green beans, drained (I use whole green beans)
1 can cream of mushroom soup
1 can water chestnuts, drained
1 can (3 1/2 oz.) French fried onions
1/2 teaspoon Cavender's Greek Seasoning
1/2 Cup shredded sharp cheese

Combine all ingredients except few onions and cheese. Pour in casserole. Sprinkle onions around outside and sprinkle cheese in center of casserole. Bake 30 minutes at 350 degrees.

Even if you can't carry a tune in a bucket, nor can you whistle or hum, you can still keep a song in your heart...it makes everything harmonize. Think about it!

Chapter 26 — Guilt Trips

Does someone put a guilt trip on you? Think about it!

Well, they can't if you don't allow it.

Ask yourself, "Am I guilty of a wrongdoing?" If your answer is "yes," then you best make amends. Apologize and get on with your life. You wouldn't want to really hurt anyone's feelings deliberately or by error in judgement, so clean that up first. You'll both feel much better afterwards.

But if you are not guilty of anything, then you have to ask yourself if that other person is trying to lay a guilt trip on you. In that case, you had better put up your guard and not allow it.

There are people in this world who are masters at laying guilt trips. They have had lots of practice. They are usually self-centered, possessive, insecure people themselves. Often they have tunnel vision and fail to see any way but their own. They fail to see the reasoning behind the motive you are doing what you do. Then the "guilt-layer-oner" goes to work doing what they do best. They pout, they yell at you, they try every way to make you feel like you are entirely at fault. They pull out all the stops to try to get you to come over to their side...but don't you let them control you, whether they be friends, relatives, co-workers, or others.

Sometimes we lay our own guilt trips on ourselves. We make the best decisions we can at the time we made them, with the information we had available. Then when we discover later that another route might have been more to our liking, we start to kick ourselves and feel guilty, guilty, guilty. This we allow too. We had better think things out again and see that we don't allow ourselves to place our own guilt trips on ourselves. For instance, we eat some "forbidden fruit" on our diet. At the time we enjoy it. Then later we hate ourselves. We feel terribly guilty. So we sooth ourselves by eating something enjoyable. What a vicious circle we are in and all because of guilt that we allow to rule our lives. Forget it already. It is done. Get on with the next phase of your life.

Be yourself and do what you know in your heart is right for you. Right or wrong, you've gotta' be yourself. I've gotta' be me. You or I must pay for our own consequences. Listen but make up your own mind, about what is right for you. Then forget it and don't accept any guilt trips or poor-me's.

Isn't it great that most of our friends are refreshing to our lives like a dip in the pool on a hot day. Or invigorating like the clean, strong Oklahoma winds on an August day. Or calming to our lives like a beautiful sunset, or electrically charged, transmitting their high-powered voltage through our minds. All these friends and families we simply love.

So...don't let that other two percent ruin your orderly life by placing a guilt trip on you. Enjoy the ninety-eight percent that enrich your life.

It has always been a mystery to me why some people are ruled by guilt trips, either by placing them or allowing them to be placed on themselves.

Speaking of mystery...here is a recipe for Mystery Pie: It is a mystery how it can taste so good and not like the crackers. It is a mystery how great it tastes.

Mystery Pie

3 egg whites
1 Cup sugar
1 teaspoon vanilla
24 Ritz Crackers, crushed
1 Cup chopped pecans
Whipped Cream (or Cool Whip)

Beat egg whites to soft peaks. Gradually add sugar and vanilla. Fold in crushed crumbs and pecans. Spoon into well greased 8" or 9" pie pan. Bake at 300 degrees about 30 to 40 minutes. When cool, top with whipped cream. Don't panic, as this pie cools it will fall. It's okay.

Don't let others control you with a guilt trip. Stay in control of your own life. Think about it!

Chapter 27 — Criticism

How do you react to criticism? Think about it!

If you are like most people...and normal...you react with hostility and resentment. None of us likes our ideas challenged or wants to be told we are wrong about the way we do something or think something. We put up a shield to defend ourselves from attack. We each like to think we are doing something of merit and in our own way at our own speed and system. We really don't like being told in criticism that we should change everything to another's way.

If we don't become defensive, then we hold it all in and hurt inside and go home and kick the dog and yell at our families. Or take it to heart and let it destroy our self esteem.

It does no good to isolate ourselves or withdraw. It is better if we can calmly discuss the criticism and see how things can be worked out the best way so all will benefit and all will be satisfied. It can be done. A touch-me-not attitude does not solve things. Only more resentment is being built up inside and you hurt even deeper.

To some people being critical is a power thing. They seem to think if they have whipped you they have won. They are not like an old dog who hangs around and then will come back and forgive you and forget the past. They seem to think that makes them a step above and they may try it again if you let them put you down. So it is best to gently stand up for yourself and let them know your true feelings. You can do it kindly, of course, but firmly.

Now critique is a whole different ball game. We all can accept suggestions when they benefit everyone. We all have ways of improving what we do. That is part of learning, to improve our ways and become more efficient or find a better way to do things. Any artist or writer or singer needs helpful critique along the way to develop their talents to the best of their ability. And many times we cannot see the forest for the trees so need some gentle guidance along the way. This kind of critique we readily accept, or should accept anyway, because it is meant to be helpful, and not bossy or hateful.

Critique, if it is given in the right frame of mind, and accepted in the right frame of mind can actually build our self esteem. It helps us look at ourselves in a clearer light. It is not a matter of right or wrong, it simply helps us stand back and take a positive view of things. This loving critique makes us a better person.

No one likes to be **TOLD** what to do, but none of us mind being **ASKED** to do something. Even little kids like to be asked to do their chores, not ordered to do them. We all dislike the saying, "DO as I say; not as I do".

I was lucky. I had two older sisters and one older brother. They showed me how to do things instead of just telling me. It was a great way to learn. My parents and grandparents used gentle critique and showing as a means of teaching too. As they showed, we also worked together. We made enjoyable fun out of everyday work.

If you want praise and no criticism, serve your family or guests this Broccoli Salad. We can make an entire meal of it with some crunchy bread sticks and a tall glass of ice tea. It is a perfect summer supper.

Broccoli Salad

one bunch broccoli, cleaned and cut up
1 pound bacon, fried crisp and broken up
1/2 Cup salted peanuts (no skins on)
1/2 Cup golden raisins
One small red onion, chopped (or use any sweet onion)

Dressing

1 Cup mayonnaise
1/4 Cup sugar
2 tablespoons red wine or cider vinegar

Toss together with dressing and serve immediately.

A person who thinks that he/she is all that he/she should be obviously is not what he/she should be, so be open to criticism and critique. Think about it!

Chapter 28 — Trust

Who do you trust? Think about it!

There used to be an old TV show named, "Who Do You Trust?" It was sometimes full of surprises. It is the same with our lives sometimes, we trust that things will turn out a certain way and then we are surprised.

But no matter, we must continue to trust. We've got to first trust ourselves that we will always do the right thing. We've got to trust in our fellowmen that they will do the right thing also. We can't go around being leery of everyone all the time. We soon become paranoid if we do. Then we fail to trust in ourselves too.

We can be disappointed in some of our elected officials at times, but they are all striving to help our country, state, county, or town. And they are not all untrustworthy. Most of them are just like you and me, truly caring for their people. Remember one bad apple in a bushel does not spoil the whole bushel. We just have to get the bad one away from the good ones. That is why, in this wonderful country of ours, we have the right to vote out a person if the majority does not care for him/her.

And are you yourself truly trustworthy and dependable? Would you cheat if you had the chance and no one was looking? Or would you steal? Most of us would adamantly deny we would steal, but when the boss is away would we waste time? It is the same thing. Stealing time from the boss is the same as stealing money, if we get paid for that lost time. We have all heard, "While the cat's away, the mice will play". This may be true, but is it really the way we want to be? What if we were the boss who was paying the labor bills?

In this world are lots of crooks, thieves, liars, cheats, and criminals. It seems like that is all we hear about sometimes but the world is full of wonderfully honest people who are the same when being watched as they are when no one is looking. I think it is just because now we have such widely read newspapers and television that tells us everything, that we feel like the world is going to the dogs. But things were the same when we used to gather around the radio and listen to the news, we just were not able to gather the news as quickly so didn't learn about it until quite a bit later or never.

When people used to visit only once a week or see outside neighbors or friends as often, they didn't waste time with bad news or gossip, they spent it in good news and reminiscing about better times or the good ole days and ways.

We are more or less on the guard with a new acquaintance, knowing nothing of his background of thought, his mode of life, or his outlook on life. If the acquaintance continues and we come to know the person better gradually we lose all inclination to which his habits and expressions and as real friendship develops we accept the whole of him, the bond often becoming so close that we are thinking and acting alike. This is the development of trust...trust in ourselves and in the other person also.

Here is a recipe you can always trust to be a hit when served.

Honey Crunch Cookies

2 Cups all-purpose flour
2 teaspoons baking powder
1/2 teaspoon salt
1 Cup butter or margarine
1 Cup honey
2 eggs
1 Cup shredded coconut
1 Cup butterscotch chips
4 Cups Rice Krispies

Sift together first three ingredients and set aside. In a large mixing bowl, cream butter. Add honey a little at a time and mix well. Add eggs, beating well. Mixture will appear to separate. Gradually add dry ingredients, mix until moistened. Fold in coconut, chips, and cereal. Drop by teaspoonfuls onto greased cookie sheets. Bake at 350 degrees for about twelve minutes until golden brown. Remove cookies to cooling rack. Yield: about 5 dozen.

Some wise person said, "It's a greater compliment to be trusted than to be loved." He may be right. Think about it!

Chapter 29 — Storms

Are you afraid of storms? Think about it!

There are some people who actually panic at the first sign of a few puffy clouds or hear a report of thunderstorms approaching. I feel really sorry for these people. They probably don't even know why they go into a panic. Perhaps they have been in a terrible destructive storm at some time in their lives. Certainly, in this part of the country, we have all been touched in some way by a storm and had someone we love involved either personally or their property damaged.

But when the radios and televisions tell of pending thunderstorms, that means rain...not necessarily tornadoes.

When I was a kid on the farm, we had what were called "cyclones." I guess they were just small tornadoes. Anyway, when it would be real stormy and strangely calm and the sky looked angry, we would go to the cellar for protection. If it was night time, we would each wrap a blanket around us and go to the cellar. In the cellar where we kept all the canned foods, was also a cot or two, and watermelons, or potatoes, etc. for storage. We simply went to the cellar and continued our sleep on those cots until it all blew over. I remember many times when morning came several of the chicken houses and barns were gone or the roofs were gone. The tree limbs would be everywhere. Barrels and equipment everywhere. Yet I don't remember that we were frightened excessively. Maybe it was because the folks were so calm about it all. If all of us kids had started crying and screaming, they would have had their hands full just transporting us the few steps from the back door to the cellar.

I work with a girl whose husband played a part of an extra in the movie production, "Twister", filmed in Wakita. He said they did the same scene about ten times to make sure they got it correct. It is not that way in real life. We have only one split second to protect ourselves and take cover for ourselves and our families.

We are so fortunate now that there is radio and television coverage to track storms and warn us long in advance of any expected storms of a destructive nature. We can plan what we will do if and when it gets to our area, things like put the cars in the garage, bring in plants, cover plants, get livestock in safe barns, etc. We used to have to rely on our own knowledge of what the sky looked like. Some people can still tell pretty closely by the sky signs and how the air pressure feels around them. Some even say their ears pop or they feel a vacuum. I don't know how to rely on my own instincts so am grateful for weather coverage by the media.

Oklahoma and the midwest was once known as tornado alley but now, it seems, they happen all over the southern part of the nation as well as the eastern and northern portions. It seems no area is completely safe from the ravaging effects of mother nature.

It is best to stay ready so that you can grab the essential things at a moment's notice. Keep flashlight, candle, matches, crackers, a bottle of water and any medications where you can quickly take them with you to the cellar or to an inside, supported area in the center of your house.

When it isn't stormy but just a gentle rain it is fun to bake something like ginger bread to make the house smell wonderful, and enjoy the comfort of your home and listen to the patter of the rain. It can be so relaxing.

Ginger Bread

1/2 Cup soft shortening
2 Tablespoons sugar
one egg
1 Cup dark molasses
1 Cup boiling water
2 1/4 Cups flour
1 teaspoon soda
1/2 teaspoon salt
1 teaspoon ginger
1 teaspoon cinnamon

Mix shortening, sugar, and egg. Blend in molasses and boiling water. Sift dry ingredients and stir into other mixture. Pour into greased and floured 9 inch square pan. Bake 45 to 50 minutes in 325 degree oven. Serve with apple sauce or whipped cream.

In life, as in a storm, watch for those dark clouds, but also look for that silver lining that surrounds them. Think about it!

Chapter 30 — Time

Doesn't time fly? Think about it!

It seems like only yesterday that our granddaughters were babies. Now they are both teenagers. Thank goodness we adults don't age as fast as kids do. All we did was blink and they are grown, or as the song says "Turn around and you're a young girl going out of the door".

What is even worse is that it seems like only last week that I was just a young girl myself. When I go back home, I can sit on Daddy's footstool and talk to him and feel like a little girl again. I can walk where I used to play and remember all the fun times my sister and I had playing. I remember the old songs we sang and the old games and make-believe we played.

It is strange but when we are young we feel that time will never pass and that we will take forever to be 16 and drive, or 18 and an adult. But as we look back it passed so quickly and here we are grown, with children and grandchildren of our own. Boy, where did the time go?

I am a great believer that age doesn't mean much. We are as old or as young as we feel. Some days I feel old and some days I am like a kid. Age has little to do with what we do with our time or how we react to life around us. Some kids never grow up and some people are old even when they are little kids. They never learned how to have fun or be free.

I love to collect old things, old dishes, old quilts, old furniture, old books, old stuff. It takes me back to a happy time in my memory, a happy time at Grandma's house or home where I grew up. I wouldn't go back to those times but they do make sweet memories. Our yesterdays are the memories on which we build our future. Those were the days that molded our lives into what they are today. Those memories shape our tomorrows. Thus our future is not in the hands of fate, but in ourselves.

I love old traditions. I love the stories of our ancestors settling this great land. I love the family customs of Scotland and my heritage. In knowing our past, we can dream of our future.

We can dream of the past or look to the future, but all we really have is today. We can do nothing about our past or our future, but we do control today and what happens with it. We can make sure that we pass today fruitfully, so that we do have pleasant memories of what happened. Today is the tomorrow you worried about yesterday. That worry didn't help a thing, all it did was consume part of yesterday.

Don't hurry through life. Take time to smell the roses, to hear birds, to talk to people you love, to feel the air around you, to see the beauty of nature and the kindness of people. Absorb the moment. Drink it in. Think about what you are doing to start the rest of your life, which begins today.

I can close my eyes and remember the way home was when I was a child. We used to play upstairs at Grandma's house. The upstairs was full of old clothes and stuff that was from my grandma's childhood. We loved that old stuff. It was part of our seeing our grandma as a young child. She may have felt the very same way, watching us.

Times were hard in the early days. No one had any money but we certainly did well with what we had. I remember Grandma making cookies that I thought were wonderful. She called them "Sweet Nut'ens" and that was about all they were...sugar, nuts, and egg white. It was the way she put them together and made cookies, and a memory, for us that was important.

Grandma's Sweet Nut'ens

1 Cup brown sugar
1 Cup ground pecans or peanuts
1 egg white
1/2 teaspoon vanilla
1/4 teaspoon cinnamon

Mix the ground nuts and sugar together in a bowl until they form a smooth paste. Make a well in the center and add the egg white (unbeaten) and vanilla and cinnamon. Using a wooden spoon knead the mixture together until it forms a smooth ball. Use buttered hands, form dough into balls about the size of a large pecan. Flatten onto a well oiled cookie sheet. Bake in a moderate oven, 350 degrees for not more than 12 minutes. Cool. This makes enough for a tea party and many memories.

When saving for old age, be sure to put away a few pleasant thoughts, because time flies. Think about it!

Chapter 31 — V.I.P.'s

Are you a V.I.P.? Think about it!

Either you are a very important person to someone or you have someone who is very important in your life. Ideally, life is like that. However, in this world are sad situations where there are lonely people who really have no one who cares or knows about them. These people need our caring too.

We recently returned from a Command Visit to Jim's old Marine base in San Diego. Here is where he was in boot camp at the Marine Corps Recruit Depot. Here is where he had his first real taste of "family". He was reared by his father who traveled in the oilfields in Oklahoma and Texas after his mother died when Jim was tiny. Times were different then and his father did the best he could to keep him in a school, even though he was in many towns in just one year. But when Jim joined the Marines, he had someone who cared when he was "in", that he ate three square meals a day, instead of just peanut butter sandwiches, and that he was accounted for. The Marines made all the difference in his life.

I was so glad to get to go on this trip with him as it gave me such a good insight into what makes him tick. The Marines was, IS structured and that was good for Jim. He still is structured in his everyday life. In fact he is almost regimented...and he likes it that way.

Because of Jim's involvement in Tarawa, Guadalcanal, and Iwo Jima, Jim was treated like a very important person. The young recruits and officers, including the general, payed him great respect. Just because I had the good fortune to marry Jim, I was treated with the same honors. It was very humbling.

Our flight out to San Diego in a DC9 USMC plane was a great experience. Young Marines were the stewards. I was amazed and pleased at the fine service. They were at our beck and call and tended to our every whim. I was struck by their posture, their demeanor, their appearance, and their courtesy. I knew Jim must have been just like that when he was a young recruit, for him to still be so clean and tidy and courteous, and thoughtful as he is. These traits were instilled in him as they are the new recruits on base.

At graduation on Friday, we saw the finished product of the scared, nervous, unsure recruits as they became Marines. There was such a striking contrast between the graduates and the ones who had just stepped off the bus to begin their new life in the Corps.

I am thankful that Jim became my very important person. I wish everyone in the world were so lucky and fortunate.

In our daily lives, we can make people feel important and necessary by the way we treat them and by how we talk to them. A simple greeting can make a person's day turn brighter. A smile can go a long, long way to make a person's attitude change from gloom to bloom. We can help a very insignificant person feel like a very important person by the simplest remarks and actions.

When you have someone you want to make feel important, serve them Coconut Dream Pie.

1 1/2 Cup milk
3/4 Cup sugar
1 Cup shredded coconut
2 eggs
3 Tablespoons flour
1 teaspoon vanilla
one unbaked pie shell (9 inches)

In large bowl stir all ingredients. Pour into pie shell. Bake at 350 degrees one hour. Cool before serving. Refrigerate leftovers. Serves eight people. We think it tastes better the second or third day.

Treat everyone you meet like a very important person. They are, you know. Think about it!

Chapter 32 — Picnics

Isn't life a picnic? Think about it!

Remember in the "olden days" when a picnic was really a picnic! We spent all morning getting it ready. First we had to dress enough chickens to fry so that everyone had much more than they needed, plus enough to share with anyone who joined our group. Then it was fried crispy in lard, but it had such a great crunch and flavor. Then there was potato salad. It was so freshly made I never remember anyone getting sick from the eggs or mayonnaise. Then there were baked beans, but these were truly baked beans started from dried beans and nothing of the pork 'n bean stuff. Tomatoes were sliced fresh from the garden along with onions that were hanging up to dry in the granary. And then we had homemade bread sliced thick and spread with butter. To top it off there was either watermelon or crank ice cream.

You packed the meal in a big basket or wash tub and went to a cool shade tree and spread out the picnic on the tablecloth spread out on the ground. You didn't spread it out until you were plumb ready to eat because the ants would take over. When you were starved beyond the limit, the picnic was served along with lots of home squeezed lemonade. You filled your plate and either sat around the tablecloth or took your plate elsewhere to eat. Either way it tasted wonderful and was all worth the effort.

Picnics like that are a thing of the past but when the girls were little we went to a little hill near our house and took a simple picnic lunch and felt like we had had an outing. We feasted on a peanut butter sandwich, a cookie, a half a banana and something cool to drink. We blotted our chin with a fancy napkin and went back to the house, refreshed and ready for our afternoon naps. Those picnics were full of memories too.

Now, sometimes we have a grocery store picnic if we go fishing or decide on the spur of the moment to leave the city limits. We stop by the market and buy cold cuts, a loaf of bread, a package of cookies, some fruit and pop, and away we go. Those picnics are fun too.

Come to think of it nearly every kind of a picnic is fun. Only nowadays more cookouts are taking place so there are less real picnics but the feeling is the same. Even though we seldom have a cookout, they can be planned in advance or can happen on the spur of the moment. One sees elaborate tail gate cookouts at ball games that took lots of planning. But a pick-up hamburger tastes pretty good too.

The whole idea is that you eat out and get away from the conventional kitchen and into less formal surroundings where you can relax and enjoy. It is easy to forget the work it took to get things ready and to clean up afterwards. I love picnics, yet I have always wondered why we leave our air-conditioned kitchens to eat with the bugs and in the heat. The answer is simple: It is because of the freedom and the fun and our fascination with the outdoors.

Life is somewhat like a picnic. It can be comfortable, and cordial, and cozy if we make it that by appreciating the simple, rewarding things about our daily lives.

Like a picnic with its ants and flies and bugs, life has its own pests and problems but it is still a wonderful experience and we wouldn't want to miss a thing about it. We'll just arm ourselves with bug spray, sun lotion and have a picnic, just like we protect our lives along the way with proper guards and planning.

Every picnic has deviled eggs on the menu. Here is a hot but good and different recipe that sure adds a spark to picnic fare.

Tex-Mex Deviled Eggs

6 hard cooked eggs
2 slices bacon, cooked real crisp, then crumbled
1/4 Cup picante sauce
1 Tablespoon mayonnaise (or more if necessary)

Cut eggs in halves and remove yolks. Mash yolks and blend in picante sauce, bacon, and mayonnaise. Add salt to taste. Refill whites and garnish as desired.

Now spread an old quilt on the ground, open a basket of goodies and enjoy the outing. Take a deep breath and look at the great outdoors. Ain't life grand? Think about it!

Chapter 33 — Liking Yourself

Do you like yourself? Think about it!

If you don't like yourself, how can you expect others to like you? We are taught to love our neighbors as ourselves but usually we love our neighbors and friends more than we love ourselves. And we are much more forgiving of our neighbors and friends than we are ourselves. We can despise ourselves for some silly thing we've done, like forgetting a name or other minor something, yet when our neighbor does it we simply laugh it off and forget it.

We need to back off and take a hard look at ourselves and learn to love ourselves. If we don't, then we need to take inventory and see why not. What do we wish to change about ourselves? When we were kids we could blame our parents, teachers, friends, and others for the things about us that we didn't like. But now that we are adults, we can no longer pass blame to others. We have to be accountable for our own actions and what we are. If we don't like what we see, then we have the power to change it.

After we have taken a thorough inventory, then we need to work out a plan of action to see what we can do to improve ourselves. Sometimes we discover hidden powers in ourselves that we scarcely expected. We are simply amazed at what the inventory brought forth. We discover strengths and weaknesses we hardly knew we possessed. Then we take those strengths and weaknesses and discoveries and build upon them until we have achieved the kind of person we want to be.

Beyond the inventory and makeover is something we need to consider called acceptance. I'd really like to be tall, and blond and small featured...but that will never happen. You could put me on a rack and stretch me for a year and I'd never be tall and willowy. As the days go by I can see myself becoming more blondish, but gray is more like it. These things I have come to accept. They are really not that important any more. I am more satisfied with the way I am and just thankful that I am not grotesque or crippled. I really have a lot to be grateful for.

In accepting ourselves sometimes we have to be content with small means and think of wealth in other areas. I have many blessings, so many my cup runneth over, but I am not rich in money, just things.

Elegance is more important than luxury, and refinement rather than fashion. And as we were taught at our mother's knee, cleanliness is next to godliness.

We need to act frankly, but speak gently and listen as we go. We need to be more cheerful and more brave and more tolerant and more understanding.

We need to count our blessings and not dwell on the few things we don't possess.

After inventory and planning comes action. Just do something about the things you dislike about yourself. It can be done but only you can do it. Get going! We're not getting any younger. There is no time like the present to mend our ways, and make a newer self.

When I want to reward myself, I make just for me the cookies I call "Three for Me Cookies" as they have peanut butter, oatmeal, and chocolate chips, all of which I love.

Three for Me Cookies

1 Cup butter or margarine
3/4 Cup sugar
3/4 Cup brown sugar
1 teaspoon vanilla
2 eggs
1 Cup Crunchy peanut butter
2 Cups flour
3/4 teaspoon salt
1 teaspoon soda
2 1/2 Cups oatmeal
1 1/2 Cup chocolate chips
3/4 Cup chopped pecans

Cream butter and sugars. Stir in vanilla and eggs and peanut butter and mix well. Sift dry ingredients and stir into creamed mixture. Stir in nuts, oatmeal, and chips. Drop by spoonful onto cookie sheet. Bake at 350 degrees about 12 to 15 minutes until golden brown. Makes about six dozen cookies.

Accentuate the positive, eliminate the negative, latch on to the affirmative about yourself. You're bound to like who you see. Think about it!

Chapter 34 — Games We Play

What kind of games do you play? Think about it!

Remember when we were kids and played all those games like: Blind Man's Bluff, Red Rover, Annie Over, Kick the Can, Follow the Leader, London Bridge, Hide and Seek, King of the Hill, and other active games? And when it rained or was real stormy and we couldn't go outside for recess or noon at school, we played games like: May I?, Red Light/Green Light, Simon Says, and had ciphering matches, spelling matches, etc.

There were also games that were reserved for girls like Jacks, Jump Rope (with hot pepper), and Hop Scotch. The boys honed their skills on marbles, spinning tops, and Mumbletypeg.

Mumbletypeg, which we just called "Mumbly-Peg" was played with pocket knives. All the boys in school carried them, from the oldest in the eighth grade to the kindergartners. All of the ages played together and spiked those knives but not once do I remember that anyone was hurt by one of those knives. And certainly no one would dream of attacking a teacher with a knife over discipline methods or an unwanted assignment. It was simply unheard of in "My" day. It was a great way for the older kids to learn how to care for the younger ones, and for the younger kids to learn to respect and admire the older kids.

We all tried stilts. Now they will teach you coordination if anything will. I believe I could still do it but I might be hesitant, since my bones are more brittle now than they were years ago.

We played softball and some basketball and had playground equipment like: the giant stride, swings, merry-go-round, teeter-totter (I don't recall we ever called it a see-saw), and monkey bars. I have vivid memories of the slipper-slide when I went down it once and failed to stop in time and really had a hard fall. I just skipped like a stone on water. Ask my brother for the details. He was supposed to catch me. He didn't!

From those childhood games we learned fair play, watching out for someone smaller than self, how to share, good sportsmanship, and how to win and lose. We knew what it felt like to be chosen first for some games and last for other games.

Well, we still play games...only now they are a different kind.

In some of our game playing we want to be "It" all the time. This says to the other players, "Look at me. I'm a winner, You're the loser. I will win at any cost and you will lose at any cost." Being "It" satisfies our desire to be recognized and to be dominant over others. Then suddenly the game shifts and someone else becomes "It". Then we have to do the lesser things.

Many activities we do in our daily living are much like the games we played in school. We may swing high or low, fast or slow but just never really go anywhere. We may teeter-totter all day, and remain in balance. We may be on a merry-go-round and spend our days going in circles. In the end all we have accomplished is a lot of exercise. But exercise is fine...it is better than doing nothing.

The name of this pie stirs memories of those wonderful days in that one-room school, and the games we played.

Hop-Scotch Pie

1 Cup butterscotch chips
1/2 Cup brown sugar or honey (I like honey best)
1/4 Cup flour
1 teaspoon cinnamon
3 Cups chopped raw apples (I like Jonathan best) Peeled.

Mix all together and pour into uncooked 9" pie crust. Bake at 350 degrees for 30 to 40 minutes. Remove from oven, sprinkle topping on top, and bake another 15 minutes at 350 degrees. Allow to cool some before cutting.

Topping for Hop-Scotch Pie

1/2 Cup flour
1/4 Cup butter
3/4 Cup chopped pecans
1/4 Cup brown sugar

What games do you play? And whose rules do you play by? Think about it!

Chapter 35 — What We Do and Why

What ya' doing?...why? Think about it!

How many gillion times has some small child asked that very same question? First: "What ya' doing?" and as soon as you give them any kind of answer, their next question is "Why?"

I think they ask two questions that we need to think about and reflect upon. Most of the things we automatically do require very little thought. But still, why are we doing them? Do we have GOOD answers to what we are doing and why?

The story is told of the man who was building a huge building, laying stones. A passerby asked him what he was doing. His answer was that he was building a great cathedral. The passerby asked a co-worker what he was doing and his reply was just putting up stone after stone after stone. It is all in the attitude of what he was doing and why. Do we just muddle through life washing dish after dish, and dusting over and over, and doing laundry and folding clothes by the tons with no real purpose or do we keep in mind the reason behind all the housework is to make a comfortable, happy home for our family?

Some people never get things completed so always feel they are over-worked and overstressed but see nothing accomplished or finished to the end. Too bad, as there is such satisfaction and joy in a job well done and achieved.

Do you complete a list of things to do every day? Maybe you don't actually make a list but at least you surely have a plan of action, something you wish to accomplish. If you don't have a plan or goal, how do you know when you are finished with a job? My mother was a hard worker. She got many things accomplished in her life time, but she always had something else exciting she wanted to do or try just in front of her, like a bunch of carrots in front of a donkey. She felt that we never live long enough to do all the fun things we want to do. She started painting when she was about 65 or 70. She always had an interesting project in the works so she always had something fun to do to spice up her life. She was an interesting, interested person who was never too busy for her friends or family. She always thought of others first.

I have a friend who was planning to entertain her little club at her house. She vacuumed the entire house, under every bed, behind every stick of furniture. When the day of her meeting came, her arms hurt so badly she could not enjoy her friends. And they probably didn't even look behind the piano and under the beds, so how futile were her labors. What a shame that she missed the point of having friends over...to enjoy their company and have made a sweet memory.

Here is a simple dessert that takes little effort but is oh, so rewarding: Pineapple Up-Side Down Cake.

1/4 Cup butter
1/2 Cup brown sugar
one small can crushed pineapple, drained well, save the juice
2 eggs
2/3 Cup sugar
6 tablespoons reserved pineapple juice
1 teaspoon vanilla
1 Cup flour
1/3 teaspoon baking powder
1/4 teaspoon salt

Melt butter in 9" skillet. Sprinkle brown sugar evenly over butter. Arrange pineapple over butter/sugar mixture.

Beat eggs until thick and lemon colored. Add sugar, flavoring, and pineapple juice. Sift dry ingredients together and add to sugar/egg/juice mixture. Pour batter over pineapple/brown sugar mixture in skillet. Bake at 350 degrees 45 minutes. Immediately turn upside down on serving plate. Do not remove skillet for a few minutes. Brown sugar mixture will run down over cake instead of clinging to the pan. Serve warm with plain or whipped cream.

Today is the first day of the rest of your life. Do something useful with it. Think about it!

Chapter 36 — Courage

Do you have courage? Think about it!

The granddaughter of a friend of ours just received the Jim Thorpe Award for Courage for her fight back from a traumatic car accident. That is REAL courage, and I hope we never have to endure what she and her family have gone through and are still going through with this ordeal.

Jim, and others like him, showed real courage in battle. Many illnesses require true courage to withstand. So does the loss of a loved one.

But in a way many of the things we do take a certain amount of courage. Remember your first day of school, the smells, the echoes in the huge halls that seemingly reached to the ends of the earth. And it was that first time away from family and home comforts. Of course you were a little timid and that took courage to stay there and not cry. It also took courage for that parent to leave you there too.

Then you advanced to junior high or middle school. You went from feeling you could conquer the world to feeling very insignificant. You soon learned how to change classes and get from building to building or classroom to classroom without being late, or lost. Then it was a big transfer to high school. It takes courage to be a lowly freshman among all those upper classmen.

The BIG step was when you went away to college. Suddenly all those things you thought you knew needed a little more detail. Things like laundry, cooking, caring for your car, ironing, planning for dates, etc. It takes courage to choose a career and plan the classes toward that life's work you have selected.

When the final alma mater is sung at your college graduation, you had a sudden lump in your throat, knowing that this was the end of a very special era and you would be starting a new job or career and on your own when you walked out that auditorium door. What a feeling of joy overtakes you. You have accomplished what you set out to do...graduate. Now for the part that takes courage,
a new job.

Marriage takes courage. Setting up a new home takes courage. Buying that first house takes courage.

Bringing a beautiful baby into this world takes courage. We pour our life into raising that child and many decisions regarding that young life take courage. To stand up for what you believe and teach it to your child takes a great amount of courage and effort but it is all worth it when that child becomes a useful, participating part of society.

One who's suffered through the severe illness or loss of a loved one certainly knows the meaning of courage. It must be almost unbearable at times. Yet these people carry on and must go on.

We mostly fear the unknown. When we know what we have to do and how to go about it, we step forward with courage and determination.

Don't be afraid to have friends and family over for a meal. If you're new at entertaining, try something very simple like Taco Salad and a special dessert or even ice cream with purchased sauce. The menu is not the most important part, the company is.

Taco Salad

1 pound coarsely ground hamburger (or round steak cut into 3/4" cubes)
one medium head lettuce
1 large tomato
1 medium onion
1 medium green pepper
1 Cup (4 ounces) sharp cheese, shredded or cubed
11 oz. package Fritos Brand corn chips (small)
1 can Ranch Style Beans (drained)
French Dressing or dressing of your choice

Cook hamburger or steak until done and drain on paper towel and cool. Dice onion, pepper, tomato. Break lettuce into bite sizes. When ready to serve, toss all ingredients with salad dressing.

It does take a certain amount and kind of courage to face any changes, but hang in there. What does not destroy us, makes us strong. Think about it!

Chapter 37 — Pretending

Do you pretend? Think about it!

I'll bet you do more than you think you do. We all pretend we are a little prettier, a little braver, a little smarter, than we truly are at times. That's okay. A little pretend is good.

My sister, just eighteen months older than I, used to play house with me for hours, weeks, months...forever. We saved choice tin cans and chipped dishes for our kitchen. We used old wagon seats, orange crates and great boxes for our furniture. We picked wild flowers and put them in jars to decorate our houses. We sneaked things out to enhance our pretend living quarters. We lined our dolls up as our family.

Our favorite playhouses were the wooden granaries when they were emptied of the oats or wheat. The floors were so smooth and they were cozy and smelled wonderful. Another neat spot was under the grove of hackberry trees by the smoke house (called that because that was where we kept the hams, etc.). The dried leaves of the hackberry trees smelled exactly like tea so we made pretend tea. We never had the nerve to taste it, but we served gallons of it to our "guests" at high tea, sipping and chatting away for hours.

Little girls in playhouses aren't the only ones who pretend. Young men do it also when they imagine they are a noted lawman, a brave soldier, or a hero of some sort.

Then we grow up. There is still a limited amount of pretend to what we do. We pretend to be happy when we are sad. We pretend to feel great when we are under the weather. We pretend to be glamorous when any mirror tells us we are not a raving beauty.

It is our attitude that gives us this edge to pretend, and imagine, and dream that things are better than they really are. And isn't it great that we can rise above a situation by imagining things the way we want them to be instead of the way they actually are.

Close your eyes and imagine yourself on a desert island or on a great vacation somewhere, or fishing on the bank of a bass pond or a trout stream in the mountains. You are transcended by your thoughts to a wonderful world of make-believe. And what a wonderful world it can be. We can go where our minds take us at absolutely no expense. It is a free vacation.

Children have an advantage over big people because they are expected to pretend play. Some of us adults have forgotten how much fun it is to pretend and let our minds wander to a far-off place of fun and relaxation. Somewhere along the line we forgot how to have fun pretending.

I can remember Mama baking these brownies and bringing them out to the playhouse warm, using the corner of her apron as a potholder. I hope you enjoy them as much as Marianne and I did (do).

Butterscotch Brownies

1/4 Cup butter or margarine
1 Cup brown sugar (firmly packed)
1 egg, unbeaten
1 teaspoon vanilla
1 Cup sifted all purpose flour
1 teaspoon baking powder
1/4 teaspoon salt
1/2 Cup chopped pecans

Combine butter, sugar, egg, and vanilla in mixing bowl. Beat well until light and fluffy. Stir dry ingredients together and add to egg/sugar mixture. Mix in pecans. Spread in greased 8" square baking pan. Bake at 375 degrees for 25 to 30 minutes, or until done. Let cool in pan and cut into squares while slightly warm.

A child is a bundle of mystery, enchantment, magic, and fantasy all rolled together, in a world of pretend. Be a child again. Pretend. Think about it!

Chapter 38 — Fork in the Road

Have you come to a fork in the road? Think about it!

Whether you are in mid-life crisis, a late bloomer, or just by choice, being at a cross-road, or fork in the road, is a time of decision making. Sometimes we come to that fork in the road through circumstances beyond our control like a car wreck or other accident, illness, the shut-down of a job due to automation or drastic changes in policy, or some other unforeseen happening.

Whatever that reason for change, it is important to weigh all pros and cons and even list if necessary the assets, strengths, positives, as well as weaknesses and limitations. When we really look deep within ourselves, we find talents we have not used for a long time or positive things we had not really recognized.

There are people who have abandoned professional, high paying, jobs to live in the wilderness. They dislike their situation and the rat race, and long for a calmer life with different rewards than only money. These people are doing what they have always wanted to do and going where they have always wanted to go. But they are happy in their choice and wouldn't turn back for anything.

We might not choose to make such a drastic change and life has not forced us to come to a fork in the road if we are lucky. But many of us may want to make some subtle changes in our lifestyle or try something we have never done before. We may want to change careers or enrich our life by adding to what we already do. Many older people have taken up the computer. They are having a ball. My mother started painting when she was almost 70. She had always wanted to try her hand at it and had looked longingly at paintings and thought to herself, "I can do that." Then she got a paint set for a birthday present and the rest is history. She painted every chance she got, which was often.

Many churches offer classes in simple (and not so simple) crafts such as paper capers, cooking, knitting, quilting, painting, trunk refinishing, etc., etc. The list is endless. Just watch for those wonderful classes.

Take up a new sport or activity. Many enjoy golfing, tennis, or simply walking or jogging when they feel the need for a change. These are all good, and they make you feel so great and like you have accomplished something.

Don't be afraid to try new, different things. Age has nothing to do with change, but desire does. Go for it!

When you can't decide what to serve guests or family that will really hit the spot, serve Kahlua Chocolate Cake.

one box German Chocolate cake mix
one box (3.5 oz.) instant chocolate pudding mix
4 eggs
1/2 cup cooking oil
1/2 cup Kahlua
1/2 cup water
1/2 cup finely ground pecans

In large bowl of electric mixer, combine cake mix, pudding mix, eggs, oil, Kahlua and water. Beat on low speed until moistened, then beat at high speed two minutes. Generously grease a Bundt pan or tube pan. Place nuts in the bottom and roll pan around to cover the inside with nuts. Pour batter on top of the nuts and bake 40 to 45 minutes at 350 degrees.

Sauce

1 cup sugar
1/4 cup water
1/4 cup Kahlua
1/2 cup butter

Combine all ingredients in a small saucepan. Bring to boil and boil two minutes. Start timing after it reaches a boil. Pour cooked sauce over cake while it is still in the pan. Let stand 30 minutes before removing from pan. As the cake cools, it will pull away from the sides of the pan, but you'll still need to run a flexible spatula all around the sides before turning it out.

Make the cake 24 to 36 hours before planning to serve it.

If and when you do come to a fork in the road think of it as a new adventure, a challenge, a positive action. Think about it!

Chapter 39 — Rejection

Have you ever felt rejection? Think about it!

"What doesn't destroy us, makes us strong," sounds great but if one has ever felt left out or rejected, it is not easy advice to accept at the time of rejection.

Everyone at some time or other has felt left out of a closed situation when someone whispers in their presence or they feel that plans are being made without them. It can destroy self esteem, even if it is recovered later and overcome quickly. It still is devastating for that brief moment and it hurts.

I am not athletic at all. I can hardly throw a soft ball to my youngest granddaughter. So you know that when I was in school and they chose up sides for a game of ball or something, I was always last to be standing to be selected. In a way I really didn't care, because I didn't care if I played ball or not (I would have much rather been reading or writing) but for a little while I felt that nobody wanted me. It went much deeper than just playing ball. I still hurt for the last person chosen in any situation where "sides" are chosen. No matter who is last, they feel left out and temporarily unwanted.

This is supposed to really build character. It may, in the long run, but for the moment it can destroy a person's good nature and character. Later on down the line, it may create within them an empathy for a person who is left out.

Cliques can be a real hurting thing to a teenager who is omitted from the clique. Someone is always hurt. And the clique doesn't have to act snobbish for someone to feel pain on the inside.

I have always been inspired by my husband's childhood. His mother died when he was only two years old. He was raised by his father who traveled from oilfield to oilfield to make a living. Jim stayed with numerous families who cared for him while his dad was away on a job. Most of these families kept him so short a time he hardly got to know them. Then when he was 16 he joined the Marine Corps, the first taste of "family" he knew. They cared whether he was home at night, or whether he was fed. He never quite understood why all the other young recruits were so homesick. He had spent many nights when he was small, sitting on the front steps of whichever house he happened to be at, crying, wondering if anyone would ever come for him. And many nights he stayed alone, eating peanut butter sandwiches, and going to bed in a house alone, even when he was eight years old. With this tragic childhood, one would think it would have left many deep scars, but he pulled himself up by his bootstrings and made something of himself. I have never heard him complain or blame anyone. It certainly built character within him, and I admire him for what he became in spite of the way he was raised. It certainly gave him an inner strength and appreciation for life that few people possess.

Suffering can produce endurance, that can produce hope, which can make a person courageous and steadfast. It can make their armor thicker somehow. I feel sure that Jim hurt on the inside, but he never showed it. It made him a stronger, better person, and one who has become a peacemaker to others.

This bread is like some rejected people: hard on the outside but soft on the inside.

French Bread

1 package dry yeast
2 1/4 Cups warm water
1/4 Cup shortening, melted
1 Tablespoon salt
1 Tablespoon sugar
7 to 7 1/2 Cups flour

Soften yeast in 1/4 Cup warm water. Put 2 cups warm water in large bowl. Add yeast, shortening, salt, sugar and 1/2 of the flour. Beat well. Add rest of flour and knead smooth and elastic. Put dough in greased bowl, turning greased side up. Cover and let rise in warm place until double. Punch down and let rise again. Turn onto floured board. Divide into 3 parts. Roll into long loaves and put on greased baking sheet. Let rise. Bake 15 minutes at 450 degrees; reduce heat to 350 degrees and bake 20 to 25 minutes more. If top browns too fast, lay a piece of aluminum foil over loaves.

Take care that you don't leave anyone out. That is the worst kind of hurt and abuse. Think about it!

Chapter 40 — Letters

Don't you just love to get letters? Think about it!

Because of this little column I have received some of the nicest letters, correspondence from some wonderful, faithful readers. Some have nice comments and some make suggestions, and some submit recipes. Also I have received phone calls which are also appreciated. All those letters and phone calls are welcomed.

I cannot think of a letter in my life that I received that I wish I hadn't gotten. However, I did not have to register with the Draft Board so I never received a "Greetings" letter during World War II.

Jim volunteered for the Marines so he didn't get one of those letters either. But one he did receive, which we still have, is a letter from a friend that he had in his dungaree jacket when he was shot on Iwo Jima. The bullet went right through that letter and left a hole the size of a nickel. Of course where the bullet came out of him was much larger than that and did a lot of damage to his "innards".

During the war Jim got many letters from his jolly old Scottish grandpa, who encouraged him to "mind his officers and be a good boy". We still have all those letters, along with the others he received while in the Marines.

I have all the letters Jim sent when we were "courting". He kept all of mine. We have letters that Mother received from everyone. Even one from a great-great aunt written during the Civil War about brothers joining opposing sides.

I have all the valentines, Mother's Day cards, birthday cards, and other cards and letters that have ever been sent to me by our granddaughters. What a mess that will be when I die and our daughter has to sort through all the stuff I have saved all these years.

Phone calls are nice and certainly add cheer to a day, but they are not lasting and there is nothing set down for history to see.

Some people are just good letter writers. I have a friend who makes me feel ashamed of the way I write (and don't write) thank you notes and notes of appreciation and love. She has the most beautiful handwriting and ways of expressing herself. It is pure joy to receive her dear letters and I have kept all of them too.

It is really kind of sad that the only time some of us send or receive letters from dear friends is at Christmas. I guess once a year is better than none but we once had to send letters if there was any news exchanged.

Remember the black edged letters of a death in the family or of a friend? There was no way a person could attend the service as the letter usually didn't come until after the funeral. Then condolences were sent.

Remember the letters you received while you were away at college? Mine were so full of news from home and so humorous, that my suite mates loved to read them too and they didn't even know the people involved.

I took the time once to write a letter to my mother telling her how much she meant to me and that I appreciated her giving me life. She kept that letter always. I did the same thing for my Dad, and I understand that it is one of his cherished possessions and he keeps it safely tucked away and reads it ever now and then. You might try it sometime. You'll be glad you did.

In one of the delightful letters I received from a reader was this recipe for Cherry Salad. I call it "Cheery Cherry Salad"

2 cups boiling water
one 3 oz. package cherry Jello©
one 3 oz. package raspberry Jello©
Mix these together until Jello© dissolves. Add:
one can cherry pie filling
one (15 1/4 oz.) can crushed pineapple. Mix and chill.

Write a letter to a friend or relative today. Then watch the mail box for a reply. Then tuck that letter away and read it again later. It will again warm your heart. Think about it!

Chapter 41 — Those Days

Have you ever had "one of those days"? Think about it!

Think about it, but don't dwell on it or you will be crazy worrying about it. Everyone has a story to tell about a disaster that occurred on a wedding day or some special day. After our wedding ceremony, we were stopped by a patrolman for passing in a no-passing zone. We had been following behind an old car that kept signaling to turn but then he didn't. He'd go on to the next corner and again would signal and not turn. Finally Jim saw a chance to pass around him. He pulled out to pass and saw instantly the no-nonsense, flashing light to pull over. We had passed in a marked area of no passing. The officer was very, very kind and as I remember it, didn't even issue us a ticket. When he saw that we had just gotten married (by our flowers, etc.) he congratulated us and ushered us on our journey to our honeymoon site.

Have you ever had your car run out of gas, when you knew the gauge was wrong? Or the car battery was dead and made you late for an important appointment? How many times have you been delayed by a flat tire at the most inconvenient time? Or the spare tire was flat also?

Have you had buttons pop off a shirt when you had absolutely no time to sew it on? Once Jim pulled a tiny thread that was hanging on my hem on the way to church. He raveled out the entire hem in one quick jerk. I had to go back home and change clothes. Have you broken a shoe lace when you needed to be gone thirty minutes ago? And you didn't have a spare, and you couldn't sew it together and the repair knot wouldn't go through those little holes in your shoes?

Surely everyone has had a bad hair day, when it rained on the day of a special occasion and your hair either curled into tight ringlets or went straight as a string from the moisture in the air. How many times have you broken a nail on the way out the door to a special event? You knew everyone was looking at your unkept hands. Or you've lost a heel of your shoe and hobbled along to your destination. How embarrassing!

I can tell you a way to never be lonely. If you want company to come, tie your hair in a scarf and pull everything out of the front closet to clean it. People will come. Or start a messy, dusty, dirty remodeling job and everyone in the world to whom you have ever said "Now when you are in town, drop by and see us. We'd love having you anytime", will come! And probably with a suitcase full of clothes for a week.

How many times have you been met on the way out of your house as friends were coming in? "Won't keep you but a minute", they say, but minutes add up and you are late. And maybe even late to an appointment that you find out is the next day after you have rushed around and cancelled everything to get there and gave your friends the brush-off so you could run in out of breath to a scheduled (you thought) appointment. Aren't these people saints who forgive your stupidity and reschedule you?

When you do have one of those days when everything seems to go wrong, don't despair. That is the time to take out one of your frozen casseroles, dish up some of this slaw, serve ice cream with pineapple sauce for dessert and relax and recover.

Cole Slaw

one head cabbage
2 large carrots
4 small onions
3 green peppers
3 red bell peppers
1/4 cup salt
1 1/4 pint vinegar
2 cups sugar
1 1/2 tablespoon celery seed
1 teaspoon dry mustard

Chop and combine vegetables and cover with salt. Pack in large bowl and let stand at least two hours (or overnight). Drain thoroughly. Dissolve sugar in vinegar and mix in seasonings. Pour over vegetables. Cover and store for up to several months. This is always ready and handy to serve at a moment's notice.

When you do have a day of setbacks, shake it off and remember "This too shall pass". It will. And you ARE normal! Think about it!

Chapter 42 — Empty Nest Syndrome

What do you do for "empty nest syndrome"? Think about it!

Many parents and grandparents and siblings will cry at graduation ceremonies soon. These will be tears of joy and tears marking the end of an era. Things will never be the same again. Our eldest granddaughter, Jamie, will be graduating soon, and will leave a big hole in our lives and in our hearts when she leaves for college. We will rejoice with her that she has reached such a milestone, but at the same time we will miss her daily events.

We give all our energies into preparing our kids for adulthood and then miss them with they fly from the nest. We want them to be free and happy but still miss them a little bit...enough that we will bake their special meals when they do come home and plan to do the things we know they enjoy doing. And when Sunday evening rolls around and they load up clean laundry, etc., there is always a "care package" of favorite cookies and things to send back with them.

We, like most parents and grandparents, are especially proud of our graduate. We are so very pleased with Jamie's accomplishments so far. She has had many honors in basketball, track, chorus, and academics. She is editor of her school year book, and has been chosen her school representative of the principles of Fellowship of Christian Athletes. She was chosen talent winner and Miss Congeniality in her school queen contest this year, as well as being chosen basketball queen. She has been inducted into the National Honor Society.

With all of her accomplishments, she still has time to be a great friend, sister, daughter, and granddaughter. She is so poised and sweet and an achiever in so many areas, that there is absolutely no doubt in my mind that she will succeed in life and be a great contribution to society.

While Jamie, and other graduates like her, are making a wonderful new life in college, meeting new friends, getting adjusted to dorm life, and learning a new way of studying, we have got to go on with our lives here at home. We need to get busy and not dwell on the emptiness of our homes, and the clean, hollow rooms.

We've got to get a new hobby or vocation or avocation. Travel. Volunteer. Try a new schedule. Sleep late or get up real early, whatever is different from your norm. Find SELF again. Give special attention to siblings and families. Time will pass faster and a new beginning is good for us all from time to time.

Look on the bright side. Thank goodness for telephones. And thank goodness for happy memories!

One of the special things that I will cook for Jamie when she is home and has time for a meal, is chicken, rice, and gravy. The chicken is so simple to fix but she especially likes it. Here is the secret of how simple it is: Grandma's Chicken

Allow about 2 chicken breasts for each person. Skin it and remove bones. Sprinkle with seasoned salt and a tiny bit of garlic salt. Allow to sit in refrigerator at least 6 to 8 hours. Heat Dutch oven until it is hot enough to bounce water when dropped on the hot surface. Pour in about 2 tablespoons olive oil. Roll chicken in flour and brown quickly in Dutch oven. When brown on all sides, put lid on Dutch oven, and place in 350 degree oven for about an hour, (or in a 250 degree oven for about two hours if you will be busy or gone).

The rice is simpler yet: For six servings, mix 1 1/2 Cups rice (I use popcorn rice, but any rice will cook the same), 3 Cups boiling water, and 1 1/2 teaspoon salt in covered casserole. Cover tightly and bake at 350 degrees for 30 minutes. Fluff with a spoon to serve. Serve with gravy.

I've made gravy with broth and thickened it and boiled it and seasoned it and worried over it for hours, or you can simply mix a can of cream of chicken soup with a can of chicken broth, add a tad of poultry seasoning, and heat, and it is delicious and much easier.

This with Grandpa's Green beans, and banana pudding, and hot bread and my family thinks I am a great cook. Of course, feeding them when they are real hungry helps too!

Be thankful for the fact that you have a graduate ready for this big, wonderful world of discovery. Count your blessings. Think about it!

Chapter 43 — Halloween

Do you remember the Halloweens of yesteryear? Think about it!

When the frost is on the pumpkin and the fodder's in the shock, the goblins 'll git ya, if ya don't watch out! I remember saying that from "Little Orphan Annie" as a musical reading when I was a little girl. It always reminded me of a Halloween with ghosts and goblins and scary things. We always had our box supper at the one-room school to raise money for Christmas treats and other things for the school and the program always centered around the Halloween theme. That was the highlight of the Halloween season for me.

But living in the country as we did, we didn't trick or treat or do any mischief to celebrate. We heard after the fact, that in "town" there were barrels and trash cans blocking the streets, and outhouses turned over, and windows soaped, and eggs thrown, and even a goat put in the school house one time, but I cannot remember that anyone ever did any destruction of property.

Back in those days, Halloween was a time of fun for the older kids. The younger ones were hardly aware of the holiday, except for a costume party at school maybe, or popcorn balls made at home to recognize the day.

I do remember fondly, the Halloween parties Grandma and Grandpa had. Everyone in the neighborhood was invited...and came. They came in all the funniest costumes. There were absolutely no ghoulish costumes that would have terrified little kids. They were just wonderfully funny original costumes made from whatever we could scratch up. Witches, "pookie ole vitches", as my little niece called them, was the scariest the costumes ever were. Those and ghosts.

My Grandma was a ghost one year. When people arrived at the party, and they approached the door to knock, Grandma came around the house and making an eerie noise, nearly scared the daylights out of us kids. As scared as we were, we KNEW it was Grandma, and we giggled and giggled. What fun!

And we played the traditional games...like bobbing for apples, catching an apple on a hanging string, and all kinds of relays. There was always a "spook house" which was nothing like the ones we see nowadays. Ours was made up of a table with plates holding things like cooked spaghetti, peeled grapes, and harmless things like that for us to identify. Of course, they planted thoughts in our minds that they were worms and cat's eyes, but after a few years, we knew and passed it on to the little kids to scare them. Oh, yes, and remember "Black Magic" the game?

A few years ago, I took our niece, then about ten years old, to a community spook house. The things there were so horrible, with butchering people, blood, bones, screams and terrible things, that we left. I was almost too scared to go through it with her. The things were beyond funny and were just repulsive...just awful!

It is fun to answer the door to the little trick or treaters who hardly know what to say and always have a parent or adult with them at a protective distance. Their costumes are so cute and their actions are so innocent. Later in the evening, comes the older kids who are often rude, and in no costume or in appalling costumes that go beyond the bounds of good taste.

The thing that has almost destroyed the fun of Halloween, is the threat of razor blades or dope in the treats that are given to those little kids. How can those "givers" live with themselves?

To sweeten up the fun of Halloween, make Caramel Apples.

Wash, dry, and chill eight or ten medium sized apples. Insert a heavy wooden skewer into stem end.

Mix together in deep 2 quart saucepan:
2 Cups sugar
1 Cup brown sugar
2/3 Cup white corn syrup
2/3 Cup butter
1 Cup cream
1 teaspoon salt
2 teaspoons vanilla

Cook to 246 degrees (or when a little dropped in cold water forms a firm ball)...stirring constantly toward the end of cooking period to prevent scorching. Remove from heat and cool until mixture thickens slightly. Quickly dip each apple into the caramel mixture and twist until evenly and completely covered. Drain on waxed paper.

Have a safe and fun Halloween, or the "goblins 'll git ya, if ya don't watch out!" Think about it!

Chapter 44 — Health

Are you safe-guarding your health? Think about it!

Our bodies are the most delicate and marvelous instruments in the universe. We are long past the stage when the human body is neglected or starved or punished. We are taught to think of the body as fine tuned and nourished properly. Preserving health, or regaining it if it has been impaired, is not only a personal but a social obligation. There is a close relationship between mind and body.

Many of us know from experience that fear, worry, and excitement disturb the digestive system and prevent it from functioning normally. If we are teased or embarrassed, we blush. No one has to touch the body; seemingly it is not involved, yet there is a definite reaction. Every time we are cross or impatient, or think our friends have turned against us, or feel that there is nothing good in the world, if we will take an inventory of our physical condition, we will usually discover that some organ of our body is not functioning properly. Since the state of our health does affect our dispositions so definitely, shouldn't we take good care of our bodies and health?

We put our fur coats in cold storage, we put our pictures behind glass or in acid proof cardboard, we guard the temperature and humidity of our pianos, and we hire men to care for our cars. But some of us poison our bodies by consuming harmful substances, or not getting proper rest, or neglecting to exercise, and then when our health is ruined we seem so surprised that this illness hit us.

There are many, many articles and books written about diet and exercise that are easily available. But reading about them won't help unless we do something about what we read. It always feels so very good to exercise and watch what we eat and it feels so great to be in control of our own bodies. It is just the idea of getting started with an exercise regimen and special, proper eating habit that is difficult. Getting going is the hardest part.

Then there is the motivation factor to consider. What can you do to help yourself stay motivated and in control of this exercise, proper eating, proper care routine? It seems like the best motivator is to keep it fun and enjoyable. Or find a partner that has the same goals and attitude you have. Husbands and wives who feel the same way about the proper care of their bodies always seem to encourage each other and not undermine what their partner is trying to achieve.

Have a goal. If you don't have some kind of goal, how do you know when you have reached it? Then reward yourself with something special, a trip, a new outfit, or a special present just for yourself.

The bottom line is your attitude toward yourself and how you wish to maintain your health. It is a lifelong practice to keep yourself in good running order, physically and mentally. It doesn't just happen overnight. You will be rewarded with a constant size, increased stamina, stress relief, and muscle tone...and you will feel good.

Plan ahead what you will eat and when. Make time for exercise and activity. Know what you want and where you are going. When you have one of those times when you MUST have dessert, then do it...but make sure it is something that is good for you and good too.

Dreamy, Creamy Fruit Salad

1 large Delicious apple, cored and diced (about 1 1/2 cups)
1 medium banana, sliced (about 1 cup)
1 seedless orange, peeled and cut into sections (about 1 cup) save juice
1/2 Cup green seedless grapes
one eight ounce container low-fat strawberry yogurt (or flavor or your choice)

Combine apple, banana, orange sections and grapes in medium-sized bowl. Toss well with reserved orange juice and yogurt. This is good with pineapple chunks, kiwi, or other fruits added also.

Take good care of yourself, mentally and physically. You're all you've got! Think about it!

Chapter 45 — Shyness

Are you shy? Think about it!

We are more reserved about some things than others, but as a whole, are you bashful and timid about speaking up about something or are you just timid about speaking and making the first move?

Jamie just went for her freshman year at college. We had a lovely long talk before she left and she expressed concern that she wouldn't know anyone there. I told her that everyone there was in the very same boat and that not knowing anyone was no excuse to be lonely. "Go knock on a door, and introduce yourself to that person in your dorm and first thing you know, you'll know everyone" was what I advised her. On her first weekend home, she announced that she knew every girl in her dorm. I knew she would. She is genuine, and sweet and friendly. Simply making the first step got her over her shyness.

I had almost forgotten the little poem she wrote and illustrated for her grandpa, with a picture of a clown, when she was about four or five years old. It said something about, "Don't be shy. Say 'Hi,' and give a smile." She has always been somewhat that way and it is good advice. It works. It gets one over the reserved feeling around other people.

Now I am sympathetic with the fact that we can't all by dynamic, forceful conversationalists but we can look for a person standing alone, on the outside circle, at a party or event, and go to that person and at least acknowledge their presence. Nine chances out of ten that person is a great conversationalist and has a great deal to say once you get him primed. Both of you will feel better and who knows, you may have a nice new friend. There is no need to barge into a group of laughing, talking people to find someone to talk to. That group is doing just fine. It is the person on the outskirts who is a bit shy and needs drawing out. That is the road to being truly popular.

And furthermore, just because someone is mild mannered and quiet does not mean they are necessarily shy. SOMEONE has to be the one to listen in a two-way conversation. My mother always felt she was too shy, yet others said she was wonderful to visit with. This was because she was such a good listener. She knew a little about a lot of things and asked intelligent questions that helped her learn more about a topic and also drew out the person doing the talking. She was well versed on everything from football to classical music and drama. She was truly interested and consequently interesting.

I've learned so much from my readers about recipes and things. You who read this column share so many interesting things about yourselves and the things you cook for your families. I am very grateful. I am thankful you are not shy about sharing these things with me. One of these treasures is Pumpkin Cookies.

1/2 Cup shortening
1/2 Cup sugar
1/2 Cup molasses
1 egg
1 Cup canned pumpkin
2 1/2 Cups flour
1/2 teaspoon salt
1/2 teaspoon baking soda
1 teaspoon baking powder
2 Tablespoons pumpkin pie spice
1/2 teaspoon cinnamon
1/4 teaspoon ginger
1/2 Cup chopped golden raisins
1/2 Cup chopped pecans.

In large bowl, cream shortening with sugar. Add molasses, egg, and pumpkin. Blend well. Set aside.

In separate bowl, combine flour with remaining ingredients, and mix well. Gradually add to shortening mixture, stirring well after each addition. Chill. Drop by heaping teaspoonfuls on ungreased baking sheet. Bake in 350 degree oven about ten minutes. Makes 4 dozen.

Whether you are shy, cautious, demure, fearful, modest, reserved, retiring, shrinking, wary, or whatever...there are people out there just like you who are aching to visit. So speak up. Think about it!

Chapter 46 — Change

How do you react to change? Think about it!

Do you sit at the same place at the table for each meal? Or have a chair that is "your chair" and no one else dares sit in it? Does everything have to be in exactly the same place in your kitchen? Or in any room in your house? Do you move furniture around or are you content with where it is now? Do you like the things you have purchased long ago or do you get rid of everything and start over ever so often just because?

Have you said to yourself and others that you would never be caught dead in a certain attire, long or short, or something else, and then several months later you finally broke over and became one of the stylish few who wear it?

All of us have been guilty from time to time of liking things better the way they are. "Because we have always done it that way," but we really don't know why we have always done it that way. There MAY be a better way to do things if we will just look. Change, just for the sake of change is not necessarily progress. If it works, don't fix it. But sometimes there is a better, more efficient, economical way to do things. Think about it and adapt, adjust and redo. It's okay to change. And compromise is good too, so long as we do not compromise our basic beliefs and morals of right and wrong.

It is difficult to make changes in a lifelong way of living and eating. By self-searching we discover the adjustments that must be made in our lives. There are three possible attitudes that we may take after such a discovery. We may proceed to convince ourselves that our present plan of life is good enough, or we may satisfy our conscience by postponing the time for beginning our own remaking to some convenient season, or we may begin at once the serious business of bringing our own lives to conform to what we have discovered to be necessary for our new plan. There is a real joy and challenge in mastering the decision to begin now if we must, then stay motivated to continue with that chosen change in our life. Nobody ever said it was easy.

Change has to happen for growth to take place. Look at the bulbs you plant. They must change to become beautiful tulips. Those caterpillars have to change to become floating butterflies. Those blossoms must change before they become fruits that we eat. We must change before we can grow and mature and learn new things. This change sometimes is difficult because we like the status quo. We know we must, but it is not fun to change what we have always done in the way we have done it.

Change can be abrupt or gradual, like aging. It can slip up on us like the age of 30, or 40, or 50, or 60, or more. All of a sudden we awake to realize we are older and have changed. I have never quite understood why some people are so hung up on age, that they dread their thirtieth or other birthday milestones, as each age has its own rewards and bonuses. As one era ends another great one starts with new experiences and advantages and joys. Each age takes adjustment but each is a new glorious phase of life.

I've come a long way, Baby. I think it is great that the young cooks today are using mixes and frozen things and quick fixes. I even do that myself and it sure speeds up a meal. With so many people working and usually in a hurry, those helps are a great advantage. I am all for them. This recipe uses the stove top stuffing, canned soup, even canned broth and canned chicken if you don't have the time to boil and debone the chicken yourself.

Chicken/Stuffing Casserole

2 large chicken breasts (or use a can of white chicken, drained)
one package stuffing
1/4 Cup melted butter
one can cream of chicken soup
2/3 Cup evaporated milk
1/2 Cup chicken broth (reserved from the can of chicken or homemade)

Combine stuffing and butter. Press about 2/3 of this mixture in 9" X 9" baking dish. Spread cooked, boned, flaked chicken over stuffing mixture. Combine soup, broth, stuffing seasoning, and milk in a pan and heat to almost boiling. Pour over chicken. Top with remaining stuffing. Bake in 350 degree oven about 20 minutes. Cool a little before serving. Good using leftover chicken or turkey.

May the spirit of adventure keep you from fearing unexplored fields. Change when necessary. Think about it!

Chapter 47 — Victory

What is your greatest victory? Think about it!

Any victory requires a certain amount of struggle and usually a battle within your life. Victory requires bravery and a pioneering of unknown areas. It requires creative thinking and fortitude. No battle worth winning comes easy, without a certain amount of strife and growth.

For some the victory may be over their fears. Those fears may be real or imaginary. They can be as simple as stage fright when giving your first recital as a child to fear of failure when an adult. Fear can be of the dark, and what is in the dark. Or it can of the light and what that light reveals. Fears vary greatly and what is fearful to one is nothing to the next person.

Feeling of inadequacy or lack of self-esteem requires constant battling to achieve a victory. Education, training, time, looking around you for acceptance by someone you love, and looking within you for reassurance can lead to victory over inferior feelings.

Weight is a large area that requires a victory for some of us, whether it is too much weight or too little. It is a constant battle and one that we must fight all of our lives. It is very difficult to change a way we were raised with butter, cream, and sweets at the end of every meal and as a treat in between. I am relatively sure that it is difficult to be victor over eating problems or being too thin also. Both involve more than the appetite; they involve mind play and are difficult to overcome.

For some of us the simple task of driving on ice and getting to work is quite an accomplishment and we feel we have really won a victory over the elements when we have arrived safely.

Studies in experiments tell us that struggle, whether it is issued in happiness or suffering, in joy or pain, in success or failure, is essential to life, and cannot be shirked save at the expense of harmony of being, the winning of character, and any hope of attainment of cherished goals. Granting all the instances of failure, acknowledging all the chances of defeat, still the only possible pathway to peace leads that way. It is vastly better to strive and be baffled and beaten than to yield without effort. There is something noble in the overthrow of a hero who fights to the end, but only shame in the cowardice of the craven who runs away. The struggle itself is a kind of victory, no matter what the issue.

Many have been victorious over cooking for company. Start out simple. End with dessert that is easy but delicious, like Apple-Cherry Pandowdy.

4 Cups sliced, peeled cooking apples
1 1/2 cups fresh or frozen unsweetened pitted tart red cherries
3/4 cups sugar
3 Tablespoons flour
1/4 teaspoon nutmeg
1/4 teaspoon cinnamon
dash ground cloves
1 cup flour
1/4 teaspoon salt
1/4 Cup butter
1 egg yolk
2 tablespoons cold water

Combine apples, cherries, sugar, the 3 tablespoons flour, and spices and pour into 10" X 6" X 2" baking dish. For crust, in another mixing bowl, combine the 1 cup flour, salt, and cut in the butter until mixture resembles coarse crumbs. Beat in egg yolk and water. Stir, using a fork, until dough forms a ball. Roll dough into a 12" X 8" rectangle on floured surface. Place atop the fruit filling in baking dish. Fold under the edge to fit dish. Crimp to sides of dish. Cut a 3" slit in the crust to allow steam to escape. Bake in a 350 degree oven for 40 to 45 minutes until golden brown. (Better put a larger baking pan under it as it bakes, because sometimes it boils over in the oven.) To "dowdy" the crust, use a sharp knife to cut a lattice pattern in the crust. Cool or serve warm with ice cream or half and half poured over it.

May we glory and grow in our struggles and in our victories. Think about it!

Chapter 48 — Shortcuts

Do you take shortcuts? Think about it!

We do. Only sometimes we take a shortcut in the car and it ends up being not so short a cut. We then call it the "scenic route" or the "journey of discovery." Sometimes that route ends up in a detour or a road under construction or much worse roads. Those shortcuts in miles don't always save time. Usually they take more time. But at least it is something different and occasionally we will see something so interesting we are glad we took the different route.

Something I do often is write a quick note to myself about something to think about later or do later, and when I read, or try to read, the note later when it has gotten cold, I am unable to decipher what on earth I wrote. That note was a quick shortcut, but in the end it took longer to figure out.

Every time I quickly clean house because someone is coming over and dust with a feather duster rather than do it right, the first thing a guest will do is pick up a trinket to admire it and see the dust under it. The rule at our house is, "If you pick it up, put it back exactly where you got it." Otherwise people will know what dust lurks under it. There are no shortcuts to keeping house that won't be found out sometime, whether it is cleaning drawers, closets, or surface cleaning. If there is, I wish someone would tell me their secret.

When we were twelve or thirteen years old we wanted to take a shortcut to being sixteen so we could drive, or to being eighteen so we were considered adult. Then that special birthday finally came. The rest of the years go by so fast. We are sorry we wanted it to rush by. I never wish for a later time. Mother always said, "That is wishing your life away" to want the years to be here sooner, or even a weekend to come sooner. Time will pass at its own speed. If you really want time to stand still have something real exciting planned. If you want it to speed up, have a dreaded appointment facing you.

Some of the things that sure are nice to use shortcuts on are the recipes using cake mixes, ready-made pie crusts, or frozen foods that are already prepared. I have never used sauce mixes or gravy mixes but I am sure they are nice for those who are not sure how to make them, or if one is in a hurry. I think they have simplified a lot of cooking that used to frighten new cooks. They are so handy. Here is a great recipe using cake mix. We like it almost as much as pumpkin pie and I didn't think Jim would ever like anything that much.

Pumpkin Dessert (Pie/Cake)

2 eggs
3/4 Cup sugar
1 small can pumpkin (16 ounces)
1 Tablespoon pumpkin pie spice
1 teaspoon vanilla
1 Cup milk

Mix all together and pour in 9 X 13 inch baking dish. Top with 1 box yellow cake mix. Melt one stick butter and pour over top of cake mix. Bake in 350 degree oven about 50 minutes until golden brown on top. Serve with Cool Whip.

You cannot always take a shortcut. Sometimes it is not even wise to try. If you want to be happy, here is the way: Don't live tomorrow, until you've lived today. Think about it!

Chapter 49 — Making Decisions

Do you make wise decisions? Think about it!

Do you make an effort to study problems through for yourself and arrive at your own conclusions? Do you study things from all angles? Is you influence reliable, or are your decisions hasty and one-sided?

When we have to make a decision, it is so easy to spend too much time projecting what the outcome of that decision will be. We also sometimes fall into the trap of making a snap decision without thinking of all the pros and cons. Decision making is not always easy, and of course hindsight is always easier than foresight. We can look back with regrets or we can make the most of the decision we made and go on with our lives.

We have all made bad decisions at some time in our life or used poor judgement, but we probably did the best we could at the time, and thought it was the right decision.

We might have been so created that we had to react to every stimulus in a definite set way, involving no act of choice. We might even have been so created that our reactions always had to be good. But what a meaningless, insipid goodness it would have been! No stamp of divinity would dignify that sort of goodness.

People face their responsibilities by making decisions in different ways according to their temperament. Some are like jellyfish with no backbone, who go with the tide. How little respect we have for the human jellyfish.

Others feel keenly the need for making choices, but are in a perpetual state of indecision. Some of the most unhappy people are those who have the type of mind that always regrets the decisions of the day before.

The amount of time and energy necessary to make the endless choices that face us every hour of the day may be greatly reduced if we have a clear and definite life purpose, with every act in harmony with this goal.

In other words, have you made a good choice in your life work? There are people who have made career changes in their life when they were forty or fifty years old. And they are usually very happy people. You have heard of people who left the clang and noise and rat race of the big cities and moved to the country to do a completely different job, and they are happy because it is their choice and something they have always wanted to do.

Do you feel hampered or handicapped in any way? Is it something you can change? If it is, then do it! If it isn't, then better not look back and learn to enjoy where you are and what you are doing.

Better ask yourself, is it my work or my attitude toward work that I regret? Make sure we are not just seeing greener pastures on the other side of the fence.

And are we selfish or unselfish in our choices every day? Are we just thinking of ourselves or thinking of others. We are the ones who must take responsibility of making choices that control our whole lives. It takes wisdom and strength to make wise decisions.

When you are faced with the decision of what side dish to serve with your meat for dinner, consider this easy, delicious casserole that is special in our family:

Jamie's Corn

Three (16 ounce) cans whole kernel corn
8 ounce package cream cheese
1/2 Cup milk
4 ounce can diced green chiles
1 teaspoon salt

Melt cream cheese with milk, stirring occasionally. Add salt, corn that has been drained, and green chilies. Pour in buttered casserole and bake for 30 minutes, uncovered, in 350 degree oven. What could be simpler or better?

Making a small mistake in judgement is much like making a "home run." In six months or less almost everyone has forgotten it but you. Think about it!

Chapter 50 — Counselor/Friend

Do you have a reliable counselor friend? Think about it!

It is good that we have at least one friend that will tell us what we should hear instead of what we want to hear. It is much easier and more popular to agree with us all the time than it is to be honest and tell us the truth about ourselves. Although we are not wanting to hear it, it is best in the long run that a true friend tells the truth. Haven't you had some people tell you that a certain dress looks just darling on us, when we really know it doesn't, especially when we get home and try it on again in front of our own mirror. The truth hurts but it also helps when it comes from a trusted friend.

And a true friend listens to what you are saying with your heart and not just what you are saying with the lips. They feel what we are feeling and know our true emotions.

A true friend holds us accountable for change. If we say we are going to do something or not do something, they will gently remind us of our promise to ourselves. They will bring out the best of us by making us mindful of ourselves. They will help us grow by not letting us stunt our growth.

A true friend is a real support system when we are sick or grieving or hurting. They will listen, and keep us busy when we need to or make us rest when they see the need. They will take us out in the public when they know we should go and keep us home when they know it is best. In other words, a true friend and reliable counselor will know us better than we know ourselves. In the long run they are almost always right.

A true friend is not judgemental. They will not demand to know every detail of our secrets but will let us tell our problems as they develop and not pry. They will accept our telling them only when we are ready and will not ask questions but will respect our privacy and confidentiality.

Years ago I gave a little poem to a friend and had completely forgotten about it until a few weeks ago when she reminded me that after all these years she still has it hanging in her utility room. I asked her to send me a copy of it which she did. It is entitled "Friendship", and was written by Dinah Mulock Craik.

"Oh, the comfort...the inexpressible comfort of feeling safe with a person.
Having neither to weigh thoughts, nor measure words...but pouring them all right out...just as they are...chaff and grain together

Certain that a faithful hand will take and sift them...keep what is worth
  keeping.
And with a breath of kindness blow the rest away."

It is such a comfort and pleasure to have a friend like that who is
trustworthy and loving in everything. Wouldn't it be a wonderful world if
everyone were like that?

One way to cement a good friendship is to serve them your favorite
cookies and a good cup of coffee. And then talk, sharing the good things of
your life, along with the bad things and the thoughts closest to your heart. Mix
up that batch of cookies and get on the phone to extend that invitation.

Oatmeal Crisps

1 Cup shortening (I prefer butter)
1 Cup sugar
1 egg
1/2 Cup sour cream
1 teaspoon soda
1/2 teaspoon baking powder
2 3/4 Cup flour
3 cups quick oatmeal

Cream shortening and sugar. Add egg, cream and mixed dry ingredients.
Roll thin and cut in desired shapes. Bake at 350 degrees about 10 to 12
minutes.

To have a trusted friend, you must be a trusted friend. Think about it!

Chapter 51 — Home for Christmas

Do you go home for Christmas? Think about it!

I am so fortunate to still have my father living. This makes going to our home in Pawnee County, where I grew up, a real joy. We eat and tramp in the woods and gather firewood or just mostly tramp and enjoy the outdoors. Or we just sit in the kitchen and talk and laugh and remember the fun times of years past. Every year we discuss that it would be much easier to have our celebration in one of our homes where we can still find things, but every year we just talk about it and continue to go HOME, where Daddy is. He seems to enjoy us so much, seeing all the grandkids and great-grandkids and great-great-grandkids. He may cat-nap through part of the afternoon but he still is part of the fun and festivities.

I know the day will come when going home will not have that same kind of meaning, because time takes care of that, but for the time being, we will make our way over the river and through the woods.

But in a sense, even if physically we cannot go home, we still do in spirit by the traditions we observe. Every family has special things that have very special meanings attached. Sometimes it is the selection of a tree, the trimming of that tree, or the special things we hang on it. I have wonderful old decorations that the granddaughters have colored and cut out. They look like gobs of waste paper to others but to me they are like the most fancy cut glass ornaments. They are hung with paper clips. Our angel that adorns the tree top is made out of a cookie cutter. We just love her as she looks over our Christmas celebration.

Food is another area of definite likes and dislikes at Christmas. I have my grandma's recipe for Christmas goose and how to prepare it. First you've got to have a goose to fix, which is no easy task in this day and age. Then the recipe says to remove the feathers and down carefully, and then wash the goose in soap and water. I guess this is to remove part of the grease, and as a goose is greasy, in my opinion. Have you ever baked a goose? It seems dark and dry to me, but maybe I just don't know how to prepare it. Anyway, years ago, we dispensed with that tradition and went to turkey which is easy to obtain and real easy to prepare and the leftovers are as good as the turkey itself. We have a definite way we like the dressing. I make it every year, I guess because my dressing tastes like Mother's did.

With the turkey, we have mincemeat pie, pumpkin pie, cured ham, fruit cakes, cookies, and whatever we all bring in for lunch. We have no set rule of who brings what but it always goes together perfectly.

We do not give large gifts to each other, but some little remembrances. Santa still comes for the little kids and those gifts along with all the exchange gifts are distributed after we have a huge breakfast. Then the men go to feed cattle and we clear the table and start getting lunch on. This takes hours and is fun because we visit and laugh while we are each trying to be the bossy one and give advice on how to season something. It is just a lot of fun!

Our gift giving is simple but we do give from the heart. We try to find something especially meaningful for our brothers and sisters. They are always delighted with whatever they get. Size isn't important.

I am sure that your traditions are equally important to you. By all means, ours are not earth shattering. They are just a joy to us all, as I am sure yours are to you and your families. It seems real important to me to keep these old family traditions alive as this is how we "go home" for Christmas when the way is too far to travel to that destination. The main thing is that we need to keep the joy of the season and the real meaning of Christmas in our hearts. There is something about the childlike expectations of us all at this special time of year. We are more tolerant and giving, and understanding of those less fortunate.

Here is a simple dessert that a six year old child can make, yet it is so good and tastes so fitting for the Christmas season.

Fig Cookie Dessert

Cut up 16 fig newtons
Add three handfuls small marshmallows
1 Cup crushed pineapple (drained)
1 Cup Cool whip (or more if desired)
1/2 Cup chopped pecans

Mix all together and put in pretty bowl. Chill until ready to serve. What could be easier?

When you go home for the holidays, remember it is the joy of the journey, whether it is on the road, or a trip backwards in time, that makes HOME so special. Think about it!

Chapter 52 — Favorite Time of Life

When is your favorite time of life? Think about it!

So many people are devastated when they reach 30 years of age, or The big four-o, or even fifty. Maybe they don't have very interesting lives...or maybe their life is so interesting they want time to stand still. Whatever the reason, I have never quite understood their hang-up on age. What is wrong with the age, whatever it is, that we are right now?

Each year has a special fascination. I remember when the granddaughters were tiny and just laid in their cribs and smiled. I thought to myself, "I must savor this moment, because this is the best time of our lives with them." Then when they were two years old, I knew it was the "terrific twos" that were the best. No, it must be when they reached five years old and started to kindergarten, and began to read and be spellbound by numbers and words. Well, I was wrong again. Now they are both teenagers, and now is the best time. We have such lovely, close visits and can discuss so many things that we could not talk about when they were just little. We can chat for hours about basketball, cheer leading, college classes, jobs, boys, and things, and never run out of anything to converse about.

My father just celebrated his ninety-fourth birthday. We went over to see him at Pawnee and took lunch. He thoroughly enjoyed the food and the company. We could sit for hours and listen to his wonderful stories. He is so sharp, and has such a good memory and has been interested in so many things all his life, that he is a great conversationalist. He is interested in things of our lives, and is also interesting. He has seen so much history come and go.

Daddy can remember when he was one of the first to even own an automobile. Even I can remember when we used a wagon and team of horses to go places except on Sunday to church, or to town on Saturday to take cream and eggs. Otherwise it was covered and kept in a garage. We didn't just use it to run insignificant errands.

When I was small we would run outside and look up when an airplane would fly over. Usually the pilot would wave to us as the train engineers do now to thrill kids that wave to them. But today is interesting because we can travel by plane and be at our destination in the time it used to take us to drive to our neighbor's in the wagon with the team. I guess I've seen a lot of history too.

The era of computers is here. It was a big thing when I was in school to just take typing, and Daddy used a slate or a Big Chief tablet and did not waste any of the paper, front or back. Boy, we've come a long way.

Recipes can take us back to our youth. Remember those wonderful cookies and hot breads, pies and cakes, and butter and cream. I can remember few casseroles. We usually had meat and potatoes at all meals in some fashion. We ate lots of gravies made with whole milk...everything was made with whole milk or thick cream. The skim milk was for animal feed. We also had lots of home canned fruits and vegetables or fresh from the garden on the farm. We also had lots of dried fruits, raisins in particular, which made the best cake:

Raisin Cake

2/3 Cup shortening
2 Cups sugar
2 Cups water
2 Cups raisins
1 teaspoon each nutmeg, cloves, cinnamon, allspice and ginger
2 teaspoons soda
4 cups flour
2 teaspoons baking powder
2 cups chopped pecans

In saucepan combine shortening, sugar, water, raisins, and spices. Boil for three minutes, stirring occasionally. Remove from heat and add soda, mixing well. Cool completely.

In a large bowl combine flour and baking powder, mixing well. Add the cooled mixture and mix until flour is well blended. Stir in nuts. Bake in 9" X 13" greased and floured pan, about 40 minutes, in 350 degree oven. Cool and frost with light powdered sugar or cream cheese frosting.

The forties are old age of youth: the fifties are youth of old age. Think about it!

Chapter 53 — Disappointments

Do you let disappointments throw you? Think about it!

There are times when we have our hearts set on doing something or having something and things don't materialize just as we have planned. We are then disappointed, sometimes crushed. But the way we react to that disappointment can make all the difference in the world.

There are two ways of reacting to disappointment. We can accept it or not accept it. If we accept it and look for an alternative we are much happier. If we can not accept things, we make ourselves and those around us miserable.

When we had planned our trip to California, our plane was delayed a little at a time until it amounted to an entire day. We had to stay overnight to catch the next plane out. We made the most of our delay and had a lovely evening eating out and staying in a motel. The next day everything went as planned and we had a great trip.

Had we stomped and ranted and raved, things would have not changed at all, except we would have all been distressed and lost an entire evening being mad.

There is seldom anything we can do about changed plans, BUT we can change the way we react to changed plans. We can go with the alternative plan and make the most of a situation.

Somewhere in the back of my mind is a little poem I learned when I was in grade school about disappointment and how we withstand change and frustrations. I think it was by John Oxin...something. The poem went something like this...

> "The storm that tries the growing tree
> Does yet its life prolong.
> For all that fierce oppugnancy
> Roots it more deep and strong.
>
> So trials are sent to you and me
> That shall increase our strength,
> And if we bear them manfully
> We shall win through at length."

We need to occasionally face hardships and trials and disappointments and suffering that will give strength and vigor to our character. We know that most setbacks work out to the good, if we have the capacity to meet them bravely and positively. Dale Carnegie said, "When you get a lemon, make lemonade."

One of the positive things that transpired during our plane's delay was that we met and got acquainted with a lovely couple and in our conversation exchanged recipes (as I usually do). B.J. was telling about an unusual salad recipe they had tasted that they really liked. It called for dried cranberries and Champagne Dressing. I was not familiar with either so she told me where it could be purchased. Well, the next morning when we were ready to board our plane, here she came with a bag of dried cranberries and a bottle of the Champagne Dressing.

After we got back from our vacation I tried the salad and B.J. was right, it is great. I call it B.J.'s Salad.

B.J.'s salad

Lettuce or other greens, torn into bite size pieces
sliced red onion
1/2 Cup dried cranberries
Chunked apples
Walnuts

Mix as much as you will want in the proportions that your family will enjoy. Toss with Champagne Dressing. This dressing is available in local stores. The salad is so simple but so very good and different. I can make a meal of it.

Before you get all bent out of shape by disappointment, try to look at a positive side to the change in plan. Lots of lives have been saved by just such a change. And many good things come from bad situations. Think about it!

Chapter 54 — Judging People

Do you judge people? Think about it!

Wouldn't it be a wonderful world if everyone were perfect just like we are, with no faults, or shortcomings? Sometimes we leave the impression that we think if things aren't done MY way then something is wrong with that person. Well, we should not be so hasty to judge. Thank heavens all people are different. Wouldn't it be a dreary old world if everyone were the same? We'd get so sick of the sameness.

Even though we truly know that we want everyone to be an individual and not exactly like someone else, we still have a tendency to judge people by what they say or do and sometimes even condemn them for it. Everyone has hidden things we cannot see. In every seed is a flower. In every cocoon is a butterfly. We have to wait sometimes to see the finished product. We must like a person for what we can see and then give him the benefit of the doubt.

No one is all good or all bad. Even a criminal must have some redeeming qualities. Just ask his mother. And every person has some imperfections. We know few saints or few people who are rotten to the core.

There is an old saying about not judging a person until you have walked a mile in their moccasins. I am sure if we truly walked in their paths in their shoes with the same set of circumstances, we would feel differently about how we feel about that particular person. And I'd bet we would have a new empathy of their feelings and actions.

Do you judge people by their family? Every family has a few skeletons in their closets. Most of us keep them safely hidden. But even if those skeletons escape and get into the outside world, we should not judge the person too harshly. He/she cannot help what that family member has done. All he/she can be responsible for is himself. We can't even control what our own spouse or children do. It may break our hearts if they don't respect the laws of society but we still have little control over what they actually do.

It is mighty easy to just "write people off" if they clearly do something we disapprove of or if there is some hidden, or not so hidden, something that we disagree with, and it is easy to say, "A leopard cannot change his spots". At least give that person the benefit of the doubt. Maybe they are really trying hard to mend their ways...to change their spots.

Who would have ever guessed that those raw recruits that we saw who had just arrived at the Marine Recruit Depot in San Diego would, in a short eleven weeks, become polished Marines whose lives would be changed forever? Those

Drill Instructors could see potential in those young, timid boys and never judged them on their first appearance. The D.I.'s believed in them and knew from past experiences that these young boys would become Men like all those before them who had undergone this extensive training and polish. Even I was surprised when I saw those who had just arrived, how disoriented they were. Then to see the graduation on the Parade Grounds was a sight of perfection and joy. My life was changed as well as theirs. It was a proud moment.

I wish I could remember the source of more of my bits and pieces of poetry that I learned as a kid, but somewhere from the recesses of my mind comes this little thought:

" A well kept garden filled with flowers
Has no room left for weeds to share:
The mind keeps out unworthy thoughts
When loveliness is dwelling there."

Don't be too quick to judge this recipe using kraut. I ate it at a friend's house and thought it was the most moist, delicious chocolate cake I had ever eaten. Then she shared the recipe with me, so I pass it on to you.

Sauerkraut Chocolate Cake

Mix one box chocolate cake mix according to directions on box. Add 1/2 to 2/3 Cup (8 ounce can) sauerkraut, chopped, rinsed, and drained. Bake at 350 degrees as package instructs, in a 13" X 9" pan. Ice with any chocolate or mocha icing.

Don't be too quick to judge. If you look for good you will find it and if you look for bad you will find it. Leave no room for unworthy thoughts. Think about it!

Chapter 55 — Deserving

Do you get what you deserve? Think about it!

Maybe we don't feel that we deserve all the bad things that come our way but do we deserve all the good either?

My mother, who died of cancer several years ago, taught us a valuable lesson on that. People would ask her if she wasn't bitter about having cancer and the known outcome. She was a lovely lady who spent her life thinking of others and doing good things for people. Her reply was, "No, I'm not bitter, nor do I dwell on not deserving this cancer. I never questioned all the good things that came my way, my devoted family, affluence in many areas, a comfortable life and many, many blessings, so why should I question now whether I deserve this or not?

I have thought about that many times. Whether it be illness, hardship, or other setbacks, it does no good to place blame and think about whether or not we deserved such a lot in life.

We see people all the time who are prosperous who have lived lives of near criminal acts. Yet they are successful. Is this deserved? On the other hand we see people who have lived sainted lives and have hardships and afflictions bestowed upon them that seem undeserved.

Some people bring things on themselves. People who drive carelessly and reckless have accidents on the highways. But so do those who obey the laws. People who have lived lives of self neglect and abhorred habits become ill and diseased, but so do those who take good care of themselves. Is there any truth to "paying the piper?"

I look at our daughter and her thoughtful husband, and their two precious girls, and wonder how I ever in this world deserved such a wonderful "ready-made" family, as Linda is Jim's daughter and I acquired her when we married. Then people point out that I didn't deserve not to have biological children either. I never even think about it at all, since my cup runneth over with this family that has filled my life and my heart so full of joy. I have certainly never done anything to deserve being surrounded with so much love and "grandma attention". I love it!

I have made so many new friends through this little column. I certainly don't deserve all the recognition and kind words and cards that I receive. That certainly doesn't mean that I don't appreciate them though. You readers are the greatest! You keep me humble and filled with enthusiasm.

And one more thing...I don't deserve credit for so many of these recipes I share that have been handed down to me by my family through several generations. The following is a recipe that my grandma used to make, especially Sunday evenings, and then my mother carried it on, and I do the same often. We called them "Catfish". It was probably a name some tiny child called them but we have no idea of the origin of the name. Now you'd imagine maybe an afternoon on the creek bank, sunburn, mosquitoes, and wiggly worms, but not so. The "Catfish" is a fried fruit pie, made from doughnut dough and usually a filling of dried fruit, apples or peaches, or apricots. I remember apricot the best and that is the filling I use, although I can remember apples strung on a string that were stewed and used also. Anyway this is how I do "Catfish".

Snip about 36 halves of dried apricots and place in 1 Cup water. Bring to boil. Reduce heat to simmer and cook until all juice is absorbed and fruit is mushy. Add 1/2 Cup sugar. Stir. Set aside.

To make the dough

1 Cup sugar
1 Cup buttermilk
1 egg
1 teaspoon soda
pinch salt
3 Cups flour, to make workable dough
1 teaspoon cinnamon

Roll out to about 1/5 inch thick. Cut in circles 4" across. Put about 1 Tablespoon filling in center of circle. Fold over and press edges together. Make sure fruit filling doesn't leak out as it burns and makes the shortening smoke. Place carefully in hot Crisco heated to about 300 to 340 degrees. Turn when tan on one side. Remove when both sides are cooked. Drain. Roll in mixture of 1 Cup sugar and 1/2 teaspoon cinnamon. Hope you enjoy one of our family traditions. You deserve it!

There will be many unexpected, unpredictable events in our lives, events over which we have little or no control. In these areas we have the ability to determine and manage our reaction to what is happening. Think about it!

Chapter 56 — Needy or Greedy

Are you needy or greedy? Think about it!

Sometimes we just think we need something because we see it advertised on TV or hear about it on the radio. These advertisements are crafty; they know how to entice us to want something, whether we do or not.

Do we think we are really in need of something just because the television in the back bedroom is smaller than the one in the living room or den? Do we need new drapes just because the ones we have are a few years old and the vogue in colors has changed? Or our hemlines are off about two inches because the styles have changed, and now we have nothing to wear? We feel a little outdated so we think buying something will make us feel better and more fashionable.

Need, true need, is being hungry or really cold, or without a home, or with no security. Few of us know what true need is, thank goodness. We may be hungry from being on a diet but that is not a forced hunger because we have no food or water. There is hunger in this country but usually it is a short-lived situation that is remedied by a call to an agency or church. There are also shelters in this country who provide adequate warmth and protection from the elements when the weather is real cold, or shade when it is real hot. Some poverty is due to failure to manage funds to provide creature comforts.

When I was little, during the depression and following that era, no one had any money. But we were lucky. We lived on a farm and had wonderful food to eat. But it took work, lots of hard work, to provide that food. Nothing was handed to us. We picked wild blackberries and wild sand plums. We raised a huge garden and did not let any vegetable go to waste. We raised our own beef, pork, and chickens for meat. We had our own laying hens for eggs, and turkeys, and geese for pillows. We never let anything spoil or go unused. What we could not consume or can, we shared with neighbors. Nothing was wasted.

We had a roof over our heads and walls that surrounded us with love and close family ties. We did not have lots of room in our house but it was cozy and warm in the winter as we gathered around a wood stove. The rest of the house was cold enough to hang meat in. We chopped our own wood for cooking and warmth. In the summer we slept out in the yard where it was cool.

We played with used thread spools and blew bubbles for something exciting to do. We never knew we were in need or poor, because we weren't. My folks had a knack of making us feel that we were special and got to do special things like blowing bubbles. It just never once occurred to us that this was because we had few toys.

Nowadays, that would be considered poor and deprived but we never once thought we were. We have now gone way beyond that need for anything and I am afraid greed has taken over. If we don't have shoes that match our outfit, we think we are in need. We seem to forget the days we went barefooted and had one pair of shoes when school started. Our clothes were hand-me-downs and we didn't mind them at all. We were glad to have clothes. And Mother sewed so we had nice things that were sometimes revamped hand-me-downs. We didn't have the best of everything, but we did make the best of everything we had.

One of the things we used to bake out of need, and now we bake it simply to help us remember and appreciate what we can now so easily purchase at the market is "Soda Crackers".

4 Cups flour
1/2 teaspoon baking soda
1 teaspoon salt
3/4 Cup sour milk (we called it clabber milk)
1 Cup butter

Sift together dry ingredients. Cut in milk and butter, mixing well to form a stiff dough. Roll and turn over repeatedly until the dough is very stiff. Roll very thin, cut into squares, and prick with a fork. Sprinkle with salt if desired. Bake at 400 degrees until the edges are lightly browned. This makes about 5 dozen crackers.

Need makes you appreciative. Greed is like rust on metal: it will corrode your soul. Think about it!

Chapter 57 — Trading Places

Would you trade places with anyone? Think about it!

There are probably times when you would like to check it all in and trade places with someone else... anyone else. There are times that try men's souls. Which reminds us of the old story when things were going all wrong. A friend said, "Cheer up, things could be worse." So I cheered up and sure enough, things got worse. Things do go from bad to worse sometimes but would we really want to trade places with another person?

Very likely, if we knew what problems the other person bears, we would settle for our own setbacks. People do hide their troubles. They don't usually carry their feelings on their sleeves for everyone to observe.

There are times when we wish we were rich, or famous, or talented, or beautiful, or shorter or taller, or thinner or heavier, or healthier, or whatever. We wish we had more leisure time or less responsibility or less irons in the fire, or more time to do things. Of course we never wish for what we already have so we are always looking for something else to wish for.

But the other side of the coin is that every positive has a negative. With notoriety comes less privacy and less time to yourself. With money or prestige comes more responsibility and accountability. With every accomplishment, comes some problem. Every positive has a negative. Every blessing has a little setback or side step. Every choice has a curse of some kind.

Every person has an ambition to achieve, but faces staggering challenges. There is no royal road to success and happiness. The path is beset with bewildering problems which must be solved. Success is for those who have found the way to meet issues and solve problems. Success does not look for an easy way out, nor does a successful person wish he were someone else. He is content with his lot in life that he has chosen for himself. He accepts the credit or responsibility of what he has become. He is content, or he would do something about it.

Contentment is outlined in a little saying by Von Goethe which states simply (yet not so simply):

"Contentment is:

Health enough to make work a pleasure.

Wealth enough to support you needs.

Strength enough to battle difficulties and forsake them.

Grace enough to confess your shortcomings and overcome them.

Patience enough to toil under some good is accomplished.

Charity enough to see some good in your neighbor.

Love enough to move you to be useful and helpful to others."

I'd like to cook fancy, but really I wouldn't trade places with anyone because of my background and family heritage of good old plain cooking that feeds the soul as well as the palate.

My mother used to make butter beans so good they were delicious hot or cold. They cooked in the oven while she went to pick wild blackberries, or work in the garden, or sew our clothes. I can't begin to make them as good as Mama did, but here is how I cook them. Pick over a pound (about 3 cups) of white lima "butter" beans. Wash. Cover with water and bring to boil. Add scraps of good ham or a ham bone if you have one, two teaspoons of salt, one tablespoon of picante sauce, and 1/4 cup finely diced onion. Put in covered Dutch oven and place in oven at about 300 degrees for at least 3 to 4 hours. Keep covered with water until about the last hour. You don't want them too soupy.

These beans along with fried potatoes/okra/onion, some vine ripened sliced tomatoes, and some fresh peaches make a wonderful country meal I wouldn't trade for the fanciest soufflé or trifle in the world.

Don't wish to trade places with another person. You are not equipped physically, mentally, or emotionally for their problems. You've gotta be you! Think about it!

Chapter 58 — Cooking

Isn't cooking enjoyable? and fun, and rewarding, and relaxing, and creative, and satisfying, and...? Think about it!

I have always enjoyed cooking. From the time I was a little girl on the farm cooking for hay hands and harvest crews alongside my mother, I have loved the kitchen. I am so grateful I had a mother that enjoyed cooking too and passed a lot of her skills and recipes down to me. We never cooked fancy but we sure cooked filling. Cooking for a family is not only nourishing but nurturing. It is a way to express your love for your family and friends. To this day when I get word that a member of my family is dropping by, my first thought is what to serve, never what shall we talk about. Anything I cook is liked by my family. Perhaps it is because that is the food of our youth and heritage, our "soul food".

I was pleased that the Enid News and Eagle again asked me to participate in their cooking classes at the recent Home Show at the Hoover Building. I found it such fun to share my simple recipes with old and new friends. I had the best audiences who contributed to the program as much as I did with their fresh ideas and great suggestions.

Pineapple Paradise is one of the recipes prepared. It is simply an angel food cake mix prepared according to package directions, except pour 1/2 of the batter into a jelly roll pan (11 1/2" x 9 1/2") that has been lined with wax paper. Bake at 350 degrees for 15 minutes. Turn out on powdered sugar dusted towel and cool. One of the class participants suggested that I flip it over again making the brown side up to put the filling on. We did and it makes the pretty white side out when it is rolled. I am so grateful for this tip, and I didn't even get the lady's name who shared this suggestion.

I used Cool Whip with drained, crushed pineapple for the filling, but you can use almost anything your family likes, from strawberry jam to ice cream. After the filling has been put on the flat cake, roll it as for a jelly roll. Put it "seam side" down on the serving tray. Slice with electric knife. This freezes well, or just refrigerate if you don't have a frozen filling. This idea too is not original with me; it was shared with me by a co-worker who is a great cook.

That entire class was a delight for me, from the clean-up crew that was provided for me to the people who handed out the recipe leaflets, to the keeper of the door, to the entire set up with microphone and serving dishes. I appreciate all of you who attended and were such a great audience. You made me look good.

It seems that when cooks get together the subject eventually gets around to recipes or food. I can always bring a conversation around to my two favorite subjects, food and granddaughters. It is surprising how the two can be combined!

On one such occasion, my beautiful friend, Icy, told me of a recipe she had gotten from a friend out-of-state. It contains buttermilk which was a real turn-off for me and she said it was for her too. "But just try it," she said, "You won't taste the buttermilk but it is different and good." I tried it, and she is right, it is different and good. And simple to do. For want of a better name, we call it "Buttermilk Salad"

One 20 oz. can crushed pineapple with juice
2 packages apricot or lemon Jell-O (we like apricot best)
2 cups buttermilk
One 16 oz. carton Cool Whip

Heat pineapple and juice, bringing to boil. Turn off heat. Add Jell-O. Stir until dissolved. Chill in refrigerator until it starts to set. Fold in Cool Whip and buttermilk. Place in refrigerator to set.

I thank all of my readers who share with me their recipes and ideas and suggestions and requests. Part of the fun of cooking is the sharing.

I am almost convinced I live to eat, not eat to live. Are you that way, too? Think about it!

Chapter 59 — Day-Cations

What is your favorite "day-cation"? Think about it!

If you could go anywhere you wanted and do anything you wanted for just one day, what and where would it be? Sometimes all it takes is a day change of pace to feel better about everything. Lots of times we can't go on a real vacation because of other commitments but we can usually eke out one day to regroup and things look better. One day of complete rest or complete recreation can do wonders.

Just one day for self. Ah...relax. Sometimes it is more restful and relaxing to spend one day close to home, or at home, completely doing what you want to do, than it is to go on a two week vacation, because you don't have all that dirty laundry to do up, or car to unpack, or work to catch up on at the office, or work to catch up on at home, or groceries to restock, or sleep to catch up on. We thought at the beginning of that two week vacation that this time we would come home rested but many times it doesn't happen that way. Well, on a "day-cation" you eliminate all that and just have a refreshing day.

Our ideal day is a trip to Oklahoma City or Tulsa seeing museums, an antique show, eating out at some nice restaurant, and coming back home. We will be tired and our feet will hurt but we feel like we have been on vacation.

We used to pack a picnic and go over to the ranch and fish early in the morning when the fish were biting, then ride horses the rest of the day just enjoying the scenery and the cattle and the trees and the open countryside. The fishing we did just to be out and about early in the mornings. We really didn't care if we caught any because then we'd have to clean them. It was okay just to pretend to be fishing. Again we would come home dog tired but able to sleep in our own bed and take a bath in our own shower. The day was like a vacation.

I'm sure these may not sound interesting at all to you but you have your own favorite thing to do for one single day. Who would you like to spend that day with? Family is always nice, but friends are great too. And sometimes just being alone is good. One can shop, look, travel, eat, and explore alone too. Especially if you enjoy your own company. (If you don't, you'd better start to remedy that because someday you may be all you have.)

I would be perfectly happy to spend an entire day right at home in my own kitchen. I'd bake bread and make a roast or something that makes the house smell real good. Then I'd sew or sort pictures or do something else fun and restful, like write or read books or old letters. I could (but probably won't) organize recipes and put them in a more orderly file. I could go through the old cedar chest and remember and remember. I would hope that day it would rain because that always adds a special homey touch to a day off.

If you have a day at home and want to make a roast and just let the day happen, here is how I do it: Beef Roast

Buy about a 3 or 4 pound roast. Rub it good with seasoned salt, a little garlic salt, sprinkle with Worcestershire sauce. Place in covered roasting pan and add about 3/4 Cup water. Bake covered for about 3 hours at 300 degrees. Pour off all the juice and measure to make the gravy. Absorb as much of the fat off the top of the juice as you can so that the gravy won't be greasy. Add brewed coffee if necessary to make about 1 1/2 Cups liquid. Bring liquid to a boil. Stir 3 Tablespoons flour into 1/2 Cup cold water. Stir until smooth. Gradually stir into hot roast juices. Boil slowly about five to eight minutes until thick, stirring occassionally. Season to taste. It may not need any salt or seasoning because it will come from that you put on the roast. I don't sear my roasts on each side before I cook them because I like that flavor for the gravy. The roasts always turn out crusty on the top and we think that is the best part. Now make some good ole creamy mashed potatoes out of real potatoes. When you serve, it seems to taste better if you make a pond in the mound of mashed potatoes for the gravy. Slice off the roast beef and enjoy. The cooking time on the roast will depend on the size and thickness of the roast you select, and some like a roast well done while others like a roast a little rare. The hardest part of cooking is the guessing when something is done or seasoned well, but that will come with practice...and lots of tasting.

If you spend your vacation at home, your friends will know the kind of person you are: sensible, imaginative, home-loving,...and broke! But you can have a wonderful day of rest and relaxation. Think about it!

Chapter 60 — Looking Back

Do you look back with regrets and remorse? Think about it!

Then have a certain amount of regrets and remorse and then forget about it...or it becomes remission. There is no need to cry over "spilt" milk. It really does no good at all to continue to kick yourself over something that happened a long time ago.

If an apology is necessary, then do it and do it now, and get it over so all can be forgiven and you can go on with the things at hand. Sometimes a simple explanation is all that is necessary since we all make dumb mistakes from time to time. It seems to me that people who live in the past are remembering only the poor judgements they have made or the mistakes they have made, are really not very happy people. There is not one of us, if we are truthful, that has not made an error in judgement but did the best we could with the information at hand at the time. We can all look back and see some stupid stunt we pulled that made us lose money. No telling what we might have been like had our plans gone some other way.

At the end of that tunnel we just dug for ourselves is a light, if we will just look for it. No matter how rough the path we have chosen or how impossible it may seem to travel that route, we've got to keep our eyes on the prize. There is something good to look forward to.

My grandma always said "Don't look back except for inspiration." I know that she was right. It may sound easier than it is to do, but we should learn a lesson from our mistakes and then carry on, and move forward.

Don't dwell on the "What if's" or "If only's." Where will that lead you? Those "if's" didn't happen so why think about them at all? Your life took the course it did for a reason. Find out what that reason is.

Once I made a meal for guests...my delicious pork chop casserole with rice and orange sauce and nuts. I baked it just so, and served it with a salad and a rich dessert. When our friends came, they didn't even try the casserole but filled up on salad. It was then that the thought occurred to me that they were Jewish, and did not eat pork. I felt terrible, just terrible! But what could I do but apologize and make a mental note to not do that again. I am sure all was forgiven. Now I never look back on that incident, except for inspiration. I try to adjust my cooking for those who really dislike things like beets, broccoli, or spinach, or have medical problems like lactose intolerance or diabetes, or allergies. I am much happier and I know our guests are too. In the above instance, I could have just as easily made a chicken casserole, and you bet I did after that.

If you are sure of your guests and family preferences, then by all means try this Pork Chop and Rice Casserole a L'Orange:

6 pork chops (1/2 to 3/4 inch thick)
2 tablespoons shortening
3/4 teaspoon salt
1/8 teaspoon pepper
3 Cups cooked rice
1 1/2 Cups orange juice
1/2 Cup golden raisins
1/4 Cup chopped pecans
1 Tablespoon brown sugar
1/2 teaspoon cinnamon

Brown chops in shortening. Drain. Season with salt and pepper. Combine rice, juice, raisins, pecans, sugar and cinnamon. Pour into greased baking dish. Place chops on rice mixture. Cover. Bake in 350 degree oven for 45 minutes. Remove cover and bake additonal 15 minutes. Serves 6.

Don't let regrets and remorse eat away at your thinking. It will devour you and lead you nowhere. Repel it, repress it, or replace it with positive action. Think about it!

Chapter 61 — Home

What makes a house a home? Think about it!

We've been in houses that were so tiny you could hardly turn around with furnishings so sparse there was hardly a place to sit, or you sat on a box, yet that house was so warm that you felt right at home. There was a glow there that said "Welcome." You felt like family.

And we've been in houses that were so elegantly furnished, and so beautifully groomed that we were almost afraid to sit down for fear we'd wrinkle the upholstery. That house was probably expensively appointed with the finest things, and yet we failed to relax and enjoy the surroundings. Something was lacking.

I certainly have no envy for those who can and do decorate with fine possessions. I am happy for them. But I am also happy for me in my humble house where everything is comfortable, and cozy and relaxed and easy....and mine. Everything in our house has a special meaning. We remember where we bought it, or acquired it. The things that set around on the tables are mostly things that friends or family have given us and we enjoy each thing, whether we use it or not. Some of the things are just a joy to look at. Everything we have evokes a memory of some kind. Many of these beautiful things are things the granddaughters have lovingly selected for us and are very special.

I've always felt that a house should be clean enough to be sanitary but messy enough to be homey. At least the dirt that we have is our own dirt...dust and all. In fact I have a little sampler that a dear friend gave me that hangs in our kitchen that says, "You may touch the dust but please do not write in it." It has a very special meaning to me, and I am sure it does to Helen too. Living in the Enid area just naturally guarantees that there will always be dust some-where, sometime.

The sounds of a home are very special. There should be laughter, giggling (they ARE different), music, children playing, dogs conversing with their masters, talking at dinner and breakfast, excitement when one returns home and greetings on their arrival. I remember one of the joyous sounds of my home when I was young, was the sewing machine humming as Momma sewed for us. In winter there was the crackle of the fire in the cook stove and the heating stove. Ah...what memories of sounds!

Then there were the special feelings that only home could provide. The comfort of a loving family, the acceptance of you, just as you are, the encour-agement to reach goals and do what you wanted, the insistance that you be a good citizen and study hard and do your best, and respect other's property, and do your part to make a home run smoothly. We each had chores to do. Even the smallest child would gather wood chips or bark to start the fires in the stoves. What great training we had for life. I still believe in the saying, "no workey, no eatey". It was a way of life to help a home run smoothly.

Then there were the wonderful aromas of home. I can sometimes get a faint hint of the way Grandma's house smelled. It was like some sweet soap or something. I can't describe it but I know it still. And the house always smelled of some freshly baked goodies. I still think the aroma of something baked adds to the hospitality of a home. Here is one way to always be ready for company or family and to add that special touch to your reception. Keep ice box cookies ready to bake. By the time the oven is warm you can have a pan ready to pop in it, and in ten minutes you have fresh baked cookies to serve.

Ice Box Ginger Cookies

1 Cup shortening
2 Cups brown sugar
1/4 Cup molasses
2 eggs
1/4 Cup sour milk or cream
1 teaspoon soda
4 Cups flour
1/2 teaspoon ginger
1 teaspoon cinnamon
1/4 teaspoon cloves
1/4 teaspoon nutmeg
1/2 teaspoon salt

Cream shortening and sugar. Add molasses, eggs and sour milk. Add dry ingredients that have been sifted together. Form into two rolls about twelve inches long. Roll in wax paper or plastic wrap. Chill twelve hours or longer. Slice thinly and bake at 350 degrees for about ten minutes.

As someone so aptly put it, "It takes a heap of living in a house to make a home." Think about it!

Chapter 62 — Irks

What "irks" you? Think about it!

There is as much difference in irked and irritated as there is in miffed and mad. Being irked at something is just a smidgen of irritation that lasts only a few seconds as long as it is happening. My idea of irksome things is someone who fails to signal to turn. Or driving with the signal lights on. Or drivers who suddenly speed up when you attempt to pass. Or for the phone to stop ringing just as you get to it after jumping out of the shower and running while wrapping a towel around you. Some other irks: Clanging pans or dishes early in the morning. Or slamming doors or rattling papers or having the TV or radio on early in the morning. Thank goodness, I am married to someone who also likes things quiet and organized early in the mornings. We talk, but we don't have to yell above the TV or other "noise" while we are enjoying our coffee and paper and working the puzzle.

Some people have the thoughtless habit of rattling the money in their pockets while standing and talking. Or jangling their keys. Or tapping their fingernails. Or making other distracting noises while they think, or don't think! These noises bother some people to the point of distraction, while those same noises are hardly noticed by some.

It must be that we are just looking for something to be irked about. Some days are worse than others...and everything seems to bother us. It could just be that we are noticing things around us more. If we can notice the bothersome things, then perhaps we could also notice other things about people.

Maybe we just need to let our minds and thoughts dwell upon refined and beautiful things in the world around us. Good music and wholesome recreation, happy thoughts and doing things for others. For every vexing thing that person does, maybe if we looked a little harder, we could also see some thoughtful thing he/she does that makes us feel better, instead of irked.

It all boils down to the fact that we find what we are looking for. If we are looking for irritating coin rattling, we will find it. If we are looking for a kind smile and listening for a kind word we will find that too.

It is human nature to not be perfect and happy all the time. I guess we've got to have a few things that bother us somewhat, but we must not let them dominate our lives until we fail to see beauty and good around us. We might need to practice a little more patience and understanding toward others. We might also take a look within ourselves and see the real reason we let little things bother us so. Patience is idling our motor when we really want to strip our gears. We will be much happier and others will be happier around us if we ignore those irksome things and not strip our gears. Count to 10...ten times if necessary.

If, and when, you have one of those less than perfect days when things seem to irk you, cook something that is perfect and can't go wrong. It was demonstrated at the Enid News and Eagle Food Fair and many of those attending the cooking class said they enjoyed it. It is **Spicy Ricey Casserole**

3 Cups boiling water
3/4 Cup dry rice
3/4 teaspoon salt

Add rice and salt to boiling water. Bake for 30 minutes in 350 degree oven. This will make about 3 cups rice.

To the 3 Cups rice add:

1 pound hamburger, browned
1/2 teaspoon garlic salt
one can tomato soup
3 to 4 tablespoons Picante Sauce (to individual taste)
1/2 pound grated sharp cheese
onion?
green bell peppers?
green chilies?

Mix all together and bake in 350 degree oven until hot and cheese melted.

Note: instead of hamburger, you can use cooked sausage, ground turkey, canned chicken, or cut up roast beef, etc. Go easy on the Picante sauce, until you have it to your liking.

Remember, don't sweat the small stuff! You aren't hurting anyone but yourself by getting upset and is it really THAT important? Think about it!

Chapter 63 — Stage Fright

Do you get stage fright? Think about it!

Remember when you were in grade school and you had to recite a program? Little girls twisted their dresses up under their armpits. Little boys stood first on one foot and then on the other, swaying back and forth. Your mouth got dry and you went blank. Your parents and grandparents were in the audience just dying for you. Then it was over and everyone clapped and you were ready to do it again...until the next time, then it was all to do over with stage fright.

The thing that is most common in stage fright is that your heart pounds. Dale Carnegie says that is the difference in a plow horse and a race horse. It is easy once you get started and you will truly enjoy giving a speech or singing that song. Most audiences are great and would not let you fail at what you are doing. If you falter, they hurt for you. They are your friends, new or old. The audience does not know if you have added something or deleted something from your planned script.

I gave a speech a few weeks back to a lovely group of receptive ladies. I explained to them that I am not a speaker, but a talker. They made me feel so at ease that when it had ended I was ready to do it again. I actually enjoyed doing it. As long as one can talk about something of interest to themselves and their audiences, it will be a joy to speak.

For several years I have had the privilege of helping the News and Eagle with their Food Fair. It is easy and enjoyable because I am speaking of something I thoroughly love...food. Those audiences are the greatest because they also love to cook and/or love to eat. And in the audience are friends who will not let me die. It is almost like cooking in my own kitchen with little helpers at my sides.

Cooking is easy and comfortable with an apron on. Conversation seems to flow. It is always pleasant and fun to talk about something we love. Daddy talks about the old days and it is relaxing and soothing. Jim can talk about the Civil War or western lore and time stands still. They have no stage fright. They simply let the words flow and the stories develop.

If you are frightened about having people over for a meal, then do it simple with things that are easy to serve and can be done ahead of time. Serve a cool tuna or chicken salad and a fruit pizza.

Fruit Pizza

2/3 Cup butter
1 Cup flour
1/4 Cup sugar
8 oz. cream cheese
1 Cup confectioners sugar
2 Cups Cool Whip
fruits

Melt butter. Stir in flour and sugar. Pat into an ungreased pizza pan and bake for 10 minutes in 350 degree oven until golden brown. Cool. Whip cream cheese, sugar and Cool Whip together. Spread on cooled crust. Top with fresh fruits like strawberries, peaches (or use canned and drained), bananas, etc. in any desired combination. Chill. Cut like Pizza and serve.

You have nothing to fear but fear itself. Most audiences are so glad it is you and not them standing in front of a crowd speaking, that they will readily accept YOU and what you say. Think about it!

Chapter 64 — Special Pets

Do you have a special pet you love? Think about it!

We had a very special dog named Sarge. He was an English Bulldog. He never knew he was a dog. He saluted when he was fed. He stood at attention, or at ease like a Marine. The English Bulldog is the mascot of the U.S. Marine Corps, and we had always wanted one. Sarge was everything a dog should and could be. He was obedient, clean, very easily trained (he was completely house broken in three days), and a joy to be around. Last winter Sarge lost his appetite and didn't act quite normal. We took him to our beloved vet who diagnosed him with cancer of the spleen and other vital organs. We brought him home to live out his last days in love and comfort until the day came that we KNEW we had to put him out of his misery. He would just look up at us with his sad eyes, with an expression that said, "Please, help me". We could not stand it any longer. We took him to his kind doctor, and he kindly put him to sleep. We had this shared with us just before we had to leave Sarge.

A Dog's Plea

"Treat me kindly, my beloved friend, for no heart in all the world is more grateful for kindness than the loving heart of me.

"Do not break my spirit with a stick, for though I should lick your hand between blows, your patience and understanding will more quickly teach me the things you would have me to learn.

"Speak to me often, for your voice is the world's sweetest music, as you must know by the fierce wagging of my tail when your footstep falls upon my waiting ear.

"Please take me inside when it is cold and wet, for I am a domesticated animal, no longer accustomed to bitter elements. I ask no greater glory than the privilege of sitting at your feet beside the hearth.

"Keep my pan filled with fresh water, for I cannot tell you when I suffer thirst.

"Feed me clean food that I may stay well, to romp and play and do your bidding, to walk by your side, and stand ready, willing, and able to protect you with my life, should your life be in danger.

"And my friend, when I am very old, and no longer enjoy good health, hearing and sight, do not make heroic efforts to keep me going. I am not having any fun. Please see that my trusting life is taken gently. I shall leave this earth knowing with the last breath I draw that my fate was always safest in your hands."

We swore we would never never get another dog. Sarge had meant so much to us and we missed him so. However, we became lonely for a dog several months after we lost Sarge, and another precious, precious baby came into our home. His name is Brodie, named after Jim's Scottish grandfather. He is just as darling as Sarge, only in a different way. He is bright, and fun, and a delight to come home to. He has one blue eye and one black eye. One side of his face is white and the other side black. He is a great part of your family. We just adore him.

We have never had cats, but people who love cats get attached to them just like we do the two dogs that have shared our lives. I'll bet people with birds love them, or kids with gerbils, or even people who keep snakes or iguanas. Whatever the pet, they become a beloved member of the family.

Here is a special treat we occasionally make but it is not for dogs, as the name implies. It is really a great snack for our other friends...people.

Dog-gone Good Stuff

1 package chocolate chips
1 stick oleo
1 Cup peanut butter

Melt until runny. Then pour over 1 small box Crispix cereal and 1 Cup peanuts. Sprinkle with powdered sugar and shake in a covered container.

The dog is loved by old and young. He wags his tail and not his tongue. Think about it!

Chapter 65 — Bad Times

Do bad times make you bitter or better? Think about it!

We have all been through some bad times, whether it was death of someone close, a serious illness, a lingering illness, loss of resources or a position, a divorce, or the alienation of a close friend. What ever the bad times have been, they do affect our lives greatly, in different ways.

My oldest sister has lost two of her four adult sons. One would think it has make her very bitter. Well, she did go through every stage of suffering with their loss, on being struck by lightning, the other with cancer. But after she recovered, with each step she became more compassionate. Now when she hears of someone who has lost a child for any reason, she is the first to be on their doorstep with understanding and love. She had been through the worst of times and has become a better person because of it. She truly knows how those people feel and can share their grief.

I know that people who are dying with a terminal illness, are sometimes the most understanding and tolerant of anyone while they are sick. They are less demanding and more enduring than those less ill.

It may take awhile to come to the point of being better rather than bitter, but usually in the final analysis, the better part takes over. It seems to be all in the way they are thinking and in their attitude.

Everyone has been through some bad times. Some just in different ways than others, and to a different degree. We can look at some people and think they have not had bad times, but they have. They just have endured them and have grown from their experiences. You've got to admire their disposition...and learn from them how they cope.

I clipped this from some publication years ago and taped it to the inside of my cabinet door. It helps make bad times bearable and makes us better.

"During your lifetime may you have:
Enough happiness to keep you sweet.
Enough trials to keep you strong
Enough sorrow to keep you human
Enough hope to keep you happy
Enough failure to keep you humble
Enough success to keep you eager
Enough friends to give you comfort
Enough wealth to meet your needs
Enough enthusiasm to make you look forward to tomorrow.
Enough determination to make each day better than the day before."

Here is a recipe that takes something Jim cannot stand, rhubarb, and makes it better where he really likes it.

Rhubarb-Strawberry Pie

Pastry for 9 inch two crust pie
1 1/3 cups sugar
1/3 Cup flour
2 cups cut rhubarb (about 1/2 inch pieces)
2 Cups sliced strawberries
2 Tablespoons butter.

Line pie pan with one layer of crust. Mix sugar and flour and toss with rhubarb and strawberries. Pour in crust. Top with butter. Place top crust. Crimp edges together and cut slits in top. Bake at 350 degrees about one hour until golden brown. Cool before cutting, and serve with ice cream or plain.

If you can't have the best of times, make the best of the times that you have. Think about it!

Chapter 66 — New Tricks

Can you teach an old dog new tricks? Think about it!

It is rather embarrassing to have to ask our young granddaughters to come in to program our VCR or to set the clock on the VCR or in the car. We have finally mastered it, but it did not come easy. Nor was it easy to learn how to get the telephone gadgets to work. Time was when every young boy knew how to tinker with his car and get it to run, or work on it to "soup it up." Well those days are over. Now it takes a special computer to find out what is wrong in an engine. No longer can a mechanic just listen to the purr or ping and tell you what the problem is.

I am still trying to figure out what keeps a plane in the air. And I haven't solved the mystery of those little tiny people in the TV sets. When it becomes common to see the person we are speaking to on the phone, it will probably blow my mind.

My father has seen so much history in his lifetime. He has come from the true horse and buggy days to the 707 airliner for travel. When he flies out to my sister's now, he has a 30 minute layover in Dallas. He thinks it takes too long. That is the time it used to take to harness the horses and hitch them to the wagon or buggy. Those days were slower paced and people didn't even try to travel as far as we do now. And they didn't travel often either, as we do now.

I love to hear Daddy tell the stories about when the cars first came into being and when the horses were terrified of them and their loud noises. It didn't take too long to learn to drive a car back then because there were no road rules, and few gears on the cars. The hardest lesson was probably how to change and fix a tire when one had a flat tire out on the road. And cranking the car took some expertise too.

I have a new computer. I am having a ball playing with it. It doesn't always do what I think it should do, but then I remember: A machine is no smarter than the person working it. That makes me stop and think what I should do...or not do. Thank goodness, my new toy came with a lifetime guarantee of house calls if I get in a bind. So far I have had to summon help two or three times, but I keep that phone number close at hand for emergencies. It is very comforting. Word processors are a far cry from the first manual typewriter I learned to type on. In those olden days we typed with six sheets of carbon paper. If we made one mistake, we automatically made six. And correcting those little errors was messy and time consuming. Now, with this computer, I just whisk away any mistakes and insert new words. It is wonderful!

On my computer is a program of recipes. I share one of those with you now. It is for Milky Way Chocolate Ice Cream.

6 regular Milky Way Candy Bars
16 ounces miniature marshmallows
1 Cup milk
1 can Eagle Brand Milk
Milk to fill freezer to 2/3 full mark

Melt the candy bars and marshmallows in 1 Cup of milk. Add other ingredients. Add more milk to fill freezer can to full mark (about 2/3 to 3/4 full) Freeze as usual. Makes one gallon of delicious ice cream.

There is something to be said for new technology, but there is something to be said for the old, tried and true methods too. The best thing is to keep learning and combine the best of the two worlds. Think about it!

Chapter 67 — Having Fun

Are we having fun yet? Think about it!

Lucky me to have been reared on a farm/ranch. We never lacked for something to do. It might not sound exciting to some but we spent many a day catching polliwogs from the spring and transferring them to the pond. Or we fished or caught crawdads. In the evening we would chase lightning bugs and put them in a jar with holes in the lid.

One Labor Day weekend recently, about 50 of us, young and old, gathered at my brother's ranch for a delightful day of fun. The kids jumped from one large round bale to the other, or they crawled through the tunnel made by the bales stacked in rows. They climbed trees and explored the barns.

It had rained that warm day, as it usually does during the "Fair" and when school starts, so my friend, Jayne, and I taught the kids how to stomp in the soft, wet mud and make lob-lollies. It was messy but the mud felt so good oozing up between our toes. That mud washed off so easily under the pump. It was an experience I will never forget. Nor will Jayne. Nor will those kids. We were having FUN!

When I was growing up, and the weather was hot and dry the earth became a soft, fine powder that made the most wonderful flour for our playhouse baking. My sisters and I played house a lot. We imagined our houses to be the finest and most hospitable...and they were too, because of our imaginations. It is surprising what one can do with orange crates (remember them?) and old wagon seats to make a house a "home". We cooked and baked using that soft "flour" and once we used real eggs in our mud cake...but I would not recommend it. About two or three days later that Oklahoma heat brought out an aroma we will never forget.

Back then we had lots of free time to enjoy growing up, lots of time to think, and watch ants crawl, and birds make nests, or pick flowers, or watch the grass grow.

Perhaps from those carefree, enjoyable days came my love for cooking and thinking...just a variance in the ingredients and place. The joy remains the same.

Some people have never mastered the art of experiencing joy in simple things. They require an organized game or activity to have fun. They fail to find pleasure in their daily tasks and routine happenings. It is really sad because from the simplest, most ordinary things can come the greatest happiness and pleasure...and fun.

Here is a recipe that brings back memories of when we used to make fudge and dip crackers in it and let them set on wax paper. This is a simplified recipe but the taste is the same.

Soda Cracker Fudge

2 Cups sugar
2/3 Cup milk
1/2 to 1 small bag chocolate chips
24 soda crackers, broken into pieces
5 Tablespoons Crunchy peanut butter (or 3 Tablespoons smooth)

Bring to boil the sugar and milk, stirring constantly. Boil for 3 minutes, stirring occasionally. Remove from heat and add the chocolate chips. Stir to dissolve. Stir in remaining ingredients. Pour into buttered pan. Cool until set and cut into squares.

Joy is a state of mind. Most anything can be fun, if you want it to be. You ARE having fun! Think about it!

Chapter 68 — Cabin Fever

Are you getting cabin fever? Think about it!

About this time of year we get sick of cold weather and the bleakness of winter and long for those beautiful spring days when we can get out in the yard and dig in the dirt. We want to see something green for a change, or brilliant colors of blooms. We are sick of sweaters and coats and gloves and heavy clothes and yearn for something lighter and brighter. We are tired of short days with no evenings of daylight. Let's face it...we just want spring to spring forth.

Winter is wonderful. But it is difficult to make travel plans because the weather may change any second. The roads can become slick and hazardous quickly. We are afraid to go too far from home for fear we will be snowbound away from our own house and things.

The holidays are over and things are back in a routine. All the decorations are packed away and the house even looks bare and dull. The excitement of all the holidays is back to quiet and restful. All the things we wanted to do when winter set in has either been done already, or we will just put them off for another year.

We are sick of being home with colds or flu or other sickness that can keep one housebound. We are tired of running the heater and having the air dry in our houses.

The restlessness and irritability are evident from the boredom or confinement of living in a cooped up environment alone or with someone with whom we are experiencing too much togetherness. In short, we are having a bad case of cabin fever. My dad used to call it the "stir crazies".

Now sometimes it is nice to be in front of the crackling fireplace, sipping hot chocolate, going through old cookbooks or picture albums, or knitting. We have cooked all the things we really love to cook, and done all the things we really love to do. We enjoy this "time out" from the busy activities of the summer months. But after awhile we long to get out among the living, and get some fresh, outside air into our lungs.

That time of year is here. Spring, ah, Spring. We are ready for it now. There are already flowers blooming and trees in full bud. Many gardens are already producing fresh vegetables. Cabin fever will be forgotten for another year.

In the meantime, cook up a vacation and take a trip with food that is a bit different. Make this in your crock pot to have an inviting aroma around you all day.

Sauerkraut and Sausage

1 small onion, chopped
1 quart sauerkraut
1 pound fully cooked Polish sausage, cut into 1/2 inch chunks
3 large potatoes, cut in fourths
1 Tablespoon brown sugar
1 Tablespoon Caraway seed

Put all in the crock pot (or Dutch oven) and bake slowly several hours. Delicious!

Break out of that cocoon and spring forth like a butterfly. Enjoy the new season. Think about it!

Chapter 69 — Looking Ahead

Can you see a light at the end of the tunnel? Think about it!

My brother has a ranch and feeds lots of cattle in the wintertime. He will sometimes be out all day if he has trouble with frozen ponds and has to cut ice or finds a cow having trouble calving. His light at the end of that tunnel is a warm fire in his fireplace in the evening and a good warm meal.

For all of us there is a light at the end of the tunnel in a vacation after a particular confining job that lasts awhile. It may be just a short weekend of getting away, but nevertheless it is a bright light when we can look forward to it.

If you have ever been in debt for your home or other property, you know the wonderful feeling of getting that loan paid off and the light you feel and see at the end of the debt tunnel. It is such a relief to be debt free.

One of the more dim lights and the farthest away sometimes is the light we are searching for at the end of an illness tunnel. Sometimes it is so far away we can see only a glimmer, but it is still HOPE and we continue to steer toward it. Sometimes it is a long journey to that end, but we keep on trucking. Whether we ever reach it or not we have the hope along the journey to good health and freedom from disease or affliction.

If you have ever been on a diet or a new way of eating and living, you know how the end of the tunnel is approachable. It may seem like a long way, but it can be achieved. Many times there are stops along the way, but even though we may take two steps forward and one step backward, or seem so at least, we still keep our eye on the prize. That prize is feeling better, and looking better, and having a better attitude. What a light!

There are so many exercises in freedom from stress in every newspaper and magazine that you pick up now, that it is not so long a journey through a stressful situation until we can arrive at a soothing solution to a problem. The light is closer than one might think.. You just have to keep your eye on it.

When our grandparents plowed that first furrow in this great fertile soil of Oklahoma, don't you know they thought it was an impossible task with that one row plow and team of horses or mules. But they kept their eye on a sight of a stump or a tree and plowed straight furrows. Couldn't we take a lesson from their plan of laying out their fields. We must keep our eyes on one goal in the future and not just look up close.

When we need a quick supper to look forward to after a busy day, we can always have "Harmony Hominy".

1/2 Cup chopped onion
1 pound lean hamburger
1/2 package dry Taco seasoning
1 can (16 ounces) yellow hominy

Cook hamburger with onions until meat is brown and onions are clear. Stir in Taco seasoning and undrained hominy. Simmer 15 minutes. Juice will absorb. We really like it. Hope you do too.

Make sure the light at the end of your tunnel is not another train coming at you. Think about it!

Chapter 70 — Good Hosts

Are you a good host/hostess? Think about it!

I have always admired my mother and others who could see company drive in and without any advance notice create a meal that was delicious. She could always come up with something that was special, even taking time to dress and cook a fried chicken with all the trimmings, all the time visiting with her guests. I have never seen her get rattled or wish the guests had not shown.

There are people who are busy defrosting the freezer or papering a bathroom and when guests drop by, they just drop what they are doing and are delighted to have the break. My sister is like that, and I have always admired her for her hospitality. It is so warm and genuine. She just relaxes and enjoys a good visit.

I also esteem a friend who can make a banquet with fried quail, scolloped corn, fresh tomatoes, and poppy seed cake and make it seem like it was no trouble at all. She just relaxes and enjoys a good visit too with no dithering.

People who can entertain with flair are really fortunate. They make the most difficult decorations and menu seem easy. They make every meal a banquet. I, on the other hand, have to try hard to make everything ahead of time so I can relax and enjoy a group of guests. I keep things real simple so I have time for my company.

Have you ever noticed that food just tastes better if it is shared? Whether it is fancy or plain, it is just a joy to divide with friend and family. Special friends make plain food seem like a celebration. Just sit back and visit and let pleasant conversation develop.

It is not the house that makes great hospitality. A very humble home can be full of warmth that just reaches out to welcome you. And that house doesn't have to be spick-and span. I've moved lots of papers and magazines to find a place to sit down and have a wonderful time...in my own home and in others' homes. It is the hostess or host that makes all the difference by putting the guests' feeling first. Then everyone is at ease and has a great time.

Soup, salad and muffin, or a sandwich makes a good, quick meal when company drops in. Here is one we really like:

Broccoli Cheddar Soup

1/2 Cup chopped onion
1/4 Cup butter
1/2 Cup flour
salt and pepper to taste
one can chicken broth
2 Cups milk
2 Cups chopped, cooked fresh or frozen broccoli
1 Cup shredded cheddar cheese.

Saute onions in butter in a saucepan until transparent. Stir in flour, salt and pepper, and cook until smooth. Add broth and milk. Cook until mixture thickens. Add broccoli, simmer, stirring constantly until hot. Remove from heat and stir in cheese. Makes enough for four servings.

J.P.Richter says, "The best moments of a visit are those which again and again postpone its close." I believe J.P. is right. Think about it!

Chapter 71 — Beating the Heat

How do you beat the heat? Think about it!

We are so spoiled by creature comforts of air conditioning in our houses and cars and offices and everywhere that it is easy to forget how it was in the olden days in the good old summertime. We did not have air conditioning and very few fans that even stirred the air. We had to find other ways to withstand the high temperature of Oklahoma summers.

Back then we got up early and did our work in the "cool of the day." Then when it was the hottest time of the day we did easier work in the shade. In fact, we followed the shade around the house on the porch to shell peas, husk corn, or do other things to prepare for canning.

Some nights were almost unbearable, but we did now know anything else but that heat, so we made do the best we could. Lots of times we slept outside. And you know what. I never recall being frightened that someone would bother us in any way or even wake us up. Nor do I recall that there were many mosquitoes as we would have now.

Or we slept on the porch and sprinkled the sheets with water so the evaporation would cool us off. Or we placed wet cloths over the windows to let any breeze come through.

I can remember when we hoed corn in the fields, we stopped at the end of most rows to go to the creek and wade just to cool off. We really didn't hoe much corn, but at the time it seemed like a lot. Mostly I remember the wading. Aah!

When we picked plums and other fruits, we canned the juices the quickest way we could because it was so terribly warm in the house with the wood stove. Then in the winter when we wanted the heat anyway, we made the juice into jelly.

There were some things that one just had to do in the heat of the day, like pick those plums or blackberries. Then we looked forward to a swim in the pond to cool off. It was not just a fun swim. The thing I remember about swimming in the pond was that the fish would nibble at us. I am still not crazy about swimming, I think for that reason. And a pond is muddy and you can't see where you are going or where you have been...but it was cool and refreshing back then when we had nothing better.

Traveling did not have the appeal then that it does now. Those cars were HOT. The best one could do was to open all the windows for the wind, which was just hot wind. Sometimes we would hang a towel up to keep out the hot sun, but it did little good. Everyone who rode got out of the car with a huge sweat ring on the back of their shirt. It was not a refreshing vacation.

Now the churches and homes and work places are so cool we can wear long sleeves almost year around. Back then we dressed for the weather. I went barefooted and loved it. We always wore hats or bonnets when we were outside in the sun. We dressed cool.

I remember the adults would sit on the porch and follow the shade around the house in the evening after the work was done. Each would have a wet face cloth and would periodically wipe their faces and backs of their neck and arms to cool off. We didn't complain of the heat because we knew nothing different. We fanned a LOT. We looked forward to autumn or a cooling rain.

For a cool evening meal in the summer, serve this salad with iced tea, orange sherbet, and crackers. Simple and Cool.

Macaroni Salad

1 package (6 oz.) shell macaroni
1 Cup cubed sharp Cheddar cheese
1 large can (12 oz.) light tuna or white chicken
3/4 Cup diced sweet pickle
1/3 Cup minced onion
1 Cup mayonnaise
salt to taste

Cook macaroni as directed on package. Drain. Rinse with cold water. Combine all ingredients and toss to mix. Cover and chill three hours before serving.

To keep cool, think cool thoughts and don't let yourself get hot under the collar. Think about it!

Chapter 72 — Apple Butter

"Why don't you write a column about apple butter? Think about it!", so I wrote a delightful reader who lives in Medford. So I thought about it...and here it is:

I had written about apple butter when this column was in its infancy on November 17, 1993. I gave the recipe I used for apple butter. Several times I have mentioned that we picked apples and made apple butter but when I was asked about it, it brought back many happy memories of the picking of apples, the preparation, the wonderful aroma, and canning and the eating of apple butter.

When I was a kid, we gathered apples, all varieties, from an orchard we owned that must have been planted around statehood time. The trees were mature and in fact some were aging and had broken limbs like old trees have that are old and weathered. As a kid, I had visions of Johnny Appleseed having planted those apples in pioneer times. Surely he didn't, because the trees were all in a row planted around a hill, but it made a very interesting fantasy for a kid picking apples. You remember Johnny Appleseed: he was really John Chapman, who was a welcome visitor in settlers' homes all over the frontier. What a sight he must have been with his ragged clothes, bare feet, and wearing his cooking pot for a hat. He walked from settlement to settlement planting apple seeds along the way, often stopping to help build a cabin or harvest a crop before moving on. His kindness and generosity gained him the respect of everyone he met. Anyway, the story is true but the part about his planting the apples we harvested was purely in my mind. The best part was that we had apples every year to enjoy.

Of the apples we gathered, we wrapped and saved the perfect ones. We placed them in a cool place and they lasted all winter long. The windfalls and blotched ones went into canning apples and apple butter. We harvested from those wonderful trees until they all just died of old age or were split by lightning. All that remains are a few old battered pear trees and the seedling peaches from seedling peach trees.

My history of apple butter goes way back to Grandma who "canned" the dark brown delicacy in brown crocks, and sealed them with wax. Then mother always made apple butter, and now I do.

One fond memory of making it was when my young nieces were helping me. We were down on the kitchen floor tasting and tasting as you have to do with apple butter, when their mother came in. She couldn't believe that we had the kettle down on the floor, but we did. It was much easier than lifting the kids onto the cabinet. Apple butter is much a matter of tasting. The amount of sugar one uses depends on the kind of apples used and whether one likes it sweet or tart. The same goes for the spices. I don't really care for too much cloves, but that is a matter of taste and to each his own. Mother's recipe reads: "one gallon pulp, 5 Cups sugar, 1 1/2 tablespoons cinnamon, 2 teaspoons allspice, 2 teaspoons nutmeg, 2 teaspoon cloves." Adjust ingredients as you like. Bake in oven until thick. This can easily be halved and made in a crock pot. Can it and seal the jars or put it in jars and refrigerate until used up or given away.

First you make the apple butter and then make the muffins using it. They are delicious. If you don't make the apple butter yourself, then buy some or beg someone for some they have made. The muffins are worth it.

Apple Butter Muffins

1/2 Cup sugar
1/4 Cup butter
1 egg
1 Cup flour
1/2 teaspoon baking powder
1/4 teaspoon soda
1/4 teaspoon salt
1/2 Cup apple butter

Mix sugar and butter together beat in egg and apple butter. Stir in dry ingredients. Add chopped nuts if you like. Fill muffin tins (lined with paper liners) about 2/3 full. Sprinkle with a mixture of 2 Tablespoons sugar and 1/2 teaspoon cinnamon. Bake in 350 degree oven about 20 to 25 minutes. These need no butter, unless you have to have butter on everything, and they are great hot or cold.

As a tribute to Johnny Appleseed and to my kind reader/friend from Medford, make some apple butter. It doesn't have to be perfect to be perfectly wonderful! Think about it!

Chapter 73 — Warning Signals

Do you watch for warning signals? Think about it!

I don't want to sound like I am preaching, but a few pounds here and there are a warning signal that one is gaining weight and it is time to do something. It is a lot easier to lose five pounds now than to wait until it becomes twenty or more and then try to get them off. Heed those warning signals of a few ounces or pounds. Ask me how I know!

Do you have other health problems that you need to watch? Most of us have some kind of problem or at least family history of diabetes, heart disease, lung problems or something else that we know we have a tendency toward that we might need to watch, and if we are doing anything that might trigger that problem, we need to watch those warning signs now before they become real health problems. Stop or else...you will have that health problem crop up.

We have all been told by our parents that if we do a certain thing that we would reap the consequences. They said, "Do that, and you'll be sorry," or "Don't do something....or else." I never knew what "else" was but I could tell by their tone it must make a lasting impression and I really didn't want to know first hand.

This reminds me of a story when I was student teaching. We had a young man in our school that had gotten into some bad trouble at another school and in fact had been expelled from that school. Because of his young age, he enrolled in our school. Well, he got crossways with one of our teachers and she could see that he was going to try to get into the same kind of situation, so she got right into his face and whispered to him, "Do that one time in this school, and have I got a surprise for you." He backed off. We asked her what the "surprise" was, and she said she had no idea what the surprise was. She just knew that she had better get her bluff in and keep it in or she would have real troubles with this young man. The funny part of the story was that this tiny teacher was about half the size of the student. To this day, she doesn't know what her surprise would have been. Thank goodness, she didn't have to prove herself. That student listened to a warning and feared the surprise all through that year of school. All she had to do was look at him and he would get on task.

It is said that if you listen to the music you have to pay the piper. If you do it, you rue it! You've got to listen to those warnings.

Thank goodness for smoke alarms, and now alarms to let you know if gasses are in your house. I am sure those devices have saved many lives, as well as let some know when supper is ready (ha!).

When you exercise and get real sore, it is a sign that you should back off, stretch more, or take it easier. Pain is a sign that you are having a problem. If we would listen to our bodies when they try to tell us something, we would be much better off. However, the solution is not to STOP, but that we shouldn't have gotten so out of shape to begin with. Go at it gradually. Work up to your limit.

If advance notice is given when my dad comes over, I can cook him a corned beef brisket, cabbage, potatoes, and pumpkin pie. Usually he just decides he wants to drive out for an afternoon and has to take potluck. I clean out the refrigerator, and serving little dabs of things, call it smorgasbord, and we eat on that while a dessert is baking. The apples smell so good that it encourages him to stay a little longer. Otherwise he gets his visit out real quickly and is on his way. He certainly never wears out his welcome. The apples are served warm, with maybe cream or milk poured over it when served hot. Of course if you wish, it can be served cold. We like it warm.

Scotchy Apples

8 apples, (we prefer Johathan)
1/4 Cup flour
1 teaspoon cinnamon
1/3 Cup brown sugar
1 Cup water
3/4 Cup sugar
1/4 Cup butter
1 teaspoon vanilla

Peel, and quarter apples. Arrange in shallow pan. Mix flour, cinnamon, brown sugar, granulated sugar and cut in butter until mixture resembles coarse crumbs. Add vanilla and water. Mix well. Spread over apples and cover with foil or lid. Bake at 350 degrees for one hour. Makes 6 servings.

The optimist fell ten stories and at each window bar he shouted to his friends below, "All is well so far."
He should have thought ahead, and listened to the warning signals. Eventually things catch up with us. Think about it!

Chapter 74 — Balance in Life

Is your life balanced? Think about it!

Life is sometimes like a bicycle ride. You have to balance work with leisure and rest or life becomes lop-sided and, as riding a bicycle, the leaning too far to any extreme causes you to fall. I remember when Shelby was learning to ride her bicycle. We ran along beside her, holding onto the bicycle seat to keep it steady, until we were sure she had the hang of it and could handle it solo. Just as soon as we turned her loose she crashed and fell to the ground. We felt terrible about it, but she hopped right back up and got on it again and off she rode. She will never forget how to ride that bicycle. We are the same way. We could get on one right now and take off on it. That lesson never leaves us.

But sometimes we forget that life has to balance that same way. Momentarily we try to work too hard, or play too hard, or sleep too much and we crash and get all out of balance.

It has always seemed sad to me that when someone retires, in a few days or weeks he/she is already sick of retirement. Nothing was planned for their abundance of "leisure time" and they simply do not know how to handle the imbalance. They don't know when to get up, or when to do their daily chores because suddenly their schedule is all mixed up. So they do nothing. Then they become blue about it. All that play time is not so fun after all.

By the same token, all work and no play is no fun either, unless you are like my dad who feels that one must like his life's work so he never feels that he is working. Daddy was/is a rancher and still, at age 94, enjoys working with cattle. He doesn't NEED to work but he needs to work to feel useful. It gives him a purpose.

Sometimes we look around us and wonder if our judicial system is not in balance. It seems that there are more prisoners out than in but we must keep in mind that our U.S. judicial system is the best and is there really a better way?

Do you do everything for everyone else and give little time to yourself and your own family? That is easy to do if we accept every job that is asked of us to do for the community and for a "good cause". Eventually we get burn-out and decide we won't do another thing for anyone. Then we will miss one of the greatest joys of living...that of helping others. But keep things in balance and do for others as you do for yourself and your family.

Do you devote hours and hours of time and energy into preserving your outer beauty and fail to do anything for your inner beauty? Do you sit for hours in the beauty shop and fail to ever read a good book or enrich your life with culture and art and music and enjoying people? Somewhere there is a happy medium and we must find that balance.

Observe a teeter-totter. Too much load on one end and the other end suddenly goes up, or jump off one end and there is a sudden crash to the ground. I remember, as you probably do, of at least one occasion when you were playing on the teeter-totter and the school bell rang, and your partner suddenly jumped off and ran toward the school building. Where did that leave you? Ker-Plunk! A sure-fire lesson in balance and imbalance.

To strike a pleasant balance with something that is not too sweet nor too blah...try this Happy Holiday Bread.

3 eggs, beaten
1/2 Cup vegetable oil
1/2 Cup milk
1 Cup sugar
2 1/2 Cups flour
1 teaspoon baking powder
1 teaspoon soda
1 teaspoon cinnamon
1/2 teaspoon salt
2 Cups shredded carrots
1 1/3 Cups shredded coconut
1/2 Cup maraschino cherries, chopped
1/2 Cup raisins
1/2 Cup pecans, chopped

Combine eggs, oil, milk and sugar. Beat well. Stir dry ingredients and add to egg mixture, stirring just until moistened. Add remaining ingredients and blend thoroughly. Pour into greased 9 x 5 inch loaf pan. Bake at 350 degrees for 55 to 60 minutes. Cool in pan ten minutes before turning out to cool completely. Wrap in foil and store in refrigerator. Good frozen.

There are twenty-four hours in every day, eight to work, eight to sleep and eight to play. Think about it!

Chapter 75 — Problems

Do you have a problem? Think about it!

Few people are problem-free. Some have unsurmountable problems that we can't even understand how they survive with them...yet they do. Everyone has problems of one kind or another.

My oldest sister has a problem that she copes with daily and I greatly admire her stamina and fortitude. Her husband is quite ill and requires a great deal of help and observation. She has had lots of practice with problems, having lost two of her four sons, one with cancer and one was struck by lightning. She has seen a quick death and a slow death and none of this prepared her for what she is now experiencing. I am sure there are days when she just asks for strength for that one day, or that hour, or that moment. Her husband is very cooperative and that makes the problem bearable. She has returned to half-days of work which is good for her and allows him to have a quiet rest. But solving the problem does not absolve the problem. It never goes away. If one could close their eyes and wish hard, it still would not go away. People have the strength they need when they need it somehow.

How do you solve your problems? Problems of life are not like algebra problems where there is only one right answer. Every problem and set of circumstances has several possible answers and it is our chore or choice to find the best solution for our particular problem. First of all brain-storm. Think of every possible solution whether it is feasible or not. Sometimes you will be surprised that a far-out solution just might work for you.

Recognize all the facts...those that can be changed along with those that cannot be changed. Look deep and hard for every angle of the problem. Look inside out and outside in, too. Sometimes it puts new light on the problem to pretend it belongs with somebody else, then it is easier to solve. It seems we can always see the solution to another's problem, so let that system work for you, too.

After you have brain-stormed and listed all the facts then pick the best possible solution for you at this time. That doesn't mean that it is etched in stone and cannot be altered tomorrow. We may have to use trial and error, but at least you are eliminating some of the possibilities.

It is real easy for some of us who have no REAL problems to simplify the problems of others. I may have made the solutions sound so simple and solvable when in reality many problems are not easy at all. For every problem that is solved, another crops up and some are never free of them. These people I greatly admire. And have you ever noticed, they usually are the ones who complain and gripe the least. They are so grateful for any peace or bright hope that comes their way. What strong souls they are!

Adjusting is probably the most difficult part of problems. If things cannot be changed then the next best thing to do is change yourself to cope with the problems. One has to change to fit the circumstances and that is almost impossible to change a way of life. Never has it been said that to be happy, one is problem-free. Most of the people I know are happy in spite of their problems. It is a state of mind.

During the depression no one had money. That did not concern us kids at all. We didn't even know we were poor. But our parents probably spent many sleepless nights trying to figure out a budget or a way to provide money for medicines, etc. We always had plenty of food on the table because we lived on a farm. I cannot remember ever going hungry. In fact, one of my favorite foods was (and is) beans, and we ate them many different ways. One of those ways was in <u>Bean Pie</u>.

3 Cups cooked pinto beans
1 Cup sugar
3 eggs
1/2 Cup butter
1 teaspoon vanilla
1/2 teaspoon salt
1/4 Cup dark Karo syrup

Drain beans and mash thoroughly. Add remaining ingredients and mix well. Put into unbaked 9" pie shell. Bake about 45 minutes at 350 degrees. You'll think this is pecan pie. It has a different taste but you may like it like I do.

In digging others out of trouble, we find a place to bury our own. Think about it!

Chapter 76 — New Year Resolutions

Have you made your New Year's resolutions? Think about it!

Or if you have, have you broken them already? Don't even think about it!

New Year's Day is a good time to turn over a new leaf and begin anew with a clean slate. All the old is behind us, in last year, and we have a fresh year to look forward to.

Every year I, along with almost everyone I know, have made resolutions and most involve losing the few pounds we've put on eating all the wonderful foods of Christmas...well, from Thanksgiving to Christmas. Most resolutions have been kept, yet each year we make about the same ones. These involve eating right, taking better care of our health, exercising more, getting proper rest, etc. Also included are being more tolerant of others, practicing self discipline, and slowing down, among other things. I won't pin you down to revealing yours, if you won't ask me to tell mine.

Once I and a bunch of my friends listed all the things we had failed in the past year. We listed everything we disliked in our lives. Then we put them in a kettle and set fire to them...what a fire! Then we listed all the things we wanted positive about our lives. Those lists we kept to review the next New Year's day. This was symbolic, but it was a good reminder that we really wanted to change things in our lives for the better. It was real effective. It was a reminder that we could get rid of the old ways and start over with a clean slate, with closure to the old thinking.

Even if we don't keep all our resolutions, it is better to make them and not keep all of them than to make none at all, indicating that we have no goals.

One doesn't have to wait until the beginning of a new year to set goals and try to keep them, to voice what we wish for ourselves and work out a plan of action. Anytime is a good time to inventory and see what direction we are going and what direction we wish to be going. You've got to have some kind of map to know where you've been and where you're going to get anywhere in life.

Would you be willing to evaluate your assets on the basis of what you are at present? We dare to believe that tomorrow will find us radically changed for the better. Our perpetual desire is to arrive at the next station of development and achievement a better person than we started out to be. This hope cannot become for us a great incentive until we have analyzed carefully our own immediate circumstances and surroundings. All about us we hear people discouraged and not willing to look life square in the eye. We have to be idealistic enough to apply the lessons of life to our own situation, and make the most of our resolutions for change.

In moments of visions and exaltation we see ourselves free from lazy mental habits that prevent our reaching intellectual attainment. At our best we determine to free ourselves from required physical habits and excesses that rob us of the energies required for vigorous living. We are challenged when we read of great men and women of the past who have accomplished what we want for ourselves. We see elements in their lives and in their character that we long to possess.

We've cooked and eaten all the good stuff during December, now it is time to fix something simple and plain tasting that gives our taste buds a rest. Something like pea salad served with some crispy fish with lemon wedges. Here is my pea salad recipe.

One (15 ounce) can small June peas
Three hard cooked eggs, diced
Three sweet pickles, diced fine
Small onion, diced fine
1 Cup diced sharp yellow cheese
1/2 Cup low-fat mayonnaise.

Drain peas, mix all ingredients well. Chill. What could be simpler?

Our dreams and resolutions may all come true. With purpose, determination, and patience they SHALL come true. Think about it!

Chapter 77 — Poor Me

What do you do about the "poor me syndrome?" Think about it!

Each of us at one time or another has had a bad case of "poor me syndrome" where we have a pity party and think the world all hates us and we feel ugly, and unloved, and stupid, and whatever else it is that makes us feel low as a snake's belly. We think for a time that things just cannot get any worse...but they can.

Once when I was at my lowest ebb, and was having a real low-down period, I had a friend who had the wisdom to give me a call and tell me she would be by in a few minutes to pick me up and we were going to town. Well, we didn't go straight to town. She took a detour to a nursing home and we went in to make a quick call on one of her dear friends. This lovely lady was blind and yet she was an absolute delight to visit. She had come to early Oklahoma and had raised her large family in the country with few labor-saving devices. Yet she was so happy in telling us about their trials and tribulations, never complaining. And even though she could not see them, when Alma Jewell gave her some crocheted house shoes, she felt them in her hands and thanked us profusely for the "pot holder", until we explained to her what they were. She continued to speak with joy and enthusiasm about her children, grandchildren, and great-grandchildren. Never once did she complain about being in the nursing home, nor about her lot in life. I left there after that brief visit, feeling very guilty for whining and feeling so low about nothing.

Look around you. There is always someone much worse off than you are. I know it is that way for me. Most of us live in comfortable homes with warmth, food, and family. Yet we fail to appreciate these basic things and sometimes fail to look around us for someone worse off than we are.

Pity parties are inevitable sometimes but let's not let them go on for long periods of time and certainly don't let them become a habit or we get caught in a trap of feeling sorry for ourselves.

Snap out of it! Count the good things of life, the blessings that have come our way. Be positive. Look for good, even make a list of those positive things around us. If we made columns of the positives and negatives, I'll bet the positives would win hands down.

Now if you are truly blue and cannot shake it better see your doctor. But for those occasional bouts of the blues get busy and bake bread. Knead it, beat it, fold it, roll it. I maintain that our grandmothers got rid of a lot of loneliness out in the open prairies by making bread. They had little stress or time to feel sorry for themselves; they were too busy making bread for their families and neighbors. Invite someone to come over and eat the bread with you. Be sure to invite "up" people, and not those who whine all the time. Instead of us pulling them up, it seems some people just pull us down to their level, and when we have the blahs already, we sure don't need that. These people seem to always bring the conversation back to their problems and they are always the worst in the world...even worse than mine. These people need to see things in a different light and get a life!

On those cold winter evenings when we pull the world in around us and have a temporary case of feeling sorry for ourselves, we want something soothing to eat in front of the fireplace. Something like this "Pioneer Porridge" (Beef Stew).

1 pound hamburger, browned
5 medium potatoes, cut up
2 Cups carrots, cut up
1 Cup celery, cut up
one onion, coarsely chopped
One (15 ounce) can tomato sauce
1 1/2 teaspoon salt (or to taste)
1/4 teaspoon pepper (or to taste)

Combine all ingredients in a 3-quart Dutch oven. Cover with lid and bake in 325 degree oven for at least an hour or until vegetables are tender. Serve with hot corn bread.

Surely there is more to life than thinking of self only. What poison is to food, self pity is to life. Think about it!

Chapter 78 — Peace

Are you at peace with yourself and with the world? Think about it!

At this time of year when we have just been talking about and singing about peace on earth, do we really have that peace? It is much easier to think about peace in the world and to ask why countries don't get along and stop warring, than it is to see within ourselves that we are not altogether peaceful. We think that different races or nationalities should be undisturbed, yet within ourselves is a measure of unrest. It is easier to look "out there" and see how things should be worked out than it is to look "in here" and see how things are in turmoil.

Isn't it awful when families get together and there is strife, and certain family members don't get along with other family members. Families can provide the best of times and the worst of times. There is nothing better than a happy, congenial family for support and unconditional love, and there is nothing sadder than a bickering, judgmental family. If there is to be peace within ourselves and the world, we must learn to accept the differences of opinions, of customs and traditions, of political preferences, and religious choices. We must love the family members for the ties that bind.

That same philosophy applies to keeping friends. Look at your dear high school friends and see how they have changed as they have matured and gone on with their lives and careers and adapted a certain life style. Either we grow closer to them or we have little in common with them when we again meet. Seldom do these "best friends" remain the same socially, financially, and emotionally. Time just has a way of taking care of that, but families.....with the same heritage and ancestors in common brings people closer together (or should at least). As our roots are explored and the family trees cultivated, this closeness takes on new and deeper meanings.

Take a picture album to your next family gathering. Remember the good times with laughter and nostalgia and remember the bad times with understanding and patience and empathy.

However, sometimes it is beyond all human possibilities to have peace with family members...much less the world. But you've still got to create within yourself a calming peace. You must ask forgiveness and accept forgiveness to make things work out. When all else fails, one must know when to hold on and when to let go, and to have the grace to make the right decisions with dignity. So often we say things to family and close friends that we would never say to enemies or causal acquaintances. We need to guard against saying things in haste. It takes a truly great person to say, "I'm wrong, and I'm sorry." But when we are wrong, we must apologize and make amends. Only then can we have peace within.

We are harder on ourselves than we are on others. We never forgive ourselves when we have wronged someone else, yet we readily forgive any transgression by someone else. Why?

There is nothing like an evening of visiting and sipping hot chocolate that works like a peace pipe ceremony to bind a friendship in love. Add a great cheese dip and some crackers and you have a party. One of the girls I work with gave me this easy recipe.

Becky's Cheese Ball

2 (eight ounce) packages cream cheese
1 (8 ounce) can crushed pineapple, drained
1/4 Cup green Bell peppers, chopped fine
1/4 Cup finely chopped onion
1 tablespoon Lawry's Seasoning (or seasoning of preference)
1 Cup chopped pecans.

Soften cream cheese and add drained pineapple with other ingredients. If this is used as a ball roll in chopped nuts, otherwise add them to the dip. Serve with assorted crackers.

Be too large for worry, too noble for anger, too strong for fear, and too happy to be submerged by trouble. That is peace. Think about it!

Chapter 79 — Millionaires

Are you a millionaire? Think about it?

What if you won that eleven million dollar sweepstakes or a lottery and became wealthy overnight? Wouldn't your life change drastically, or would it? Would you be the same person as you are now? It is hard to say how we would react because it probably won't happen but it is something to think about anyway. It is nice to have sufficient money for comforts and extras too but the things in life that REALLY matter in the long run are not things that can be bought with any amount of money.

Money cannot possibly buy the love of family and friends. Oh, there may be lots of people gather around us at a time of wealth, but are they tried and true friends or people wanting to borrow money or be seen with the rich. To real friends our income doesn't affect how they feel about us.

Money cannot buy health. It can pay our doctor bills and medical bills, but the health itself comes with another price and not money only. If that were true, there would be no sick people, because we would all buy our way out of illnesses. When one is against the wall with some tragic illness, it would be nice if we could purchase sound health but it just doesn't work that way.

Money cannot buy peace of mind. There are many wealthy individuals who are a wreck mentally. They cannot cope with life in its simplest forms. They are constantly seeking something or someone who will bring them the happiness they so desperately crave. They fail to enjoy the simple life of simple foods and simple friendships, and simple everyday joys. They long for genuine pleasures and restful sleep and it does not come. Turmoil abounds.

Money cannot buy class. People who have inherited money or have acquired "new" money, often do not cope with their wealth and fail to have the elegance and grace to use it properly or with style. Thus class is not something you purchase but something you acquire with proper upbringing and caring for other people. It is the art of putting other people first and really has little to do with money for the sake of money. There are people who have very little riches who have a great deal of class and exude elegance in their way of life. Simplicity is class. Showiness is not class.

Money cannot buy happiness. Happiness comes from within one's self and not from their pocket books and wallets and bank accounts. Happiness is a state of mind of being content with what we have with enough to share with those less fortunate. Some of the happiest people are those who have the least money because they look around them for beauty and love. They find pleasure and satisfaction in their humble surroundings. They appreciate what they have and how they got it.

I am not putting down people with money. I am happy for them and this is not sour grapes. I have enough to be comfortable and fed and I am grateful for that. However, even if I were to become an overnight millionaire, I would continue to work and to cook and to care for my family and things as I have always done. I can't imagine that it would change me or mine all that much. I am content with what I have and I think most people feel the same way I do. Would you really change that much? Maybe for a short time we would bask in our glory and money but then we would settle back to the norm of things. This norm is our happiness.

Even if we can't live like a million, we can eat like a million with this Million Dollar Pie.

One large Cool Whip
1 1/3 Cup lemon juice
1 Cup chopped pecans
1 can Eagle Brand Milk
1 Cup drained crushed pineapple
Baked 10" pie crust

Stir lemon juice into milk. Add pineapple and nuts. Fold into Cool Whip. Pile into pie crust and chill.

Sometimes the world seems to be luxury mad and money crazy. Money is a great power. Properly handled it accomplishes modern miracles. Used for the wrong purposes it can wreck the whole social order. What should be our attitude toward it? Think about it!

Chapter 80 — Solid Foundations

Do you have a solid foundation? Think about it!

Much of our foundation goes back to the way we were reared by our parents and families. Through all the years they have loved us, cared for us, sacrificed for us. Our first standards of conduct were patterned after their lives. They gave us our first moral concepts and ideals. Much that is best and noblest in us is a heritage from our parents.

And can a leopard change its spots? Or would it want to? The moral standards and beliefs are so ingrained in us that we probably couldn't change if we wanted to. That code of ethics was instilled in us by example of our parents and family and associates and is US. It seems to me that it is as difficult to speed up a slow person as it is to slow down a speedy person. Those work ethics are also a part of the individual person's basic makeup.

So are honesty, and loyalty, and punctuality. These are a basic part of our personality and it is almost impossible to change, unless we really want to, then anything is possible.

I am very grateful for parents and family who taught me the basic behavior and caring for others. I know it would have been much easier if they had just let me go my own way of least resistance, but they felt the responsibility to teach me the code of ethics of honesty and fairness. It does not always make parents popular when they must say "No", but it sure makes for good kids and I think most kids really appreciate the true caring in the long run.

Even with little training, a child knows right from wrong. They may not always do the correct thing, but basically they KNOW what is right and what is wrong and dishonest and taking advantage of others. Thank goodness, most of us had a family who trained us in the proper ways of society and decency. When these attributes have become a part of our basic philosophy, they will stay with us all our lives.

Whatever virtues of character we may possess, their roots run down into the unselfish and tender loyalties of home affection. We can only repay so great a debt by keeping the fire burning, remembering those teachings and living in a way that will justify their trust in us. How can we fail them in even the small ways? They trust us so much and have such great expectations from us.

Are we conveying these same standards of moral fiber to the next generations? Sometimes it is so easy to be permissive and think that kids will learn by their mistakes. True, in a sense, but isn't it our responsibility to teach them, too? Why should a child get burned in order to learn that a stove is hot? Is it not our responsibility to tell them and save them the pain of a burn?

We are molded by our teachers, our families, our neighbors, and all of those we associate with. Each of them influences our life in some way...good or bad. As the song says, "Be true, because people trust you, Be pure for there are those who care".

When you want to begin your day with a good foundation think about it the night before and make this Hot and Hearty Breakfast. All you need to go with it is juice and muffins of some kind: We serve it for our open house every Christmas and most seem to like it.

Hot and Hearty Breakfast Casserole

3 cups dry bread cubes
6 eggs, slightly beaten
1 teaspoon salt
1/2 small can chopped green chilies (drained)
1/4 onion, chopped real fine
one pound sausage, cooked and drained
2 cups milk

Mix all ingredients together and pour into greased 9" x 13" casserole. Top with 4 ounces grated sharp or mild cheddar cheese. Cover and refrigerate overnight. In the morning, bake in 350 degree oven about 45 minutes. Let set 5 minutes before serving.

Frederick Starr said, "Strive for the approval of your companions but do not be too easily moved by ridicule. When you know what you ought to do, permit not the laughter of others to deter you." Think about it!

Chapter 81 — Valentines

Who is your favorite valentine? Think about it!

Remember when you were a kid in grade school and you sent a valentine to every kid in your class. Or in my case to everyone in the entire school of probably twenty-one or so kids. In this little eight grades/one room school house, the teacher would not let us omit anyone. This was awkward to some of us as we didn't want the world to know that we disliked or liked a certain person.

We spent days before Valentine's Day making a box to hold all our valentines. Lucky was the person who could talk their big sister or mother out of a heart shaped box to make an opening in the top to slip the valentines in on the day of the party.

We also spent days or weeks making our own valentines of bits and pieces of materials of every kind. Some of those valentines were downright beautiful and some were awful, but we gave them anyway.

I still have some of those valentines. In fact, I still have a valentine that Daddy gave to Mother when they were in grade school together. What a treasure.

Do we still send valentines and keep them and enjoy them like we used to do?

I receive a valentine every year from Jim. I have kept all of those of course, and any that the girls have given me that they have made with loving thoughts. I treasure all of them.

I live with the thought that we should never pass up a chance to tell someone that we love them. The opportunity may never come again. We just never know. When my mother was so ill with cancer I went over to visit her. I had all my stuff already in the car and I told Jim I wanted to run inside one more time and see Mother. I went in to her room, and knelt down by her bed and told her I loved her and thanked her for giving me life. She told me she loved me too. Well, that was the last time I saw her alive. How glad I have always been that I took the time to again tell her what we already knew, that we loved each other. But it is nice to hear the words and to say the words. What a good feeling to be loved and love somebody.

Love is the greatest force in the universe. Even when our astronauts were on their space missions, when there was no gravity force, there was still love and they could feel it that far away. There is no love without faith, no love without hope, no love without loyalty.

Make a special recipe for that special valentine to express your affection. It needn't be something elaborate. Strawberry Trifle is easy and Jim calls it "Sweetheart Trifle".

One medium angel food cake
14 ounce can sweetened condensed milk
1 tablespoon lemon juice
large carton Cool Whip
2 Cups strawberries (may be fresh or frozen that have thawed)
1/2 Cup chopped pecans (optional)

Tear angel food cake in bite sized pieces. Mix milk with the lemon juice. In large trifle dish layer the angel food cake pieces, milk mixture, strawberries, and Cool Whip and sprinkle with a few nuts in that order. Repeating until all the ingredients have been used, ending with Cool Whip. Cover and chill well before serving.

Love is the greatest thing in the world. To love abundantly is to live abundantly. Happy Valentines Day. Think about it!

Chapter 82 — Crying

What makes you cry? Think about it!

Do you cry when you are happy? or sad? or nostalgic? or surprised? or disappointed? or frustrated? There are many reasons we cry.

Sometimes we cry from mixed emotions like at a graduation or wedding. We are sad for the era that is ending but happy for the era that is in its new beginning. What mother has not cried when her small child started to kindergarten? It isn't that she wants that child to stay small the rest of its life, it is just because...well, it is a real mixed emotion.

All of us cry when we have lost a dear, close relative or friend. That crying is more because we are left alone without that person. It is a healing part of the grieving process. We need that crying to wash away our sorrow. In time the tears come less and less.

Do you cry in solitude when your feelings are really hurt? It is not always a matter of low self esteem. Sometimes things just hurt our hearts. Then we cry. And very likely the person who hurt us did not intentionally mean to do it. Forgiving comes into the picture here. After we have forgiven, we forget and then we feel much better. Those tears just cleansed away the bad feelings.

No use crying over spilled milk. True. There is no need to cry over something that cannot be under our control. But we do cry anyway sometimes. It doesn't help the situation...but it sure helps us feel better.

Jim's Marine Corps Reunions after 53 years is always a very joyous, happy occasion. But there are many tears shed here. Some out of sorry over someone lost but most because of shared memories of combat and the things that happened to bind them together. We always come away cleansed and refreshed and feeling wonderful. All these great strong terrific Marines who have been through so much are so tender and caring for each other. In fact, I wouldn't give you ten cents for a person (men included) who can't or won't show their true emotions and cry when they feel like it. It is truly a sign of great strength and purpose that people can cry. Why try to hide one of the greatest emotions there is. It is perfectly normal and one of the first emotions we show, even before laughing.

Have you ever served a loaf of bread that was dough on the inside? Or served a cake made with a cup of salt instead of sugar? Or made a pie crust that had to be cut with a hatchet? Well, everyone has had a failure at one time or another. Don't let it make you so frustrated that it ruins your day. This too shall pass. In time, it will be funny!

Have you watched a show on T.V. or in the theater that made you laugh until you cried? Your eyes teared up and your sides ached and you couldn't stop the downpour. These tears are cleansing too. Laughter is so good for the soul.

What is the story about the princess that wouldn't cry? Finally they tried onions and it worked. Then she was a complete person again. Tears did it. I can't remember if she married the handsome prince but I bet she did...And I know she was happy because she cried.

When you want a "comfort food" try something chocolate...it's gotta be chocolate.

Chocolate Crinkles

1/2 C. shortening
1 2/3 C. sugar
2 t. vanilla
2 eggs
6 T. cocoa
2 C. flour
2 t. baking powder
1/2 t. salt
1/3 C. milk
1/2 C. nuts, chopped
powdered sugar

Cream shortening and sugar. Add vanilla and beaten eggs. Sift dry ingredients and add alternately with milk to creamed mixture. Stir in nuts and chill dough at least three hours. Shape dough into small balls. Roll each in powdered sugar. Place on cookie sheets about two inches apart. Bake in a 350 degree oven 10 to 12 minutes.

These and a glass of milk will make all the bad things go away. You'll feel so much better. Smile and the world smiles with you. Cry and you cry alone. Think about it!

Chapter 83 — Stupid Things

Have you ever done something really stupid? Think about it.

If you are a member of the human race and anywhere near average, you have! We all have. Or will. Some of us more than others. One always feels so foolish afterwards. For example, someone tells of a pending funeral. "Oh, did he/she die?", you've heard asked.

Have you ever licked frost off a pump handle? Ask me how I know.

Have you ever taken someone "snipe" hunting? or been taken on a "snipe" hunt yourself? Boy, that brings back the old days when we were silly.

"Wet paint" signs just announce to the world the compulsion to touch the paint and see just how wet it really is. Surely the sign is wrong.

Have you even ran up to someone on the street and hugged them and greeted them warmly while they backed off and looked at you like you were some kind of nut? Only then did you realize it wasn't the person you thought it was. You felt so embarrassed. Again, ask me how I know. I am the master at that and have done it several times but not to the same people each time.

Jim tells of a time he felt really stupid just after he had returned from combat in World War II. He was standing on the street corner with a buddy when a car back-fired. Instinctively they hit the ground for cover. Only then did they realize it was only a car. They got up as quickly as they could, looking around them, hoping nobody saw them.

Have you ever gambled with the gas gauge all the time knowing that the gauge allowed extra miles after it hit the big "E". You were positive you had enough gas in that tank to get you where you were going...WRONG. Our philosophy is it takes no more money to buy two half tanks of gas than it does one whole tank and it sure saves a lot of embarrassment and shoe leather.

Have you ever mis-read the clock and scurried around in the morning and went to work only to find that you had looked wrong and had arrived an entire hour early? Where was everyone? Or have you ever gone to work on a Saturday or a holiday? These things we quietly keep to ourselves, hoping no one finds out and thinks we have slipped another cog.

How many times have you locked yourself out of the car? or out of your own house? You knew the very instant the door clicked that those keys were INSIDE and you were OUTSIDE. You grabbed for the door but it clicked just as you touched it and you had done it again!

I don't expect anyone to own up to this, but how many times have you walked into a room and forgot why you came...then you have to go back where you were to remember what it was you were supposed to do or get. It is so easy to do (forget, I mean), and few of us are exempt from it.

As bad as anything is to be talking and be distracted and completely forget your place in the conversation or your train of thought. Your mind just goes blank. I'd hate to be on the stage right then...only perhaps it would help if we had those prompters after all.

A recipe that is kinda odd but is really easy and delicious is:

Upside Down Fudge Cake/Pudding

Sift together into bowl:
1 C. flour
2 t. baking powder
1/4 t. salt
3/4 C. sugar
2 T. cocoa

Stir in:
1/2 C. milk
2 T. melted shortening

Spread in 9" x 9" pan.
Sprinkle with mixture of:
1 C. brown sugar
1/4 C. cocoa

Then pour over the entire batter:
1 3/4 C. HOT water

Bake at 350 degrees for 45 minutes. During baking the cake mixture will rise and the chocolate sauce settles to the bottom of the dish. Serve warm, dipping sauce over cake as served. Wonderful with a dollop of ice cream.

Sit back and enjoy this dessert with a cup of coffee and laugh at all the stupid things you have done. You're not alone. Everyone does something stupid sometime. Think about it!

Chapter 84 — Illnesses

Have you ever had a serious condition or illness? Think about it!

If you have, you can probably recall the friend that stood by you for comfort and strength, or you offered the same support system.

At first, you were probably devastated when you heard that you or someone you love was seriously ill. Then you regrouped your thoughts and counted the positives and blessings. You wanted to share it with family and friends because from them comes your security and strength when you are surrounded by love and caring.

We direct all our energies to feeling better. We never give up. We have a will to live, to survive, against all odds.

When my husband, Jim, was shot on Iwo Jima and hit by a bullet through his mid-section, he said the thought never occurred to him that he would die. He tried to run and collapsed and was finally carried off the battle field to a safer part of the island. There he was "passed over" for those the surgeons thought had a chance for survival. He begged that they accept his case and operate on him. The surgeons finally agreed. He was so grateful that he was accepted and not left alone to die. The surgery was performed in a tent set up on the beach, with little equipment and less than sterile conditions.

His survival left Jim with the attitude that he was "spared" for a certain purpose, for some reason. The experience made him a better, stronger person with goals and determinations that few people feel.

Jim knows what it is like to hit bottom and bounce. We've heard it said that a ball does not bounce in mid-air. It has to hit bottom before it bounces. This can be said for many severe illnesses. One has to be very ill before they get better. Then they really appreciate good health and a whole body.

Remember when you were a little kid and cut a finger or fell down and hurt yourself? You thought, and you were right, that a kiss would make it bette and make all the bad things go away. It was that support system, usually your Mom, that made all things better. You felt better all over. Things don't change that much from when we are kids and when we grow up, especially when we are hurting. We still like that good feeling that someone who cares gives to us in support and love.

Bet you thought I was going to share a sickie recipe for broth or green gelatin. Tain't likely! Here's a recipe that makes you feel better...to take to a sick person or eat at home with a fresh cup of coffee.

Pumpkin Bread

2/3 C. shortening
2 2/3 C. sugar
4 eggs
1 can (16 oz.) pumpkin
2/3 C. water
3 1/3 C. flour
1 T. pumpkin pie spice
2/3 C. chopped nuts (optional)
2/3 C. raisins (optional)
2 t. soda
1 1/2 t. salt
1/2 t. baking powder

In large bowl, cream shortening, sugar, and eggs until fluffy. Stir in pumpkin and water. Stir in blended dry ingredients. Add raisins and/or nuts. Pour into two 9 x 5 x 3 loaf pans. Bake at 350 degrees for 70 minutes.

Illnesses are bearable because of support systems of friends and family. Sometimes the magnet that pulls them closer together is an illness or serious condition. Think about it!

Chapter 85 — State Fair

Hi, Ho, Come to the fair! Think about it!

When the September rains come, it is time to begin making plans for what we have thought about for the past year...the State fair. Isn't it fun?

The fair has its own special aroma. We go to smell the smells, see the sights, hear the sounds, eat the stuffs, and be a part of that festive time of year that brings city folks and country folks together in a special time of celebration.

When I was a kid, we always went to the fair. Daddy and Mother believed that all learning did not come from books so insisted that we be excused from regular classes to attend the fair. We were expected to observe the livestock around us, as well as show the ones we brought. We walked around and looked at the vegetables and garden produce, and the wheat samples, and the canning, sewing, and crafts that were judged and exhibited. I don't remember that we ever went to the "midway" and spent any money, but we did go to the world exhibits and take all that in.

Now when we go, we always attend the ice shows. Of course, they are usually based on some Disney movie of current interest to the young kids, but we enjoy them too...as part of our second childhood.

We go early enough to have an early lunch in the 4-H building and then see all the sights we can work in before the afternoon show begins.

We like seeing the crowds and walking around all the exhibits.

We are constantly amazed at the amount of work that goes into the canning and the sewing and the baking and the produce. And the animals are so trained and well behaved when they are shown. They seem to realize they are on display and react accordingly. The kids who stay there in the barns seem to have such a good time with all the other kids. They are making memories of these days at the fair, whether they realize it or not.

The games and rides are an attraction to some although that has never been a passion of mine. I could live all my life and not ride a farris wheel and still have a full and enjoyable life. I fail to see the thrill of going up that high to look out over the crowds. And there is always some "comic" who rocks the thing in mid-air. That doesn't hold much thrill for me!

A few years back the big attraction and rage at the state fair was the bungy jumping. Whoopee!! But no, thanks!! That too, is not my thing.

As far back as I can remember, my grandma and mother canned for fair competition. It seems they always won a ribbon too. That prompted Mother to name her cook book, "Fair Quality Cooking". She, of course, meant competition worthy, but we always kidded her about being "so-so". But she was an excellent cook and I hope at least some of that rubbed off on me.

One of her "Fair Quality Recipes" was "Watermelon Rind Preserves":

Peel off all green portion. Cut into small chunks. Soak in mild salt water overnight (1/2 C. salt to one gallon water), Drain and cook in clear water about thirty minutes or until tender. Drain well. For 11 Cups of the melon and rind, make a syrup of 9 cups sugar, 8 cups of water, four lemons, sliced, and add 4 t. stick cinnamon, 4 t. cloves (tie spices in cheese cloth bag). Boil the syrup, lemon and spices 5 minutes before adding the rinds. Add rinds and cook until transparent and clear. A few minutes before preserves are done, add enough green or red food coloring to tint if desired. Remove spice bag. Pour into jars and seal. I hope you get a blue ribbon!

Do enjoy the sights and sounds and smells of the fair. At that time you can't convince me the lights are shinning anywhere but there! Think about it.

Chapter 86 — Tempering Temper

Do you have a temper? Think about it!

Or more importantly...do you control your temper? What's that old joke about someone having an even temper...mad all the time!

I have mellowed as I have gotten older. (Some who know me now may wonder what on earth I was like when I was younger...ha!) When I was a kid I slammed doors when I got mad and let my temper flare. I cannot tell you (wouldn't if I COULD) how many times I had to come back and close the door more gently. Once I even broke the glass out of the back door. I'd bang and slam and when I was REAL young, I'd stomp my feet. A tiny peach switch broke me of that real quickly. Those switches hummed as they went through the air. They didn't hurt but they sure stung. We even had to select and cut our own switch from the peach orchard. Not too big but not too thin either. I remember only a few times it was ever used on me and each time I am sure I deserved the punishment I received. (And I probably deserved more punishment than I actually ever got.)

What angers you quickly that you lose control of your temper? Does unnecessary tardiness? Laziness? Procrastinating? Dishonesty? Snobbishness? Self-centeredness? Inconsideration of others? Bullies? Or what? The list can go on and on.

Noise, including some "music" can irritate one to the point of agitation...then the simplest thing can overcome you and make you lose it! That's the time to be an oyster...keep your trap shut, and use the irritant to make a pearl. It is easier said than done to make something beautiful out of those situations, but with practice it can be done. You can close out the distraction and get busy to the rhythm.

Sometimes when our self esteem is threatened, we feel defensive and angry. That is why when someone criticizes us or <u>tells</u> us something to do we get mad. All of us can accept kind critique, and we like to be asked, instead of told, to do or not do something. It is a simple fact of human nature that we don't want our ideals questioned or threatened.

Coaches, who work with young people, have discovered how important it is to critique kindly and to guide, rather than yell at them in front of peers and family and friends. This can destroy their self confidence. No one likes to be made a fool of in front of others. It is bad enough in private, but at least it saves their hurt feelings. The same can be said for teachers, or any boss or personnel manager. Nothing is solved by yelling at anyone in anger to embarrass them.

Some people just want to be left completely alone when they are "riled". Others want to get busy and do something that exerts a lot of energy. Others want to be calmly soothed until they feel better.

The sad thing about the ways people get angry and over anger, is that often they hurt others in the process. If they clam up they run the risk of making those around them think they are mad at them when they probably really are not. On the other hand, those who lash out at those around them hurt others in the words they say. Either way is damaging.

If anger is excessive, better see a counselor. There may be a real deep-seated problem. Or if you cannot ever get upset about something maybe you are a little too passive. Either way you may need help.

Something that is hot like a temper but so good, is: Peppy Potatoes

Peel and slice thin, about 5 large potatoes. Peel and chop one large onion. Now layer the potatoes and onions with a layer of cheese (we like sharp cheese), salt to taste, Lawry's Seasoned Salt, and sprinkle on a little Picante sauce. Repeat these layers. Cover casserole with lid or foil, and bake until potatoes are done. Remove cover the last 10 minutes of cooking so the cheese will brown a little. This is great. Jim discovered how to make it quite by accident, and it is one of our family favorites...but then, isn't ALL food!

In a fit of rage, things are said and done that cannot be grabbed back, so temper your temper. Think about it!

Chapter 87 — Low Days

Do you ever have low days? Think about it.

I guess all of us have pity parties from time to time. Most "normal" people have times of depression from set-backs or decisions or challenges they have to face. And it is perfectly normal to be depressed because of grieving or sadness. Those people are certainly entitled to "down" times. But just being depressed because of your lot in life is another story.

How deep is your down? How long are your pity parties? There could be a medical reason so perhaps a check-up is indicated, but for brief times of depression and/or gloom, it is easier to nip it in the bud before you hit bottom.

Abraham Lincoln said, "We are about as happy as we make up our minds to be". Maybe the same can be said for unhappiness and depression.

Some people are depressed out of simple boredom. What a pity! With all the interesting, wonderful things in life there are to do, it is a shame that people are bored with themselves and others. This stagnation can be changed if one will simply get busy doing something useful for others or themselves.

If you are tired, maybe you just need more sleep. Try that and if that doesn't work, then try a change of scenery, a new hobby, or a fun project. Exercise helps too, as does positive thinking and a new attitude.

I was making Scottish Oatmeal Bread recently and when the recipe said, "Test raised dough. When the depression stays, it is ready". That is much like we are, when depression stays, we are <u>ready</u> to turn our lives around and make something worthwhile of our too short lives.

It is time to think of others, to get up, get out, and do something different, exciting, and rewarding.

Baking bread is a cure for depression. I wonder if that therapy worked for our pioneer ancestors who were miles and miles from neighbors and must have had lonely, dismal days out on the prairie. I'll bet they kneaded bread like crazy, and I bet they felt better after they did it too. There's something in the mixing, and kneading, and shaping, and baking, and eating bread that releases tensions and takes away depression...especially if you share that bread with a dear friend over a cup of hot tea or coffee, or serve it to a hungry family.

For me, Scottish Oatmeal Bread will pull me out of the mournful moods quicker than anything. As I mix and measure, I think of our ancestors who came through Ellis Island to be a part of this great country. I cherish the old recipes that have been handed down from generation to generation with the same feelings that we experience. This Scottish Oatmeal Bread is easy to make and stays moist for a long time. It tastes great.

"Brodie Bread"

2 C. milk, scalded
1 C. uncooked oats
1 T. shortening
1 pkg. Dry yeast
1/4 C. warm water (105 to 115 degrees)
1/4 C. molasses
1 1/2 t. salt
5 C. all-purpose flour

Place milk and oats and shortening in a large bowl. Stir until shortening is melted. Cover and let stand one hour at room temperature. Dissolve yeast in water. Stir dissolved yeast, the molasses and salt into oat mixture. Stir in enough flour to make dough easy to handle.

Turn dough onto lightly floured board. Knead until smooth and elastic. Place in greased bowl and turn greased side up and cover. Let rise in warm place until double. (Dough is ready if depression remains). Punch down dough. Knead again and return to bowl. Cover and let rise until double. Punch down dough. Divide in half. Shape into two round loaves. Place on greased baking sheet. Let rise covered in warm place until double. Heat oven to 325 degrees. Bake until golden brown and loaves sound hollow when tapped, about 35 to 40 minutes. Cool on wire racks.

Most depression is a temporary set-back, but forget the past, snap out of it, and start over again with an attitude adjustment. Do something nice for yourself. Just buying something doesn't seem to break the spell but the act of <u>doing</u> seems to turn things around from depression to elation. Think about it.

Chapter 88 — Apples

Don't you enjoy the crunch and taste of a crisp apple? Think about it!

Apples look so pretty in a super market or in one of those road-side stands. One cannot resist buying them. Some people like the sweet apples, some tart, some peeled and cored and quartered, while others like to take a big bite out of the apple until they nearly get their nose in the juicy pulp. Have you tried a tart apple, sprinkled a little with salt and eaten with cheese and crackers? It is delicious.

Eating apples brings back floods of memories to me because when I was a kid, we went every fall to the orchard several miles from home traveling in the wagon and spent all day in our apple orchard gathering apples. We picked and <u>placed</u> those apples in boxes and baskets, being very careful not to bruise them. When we got home, we took the very best ones and wrapped them in paper, and stored in a cool room. (Of course <u>all</u> of the rooms were cool as we heated with a wood stove and the "stove room" was the only one beside the kitchen that was toasty.)

The apples that we picked up off the ground were kept separate and used in apple butter or eaten first. As I recall, we had apples all winter and into the spring. Between times we had lots of apple butter and canned apples for pies and eating plain.

Recently some friends went with us to my sister's house in Albuquerque where it is cool and high and they have lots of apples in their orchard. Well, we gathered apples until the world looked level (that's a long time) and tucked them into every nook and cranny of our car to bring home. We put them in feed sacks and carted them all home. That is, we thought we did, until we learned just recently that our husbands had removed two sacks of apples that there simply was not room for in the car. We were so busy making apple pies, apple cakes, apple fritters, baked apples, apple butter, etc. that we never missed those two absent sacks. Now I wish I had them again!

There are so many things one can do with apples. Halloween is the perfect time to bob for apples and make caramel dipped apples. Christmas is the perfect time to put out a huge bowl of apples or to put in the socks hung by the fireplace.

There are songs written about apples..."Don't Sit Under the Apple Tree with Anyone Else but Me"... (boy, that dates us).

There are sayings about apples: An apple a day keeps the doctor away. Someone is the apple of your eye. Sir Isaac Newton discovered gravity when the apple fell on his head. Many things are done "for Mom and apple pie." We "apple polish" to get a good grade or a promotion.

Johnny Appleseed sure knew what he was doing when he spread the seeds west so the whole country could forever enjoy apples.

Nothing stirs memories like our grandmother's apple pies or apple dumplings. That cinnamony smell permeated the whole house.

Everyone has a favorite recipe for apple pie but here is a recipe that is easier and just about as good as pie. It is:

Apple Pudding

1 C. sugar
1 egg
1 C. flour
1 t. cinnamon
1 t. nutmeg
1/2 C. butter
1/2 t. soda
2 1/4 C. fresh apples, diced fine
1 C. nuts and/or raisins

Cream sugar, butter, and egg. Add apples, nuts and/or raisins and mix thoroughly. Sift dry ingredients and add a little at a time to apple mixture. Pour in slightly greased 9" X 9" baking pan. Bake in a 350 degree oven until done (about 45 minutes.) Serve with whipped topping, ice cream or vanilla sauce. May be served warm or cold or in between.

Next time you pass the apples in the produce section, stop and get some. They are full of vitamins and fiber and stuff good for you...all that notwithstanding...they just taste good!

Have you had your apple today? Think about it!

Chapter 89 — Opinions of Others

Do you care what people think about you? Think about it!

You may think you don't really care, but you do, or you wouldn't feel embarrassed when you do or say something goofy. Have you ever fallen on the ice or just over a crack in the sidewalk and the second you fall, even before you check to see if you have a broken bone, you glance around real quick to see who saw you fall? It seems to just be human nature to be concerned about what people think.

I remember my most embarrassing moment. I was at a concert in Tulsa at a beautiful auditorium. At the end of the program we all got up to leave. I felt something touch my ankle and thinking it might be someone behind me surprising me, I glanced around and there was no one I knew. I glanced down then, and could have died on the spot, because my slip had worked itself down around my ankles. The worst part of it was that I had on a rather sheer dress. Needless to say, Jim had to walk close behind me and keep me out of doorways or other sources of light. I was terribly relieved to be out of there and in the car on the way to our room. I had just quickly picked up my slip and shoved it in my purse. That slip, with its worn elastic went straight in the trash. For years I could hardly tell about it but as I have gotten older, it has become funnier. I realize embarrassing things happen to all of us and we do survive.

These best dressed/worst dressed lists are of interest to the winners only because in one way or another they are attracting attention, whether good or bad. Some of them look elegant while some look awful. But they do it because they care what people think about them.

We are also concerned about an impression we make on others. Why else are we concerned to not be too loud, or too quiet, or too silly, or too serious, or too talkative, or whatever. We aren't just trying to be like everyone else but we do want to fit into a certain group expectation.

We also want our families to behave in public and not do anything to embarrass us. But do the actions of our families really reflect on us? Can we truly be responsible for what our families do? Our friends, yes, because birds of feather flock together and that DOES reflect on us, somewhat. But we can raise our kids in the best way we know how, and we still don't know for sure how they act when we are not around. Usually they do make us proud of them...or we hear about it from another source, and fix it! The same can be said for any strange relative.

In marriage, you love your spouse more than you love yourself (or should anyway, if it is to be a truly happy marriage). This means that you love that person as she or he is. We should ask ourselves frankly what that impulse is that makes us want to redesign a person. It isn't love. We want the other person to be normal, like us! But is that loving the other person, or ourselves? We do care what people think.

If you really care what people think and want to impress them with your culinary skills, make this simple, delicious casserole for your next dinner party. It is good with any meat dish and easy to prepare. I got it from a good friend. I'll pass it along to you.

Perfectly Wonderful Potatoes

one package (24 Oz.) Orida Brand frozen O'Brien Hash Browns
1/4 Cup melted oleo or butter
1 can Cream of Chicken soup
8 oz. sour cream
1/2 teaspoon salt
8 oz. grated sharp cheddar cheese

Mix all together (except cheese) and place in large casserole dish. Top with cheese. Bake one hour at 350 degrees (covered).

Now serve it and sit back and listen to the raves. You'll have your guests right where you want them...thinking you are wonderful and talented and caring.

I think it was Queen Victoria who said, "The important thing is not what they think of me, it is what I think of them." Well, maybe so...but it does make a difference. We all want to be liked and admired. We do care. Think about it!

Chapter 90 — Making Excuses

Do you make excuses? Think about it!

Oh, we've all made excuses from time to time but if we always have an excuse instead of a reason to do or not do something, then maybe we should look into our motives. There is a vast difference in excuses and reasons. Reasons are real, actual things that prevent our doing something we might like to do. Excuses are things we contrive to explain our absence. What is the old saying about "Don't explain...your friends don't need it and your enemies won't believe you anyway," or something like that. You know what, I think whoever said that was telling the truth. Friends don't need excuses or reasons. Isn't it comforting to know that friends can be perfectly honest and everyone understands.

Have you ever told a "white lie"? Well now, I won't pin you down and make you tell. I don't think my dad will even tell a "white lie". He says where do you draw the line and know where a "white lie" and "bold-faced lie" begin and end. He has an advantage over me. He is in his 90's and people expect the elderly to say exactly what is on their mind. Boy, he does. And I don't think he ever hurts anyone's feeling, certainly not intentionally. But if he doesn't want to go somewhere he simply states that he would rather be at home in his chair. People accept that. I'm not so sure they would from me. Or maybe I am just too insecure to try to be that brutally honest. I feel (and this is MY opinion, not what I was taught at my father's knee) that a white lie is one told to save other person's feelings. It's kinder sometimes than the harsh truth.

To out and out lie, I cannot do, and I'll bet you can't either. In the first place I would not be able to keep a straight face nor look you in the eye. I could no more lie than I could cheat, or steal, or deliberately hurt someone's feelings. I would bet that 98 percent of the people feel just like I do.

Some people find it easy to make excuses for a predicament and blame others, like parents, teachers, kids, co-workers, friends, relatives, or society in general. I have heard people even blame the credit card companies for their being in debt. They say if the credit card companies didn't make it so easy to spend, that they wouldn't be so far in debt. Hog-wash. No one made them spend it. This touches our most personal habits and inclinations. The world seems to be luxury mad and money crazy. Money is a great power. People have their ups and downs...the problem of keeping appearances up and expenses down. Properly handled, money accomplishes modern miracles. Used for the wrong purposes, it can wreck the whole social order. We can use excuses, or in some cases (like unforeseen illness or emergencies) we have true reasons for a financial crisis.

We pray ardent prayers for the people who live in poverty and want. We may render some immediate assistance, but we find out that some fundamental changes must be made in the motive and organization of our economic life before permanent relief can be expected. It is easier to see the way out and make EXCUSES than it is to join the cause and have REASONS.

You will not need a reason to serve this salad, but you will be hunting excuses to go back for seconds. It is that good.

Super Chicken Salad

2 1/2 C. cold diced chicken (I use only white meat) cooked
1 C. celery, chopped fine
1 C. sliced white grapes
1/2 C. shredded brown almonds
2 teaspoons minced parsley
1 teaspoon salt
1 C. mayonnaise
1/2 C. Whipping cream, whipped

Combine all ingredients. Serve on lettuce leaf.

First and foremost, be true to yourself, and remember that honesty is the best policy...usually. Weigh your excuses and reasons. Think about it!

Chapter 91 — Perceiving the World

How do you perceive the world around you? Think about it!

The world is a place of joy and beauty for most of us. Each season brings its special gifts and seems on its coming to be more beautiful than the last. Each day brings new experiences, rich in possibilities. Our days are filled with happy fellowships. Our lives are enriched by the associations of loved ones, and are made easy by the multitudes of conveniences which surround us.

That is how most of us view our world. We look for the good and we find it. On the other hand, if we look for bad we find that too.

The front pages of newspapers and the evening news are full of stories about bombings, criminals, horrible car accidents, terrible murders and crimes against children and innocent people, but there are stories about the great kids who participate in sports and band, and academic excellence also. We just need to look a little harder for those stories.

The media is flooded with tales of drugs, gangs, and alcohol abuse. Yet out there in this wonderful world are many, many people who go about their business every day of the world making a living for their family, going to church, volunteering in the hospitals, etc. The world is just as we perceive it!

Time changes our perception of things sometimes. I remember when I was a kid doing the chores in the winter on the farm, walking to our one-room school in the snow or unpredictable elements. I thought it was awful. In fact I thought it was the worst time of my life. Boy, when I got big I'd never walk that distance again, or be out in the snow, or have to work so hard. Yet, as I look back those were the happiest days of my life. And in high school I worried over every book report, every test, every presentation I made in speech or debate. Now, as I look back those were the most rewarding days of my youth. It is (was) all in the way I looked at things.

Jim says that when he was in actual combat in Iwo Jima and other battle fields in World War II, that things were the pits. I am sure they were too, not just for Jim but for every Marine and service man who served in the war. However, since the war is back in the distance, he is able to see interesting, almost funny things that happened in combat. His reunions are not all gloom and doom. They remember happy times, a time of comradeship of depending on their buddies. It is all in the way it is perceived. Looking back presents a new view, one that they could not see at the time because of the danger they were in.

I am sure the wonderful stories that Grandma and Grandpa told and that my dad tells of settling this country are different now than they appeared then, when all those incidents were actually happening. I'll bet Grandma didn't think it was a barrel of fun to drive that team of horses to Indian Territory at age 13. But as the years went on it became an adventure and a joy to relate to her family.

Swiss steak is a great alternative to chicken fried steak and cream gravy (Jim's favorite). Yet, when I cook it and not chicken fried steak he does eat it and will agree that he really likes it.

Swiss Steak

one round steak, cut in serving size pieces
1/2 cup flour
1 medium onion, peeled and sliced
1 medium bell pepper, seeded and sliced
about 2 cups V-8 or tomato juice

Place onions and bell peppers in bottom of crock pot. Pound steak in the flour (seasoned with salt and pepper) with a meat mallet until meat is tender. Brown in hot oil, and place in crock pot over the onions and peppers. Cover with the V-8 juice or tomato juice. Set on low and cook until done (it is OK if it cooks all day). Serve over cooked rice.

We needn't be an ostrich and stick our heads in the sand to avoid seeing the world as it really is, we just need to see all sides of things and look for enough good to balance the bad. It's there. Think about it!

Chapter 92 — Superstitions

Are you superstitious? Think about it!

My first knowledge of superstitions was when I was about four years old and went fishing with my grandma. She taught me the "real" way to fish to catch them. It seemed like we always caught enough for supper. First of all, Grandma always spat on her hook before she placed it in the water. No matter how tiny the first fish was she would not throw it back. Do fish talk? Was she afraid they would tell the other fish we were there to catch them? Anyway, after the first one that she kept, she could throw others back that were too small, and she was pretty choosy about what was too small. We would come home with a nice "mess."

She had other superstitions too. If she spilled the least bit of salt, she instantly threw a pinch over her left (or was it her right?) shoulder. She was a wonderful person and had a good life, so she must have done something right.

Many of us don't think we are superstitious at all, but we quickly knock wood if we make a statement that something has never happened. If there is no wood available, then we knock on our heads, which is the closest thing to wood at the time.

Who has not eaten black eyed peas on New Year's Day, even if they didn't like them, just so they would have good luck all year? Why wouldn't beans or peas of any kind work magic just as well?

Some people are traumatized if a black cat crosses their path. It is supposed to mean bad luck. But I have heard that if you go back home and turn around three times the spell is broken and good luck comes your way. It is bad luck to encounter a black cat, but it is good luck to own a black cat. We have a darling black cat that lives next door to us and belongs to Lauren. She must be the luckiest girl in the world, because her kittens love her. She has little frilly beds for them and they have all the comforts of home. Lucky cats they are!

Recently I learned that putting a hat on a bed was bad luck. I'd never heard of that and have always put hats on beds. I might have had wonderful luck if only I'd known sooner.

Walking under a ladder is supposedly bad luck...unless the ladder is orange. Then I suppose that makes it safe and okay.

We laugh about being superstitious and have a lot of fun talking about them but to some people who believe in them they are very real and they are of a nature that you cannot prove them or disprove them. My Grandma sure believed in superstitions and I would not dispute her.

Nor would I ever dispute Grandma's recipe for Potato Salad. As with every grandchild, I thought Grandma's was the very best. See what you think!

Potato Salad

1 medium onion
3 Cups boiling water
1 3/4 teaspoons salt, divided
6 medium potatoes, peeled and sliced
6 hard cooked eggs, halved
1 cup sweet pickle cubes or relish
1 cup finely chopped celery
3/4 cup mayonnaise
2 tablespoons sweet pickle juice

Cut 2 slices from onion, place in boiling water. Finely chop remaining onion and set aside. Add 1 teaspoon salt and potatoes to boiling water. Cover and let simmer ten minutes or until done. Drain and cool. Separate yolks and whites of eggs. Finely chop whites, combining with pickles, celery and chopped onion. Mash yolks and blend with mayonnaise, pickle juice and remaining 3/4 teaspoon salt, blending well. Combine yolk mixture with egg white mixture. Cube potatoes. Blend into egg mixture. Cover and refrigerate several hours.

If a superstition is real to you it is real...to you. Think about it!

Chapter 93 — Judgements

Are you judgmental? Think about it!

We have all been guilty of saying, "I'd never do that," or "My children will never do that," and then we have to eat those words. Just about as soon as we utter those words, our kids surprise us, or we surprise ourselves. Oh, how those words of ours choke as they go down!

Circumstances alter cases and we really don't know what we would do in a certain situation until we are faced with that same set of circumstances. We can't even anticipate what our actions would be without all the details. We have to walk in their moccasins to know what we would do. What is right for one person, is not right for another in a similar plight.

The differences are what makes the world interesting. Wouldn't it be a dull ol' world if everyone were like me. The differences give balance to our lives and keep us searching for better ways.

We seem to discriminate against people who look different than we look. We automatically are against new ideas that are different from the comfortable norm we are used to. If a poor person wanders into our midst, do we treat them as we would anyone else, or do we size them up real quickly and then act busy or turn away? Are we concerned with the sociological reasons for poverty? At some time we have all been poor in one way or another, either economically or in spirit. As such we have the responsibility to treat all people alike, regardless of race, creed or wealth. We owe them dignity and respect, and a chance to be themselves without our quick judgement.

It is wise to look at the world through the eyes of those we are judging. We must do this to understand other races and genders and ages and friends and influences. We can like the person and not like what they do. We can like the person without compromising our beliefs and values. They are entitled to their beliefs also.

Never let someone else form your opinion for you, whether it is of a person, group, restaurant, part of the country or whatever. Some people have never experienced something yet they decide, by what they have been told, that they don't like a certain thing. Or refuse to try a particular restaurant because a friend said it wasn't to their liking. Even worse, we let others decide who we will like and dislike. Too bad! We miss meeting the most wonderful people that way.

Why should we judge at all, if what a person is or does, does not affect us? We should live and let live, and accept the differences as interesting and natural.

Jim is not crazy about squash. In fact, he really will hardly eat it. However, there are two ways he likes it, simply steamed with onion and celery with seasoning like a friend cooks it, or this recipe for "Southern Squash." I prepared it for the cooking school presented by the Enid News and Eagle, and almost all of those in the audience liked it too.

Southern Squash

4 slices thick bacon
one onion, cut in 1 inch pieces
1 teaspoon garlic salt
1 bell pepper, cut in 1 inch pieces
2 Cups zucchini squash, yellow squash, or combination of both
1 large tomato, peeled and cut in 1 inch pieces
3 tablespoons chopped green chilies
1 can (20 ounces) corn, drained
1/2 teaspoon salt (or to taste)
1 Cup shredded sharp cheese

Cook bacon, drain, and crumble. Set aside.
In bacon drippings, cook onion and pepper until tender.
Prepare squash, cutting in 1 inch pieces and discarding seed parts.
Add squash, corn, tomatoes, green chilies, and seasoning. Cover and cook, stirring frequently, until squash is tender (about eight minutes).
Remove from heat. Sprinkle cheese and bacon on top. Replace lid. Allow to set until cheese is melted. Serve.
Use electric skillet on about 225 degrees or a moderate heat on range.

Since our understandings of others and their situations are limited, we should be careful in our judgements. Those chickens could come home to roost. Think about it!

Chapter 94 — Apologies

How do you say you are sorry? Think about it!

We all make mistakes in judgement and lose our cool and lash out and say things for which we are sorry. We feel terrible afterwards, and wish we could reach out and grab those hurtful things we said and take them back. Too late! They can't be retrieved like that. The best we can do is say we are sorry and try to make amends.

Probably more important than how we say we are sorry, is the fact that we say it. We do something about the strained relationship. When we don't apologize, it is because our own pride has been hurt and we don't know how to go about apologizing without making it look as if we were the only one that did wrong. We see apologizing as a sign of weakness or of being soft and admitting a wrong. Not necessarily! Even if we feel the other person was in error, isn't it better to apologize for the conflict and get the situation out in the open and cleared up?

As the advertisement says, "Just do it!" It is cleansing to the soul. Offer an olive branch and see if it is accepted. Make a peace offering. Reach out in love. Even if your apology is not readily accepted, you will feel better, knowing that you have tried to make a wrong right. Seldom is a conflict entirely one person's fault. It takes two to argue or to create a controversy. It will take one strong person to lead the way to harmony.

Don't wait until tomorrow to begin the healing process of apology. Before you place your head on your pillow tonight, make that call or write a letter or go see that person to clear the air. Do it now! You may not have another opportunity.

Don't let a wrong bog you down until you need a tow truck to pull you out of the bog before you get the nerve to apologize. You will feel so much better after you have taken that first step.

While we are discussing apologizing, we need to say a word about accepting an apology too. There is an art to that and it is very important. You may not know how much nerve it took for the other person to come to you and make amends. Therefore, you owe it to them and to yourself to readily accept their apology and to start fresh with renewed love and respect.

Apologies and accepting them are the same whether it involves family, friend, or foe. No matter, the cleansing is for yourself, too. You will feel so much better, and they will too. Guilt can eat at you worse than cancer.

As part of the apology, bake a pie and take it to them. They can't possibly stay angry, and the baking of the pie gives you time to rehearse what you will say, and gives you time for true remorse of any wrongdoing. This pie is soothing and liked by young and old. Even young people get their feelings hurt sometimes and need a genuine apology.

Humble Pie

Unbaked pastry for one-crust pie. Line 9" pie pan.

For the filling:
4 eggs
2/3 cup sugar
1/2 teaspoon salt
1/4 teaspoon nutmeg
2 2/3 Cups whole milk (can be part cream)
2 teaspoons vanilla

Mix all ingredients together and pour into unbaked pie shell. Bake in 350 degree oven about 45 minutes. Do not overbake or it gets watery. It will look slightly soft in the center when it is done, but it will set later. Serve slightly warm or cold.

Life is too short for conflict. Apologize and/or accept an apology today. You will be glad you did! Think about it!

Chapter 95 — Honesty

How honest are you? Think about it!

There was a time in history when million dollar deals were made with a handshake. There were no promissory notes signed, no notarized agreements, no registered contracts. Yet those handshake agreements meant more than some documents today that are signed in blood. Why? Because those men were so honest and because when they said something they meant it. A man's word was bond.

Saying you will or will not do something is a promise. A promise should not be broken. There should not have to be a sworn statement to make it a reality. The simple truth of your word should be enough to be a promise. It is nothing more than being honest and reliable.

It is so sad that there are so many broken promises in this era. There are broken vows of marriage that affect not only the two people involved, but also friends, relatives, and most of all innocent children. There are broken promises in business dealings that hurt all parties involved, and they never recover or gain back what once was.

Somewhere along the line people have started to think of themselves ONLY, and greed took over. Then their word became worthless. They said things they really didn't mean just to make it sound good for the time being. Then they turned around and did just as they pleased, without regard to anyone else. Their word was nothing. It is like they have no conscience at all, or it was so callused that they really did not feel any pangs of remorse at wronging someone.

The honor system was in use in the classrooms when I was in school. I don't know of anyone who cheated on a test. We were duty bound to do our best and grades were not so emphasized as they are now. Those tests reflected if we needed more review or explanation before we went on to the next step. Things were better in the "olden days," when honesty was the ONLY policy.

I never thought of lying. If I had I would have gotten into REAL trouble. There was nothing worse than a liar or a cheater. Everybody knew that.

And while I am on my soapbox about honesty, let me add that there was a time not too far back when no one ever locked their doors. No one would think of coming into your house if you were not home. And certainly nothing would be stolen. Borrowing without permission is the same as stealing. It all falls under the category of dishonesty.

I can honestly say you will like this simple dessert made with cake mix. It was shared with me by a dear friend who I know is an excellent cook. It tastes like you have spent all day in the kitchen.

Rhubarb Dessert

4 Cups raw cut rhubarb
1 Cup sugar
1 1/2 Cups hot water
large package strawberry Jello
white or yellow cake mix
1/2 Cup butter or oleo

Put cut rhubarb in 9" X 13" baking dish. Pour sugar on top. Mix hot water and Jello until dissolved. Pour this on the rhubarb/sugar mixture. Sprinkle dry cake mix on top of everything. Melt butter or oleo. Pour over cake mix. Bake 1 hour at 350 degrees. Cool Whip or ice cream may be used as topping.

Honesty IS the best policy. If a man's word is no good, he is no good. Think about it!

Chapter 96 — Actions

Do your actions speak louder than words? Think about it!

We have all known people who say, "Just fine," when asked how they are feeling, when you KNOW they fell terrible, because of the circles under their eyes and their gaunt look. On the other hand, we have all known people who look great yet they always have a complaint of some kind. Their actions speak louder than words for sure.

What we do around children is much more important than what we tell them to do, or not do. It is difficult to expect kids to be well behaved and say "No" when parents are at wild parties and not being temperate. We want our kids to do as we say and not as we do.

Actions speaking louder than words came home to us when Shelby was quite young, about 5 or 6 years old. The girls have always worn seat belts in the car. We insisted on it and they never questioned it. Once Shelby said to Grandpa, "Grandpa, why do I have to wear a seat belt, and you don't wear yours?" Needless to say, we have never gone even a block without those seat belts fastened since that little lesson. She probably has saved our lives. We insist on those belts be fastened by every passenger that rides in any vehicle we drive. How loudly those actions spoke!

We have always encouraged the granddaughters to try a taste of something new, even if they don't like the looks of it. When we were in California, I experienced squid for the first time. I could hardly look at it, much less taste it, but because we had made those house rules about food, I decided it would set a good example for me to take at least one bite of squid. The more I chewed, the bigger that bite got. We changed the house rules shortly after that experience. I saw things from the other side of the fence.

If we expect our kids to be organized and on time, then we need to be organized and on time. If we expect our kids to be clean and neat, then we need to be clean and neat. The things we expect of others should begin with us. If we expect our kids to say please and thank you and be courteous and thoughtful, then we must have those traits begin with us at home. We, as adults, need to be setting examples for our kids and SHOW them how to be, and not just tell them what we want them to be like.

It is always easier to tell someone how to do something than it is to do it, whether it is how to act or how to cook. Were it as easy to cook as to tell how to cook, and a wish were a dish, we could dine from a cook book...and we wouldn't have all those dirty dishes to do.

This cake is better than it looks. A dear friend in California sent it to me. It is real moist and delicious. She calls it "Ugly Duckling Cake."

One package yellow cake mix
1 can (16 oz.) fruit cocktail
2 1/3 Cups snowflake coconut
2 eggs
1/2 Cup packed brown sugar
1/2 Cup chopped nuts
1/2 Cup butter
1/2 Cup sugar
1/2 Cup evaporated milk

Combine cake mix, undrained fruit, 1 cup of the coconut, and eggs. Blend, beat at medium speed for 2 minutes and pour into greased 9" X 13" pan. Sprinkle with brown sugar and nuts. Bake at 325 degrees for 45 minutes. Bring butter, sugar, and milk to boil. Boil one minute. Stir in remaining coconut. Spoon over warm cake. Allow to cool. Top with whipped topping if desired.

Be careful of the things you do, because someone may be watching you. Think about it!

Chapter 97 — Education

Has your education ended? Think about it!

I was fortunate to go to a one-room school that held eight grades, with one teacher. I started in "primary" when I had just turned five at mid-term, as many kids did then. I was so glad to be going to school because my brother and sisters were in the same school and I was lonesome at home.

I completed eight years there before going to town for high school. I loved it there too because there was so much to do with pep club, chorus, ball games, and activities.

Then as everyone did, I left for college. However, I quit after one year because I thought I knew more than my parents did. I later went back and graduated and I can truly say I was ready the last time and applied myself and studied and learned and knew why I was there.

I have always been grateful for the opportunity of an education. That busy teacher in grade school taught me how to plan ahead. She had to, or she never could have prepared all our lessons, plus build the fire, clean the school house, and all the other things she did beside teach us.

Even after I graduated from college, I find that the more I know, the more I know I don't know. I am constantly learning. Every day I learn something from our granddaughters. It is amazing what I have learned from them. One of the main things is how great kids are.

I also am constantly learning from my elders. Every time I visit with Daddy, he teaches me something else exciting. I am sure he feels like some of his knowledge and experiences will go to waste if he doesn't pass them on to the next generation.

About the time you learn something, something else comes along. I am always trying to stretch myself. The new computer era has kept me on my toes. It is unbelievable how much I had to learn, and how little I knew. Typing did help, but it was kindergarten stuff compared to what kids know now.

Education is never wasted. Some of the classes I took in college, or in high school too, have not been used in my career, but they are interesting to know and give one a well-rounded knowledge. I liked geometry and algebra and someday I am going to take a class in those just to see if I can still remember anything, and just for the joy of learning.

It is so much fun to watch a tiny child learning. Doesn't it bring back memories? Don't they have a lot ahead of them? Won't life be interesting for them? So much to learn!

I admire those who take classes in cooking to learn all the new recipes and methods. It is great for those with the time and inclination, but I will just stick to my old tried and true recipes that I grew up with, along with those treasures that friends have shared with me. We like:

"Gringo Gravy"

one pound lean ground beef
2 medium onions, chopped
1 can (16 oz.) peeled tomatoes, cut into chunks
1 small can diced green chilies, drained
1 Tablespoon flour
salt to taste

Brown meat in skillet, along with onion, until onion is clear and the meat loses its pink color. Stir in flour. Add chilies, tomatoes and salt. Cover and simmer until juice is thickened and cooked down about half. Serve over rice or mashed potatoes.

It is not for school, but for life we learn. Think about it!

Chapter 98 — Young People

Aren't we proud of today's young people? Think about it!

It seems that the only time kids make the news is when they are involved in crime, dope, or other mischief. It is noteworthy, and the public should know, but we also need to know when they have done something extraordinary and kind.

I have turned a deaf ear to the music the kids listen to. I thought all of it was loud and meaningless and brash. But the other evening I was watching "Les Miserables" on our VCR when our 14 year old granddaughter came in. "Has the little girl sang yet?" she asked. I was so surprised that she knew anything about the opera. In fact, she told me that she used some of her gift money to buy the disk of "Les Miserables," so she could listen to it any and all of the time. What a surprise! And I am so pleased.

Another time she and a little friend were going on a short trip with us. She brought along her tapes to listen to all the way. I wasn't ready for what I thought she was going to play over and over and over. Instead, it was the lovely music of "Lion King." It was an education for the grandparents. We truly enjoyed it.

At other times kids surprise us. They have so much on the ball. They are so busy and into so many activities. I know they are smarter and brighter and more energetic than I was at their age. They develop talents I could never have accomplished and do it with grace and ease.

I am constantly amazed at how they "take to" the computers. They have forgotten more than I will ever know about word processors and computers, and they do it effortlessly. It used to be embarrassing when I was taking a computer course and would get bogged down trying to figure out a program. Jamie, who was then about 9 years old, would press a few keys and say, "This is how you do it, Grandma." Sure enough she would be right. I felt so foolish and dumb.

Jamie is in her second year of college now. It is excellent the way she makes wise decisions. She has almost outgrown needing us to help her make choices. She hardly needs our guidance. All she needs now is our continued love and support, which she has.

Shelby is maturing into a beautiful, talented, responsible young lady. She is well on her way to being as reliable as her older sister. We are, needless to say, very proud of both of them.

We are also pleased at the friends they select. They always introduce them to us, which is a joy for us. Every one that we have met has been top-notch! I hope they are as proud of us as we are them!

I don't mean to brag, but I really think today's young people have a great deal on the ball. All we have to do is look for the good in those wonderful young people and we will find it. On the other hand, if we look for the down side and the kids that get into trouble all the time, we will find those too.

Here is a very simple cookie that is pleasing to kids of all ages.

Peanut Butter Puffs

1 egg white
1/8 teaspoon salt
6 Tablespoons sugar
1/3 Cup peanut butter

Preheat oven to 325 degrees. Beat egg white and salt to soft peaks. Gradually add sugar and beat to stiff peaks. Slowly stir in peanut butter. Drop by teaspoons on slightly greased cookie sheet. Bake at 325 degrees about 15 to 18 minutes. Let cool on cookie sheet.

Young people are our hope for the future. Whether they fail or succeed, they ARE the future of our country. Think about it!

Chapter 99 — Your Legacy

What is your legacy? Think about it!

I am very fortunate to have had passed on to me a legacy that is rich in intangible things but not in material things. Many of us in this part of Oklahoma have been given the hardy pioneer spirit which involves being frugal, and a love of the land, family, and our fellow men. I look back at my grandparents and parents and know that they passed all this on to me. We did not develop this all by ourselves. These traits came from a source other than our own thinking. I am blessed with good health and longevity of life. Many of my ancestors lived well into their nineties.

These gifts were willed to us and were warmly received. I am so grateful every day for the attitude that was my legacy. We were not moneyed people, but we were rich in many ways. We had such a close family and wonderful friends, the things money cannot buy.

The pioneer spirit that is my inheritance, was naturally brought into my life by my grandparents who made the run into Indian Territory, and by a father who was born in Indian Territory before statehood. My mother was a devoted wife and mother who dedicated her life to rearing her family and teaching us how to live. Those things cannot be taken from us, like material things can in the blink of an eye. Tangible things are nice and enjoyable but they are not the most important things in our lives.

The material things I did inherit have more sentimental value than monetary value. I have the pitcher and bowl that my dad was bathed in when he was born. There is a side of the pitcher that has a large brown area from being placed on the back of the wood stove to keep it from freezing when the winters got so very cold inside, as well as outside. That is a "flaw" to anyone else, but to me it is beautiful.

Mother's black pan that she always baked corn bread in makes my corn bread taste that much better. I am real sentimental about those things she used. When I use them to bake with, I feel very close to her. You have similar things.

Our Grandma's old spoonholder or Grandpa's bootjack brings their generation to our generation, and hopefully into the next. We cherish these old things to enjoy and use. Unless we pass them on to be enjoyed by successive generations, we have failed in what they taught me...to share and care.

Among other things, I have my grandma's old cookbooks. They have measurements like "gills" and "half an egg shell" and "lard the size of a hen egg," etc., but these have very special meanings. She, like most grandmas, cooked with a handful of this and "guestamation" measurements and her food was always wonderful. Many of my favorite recipes began in Grandma's kitchen. Here is her recipe for Blackberry Dumplings. They can also be made with wild grapes or peaches, but you may need to adjust the sugar somewhat.

Blackberry Dumplings

Part I
3 pints ripe blackberries
3/4 Cup water
1 Cup sugar
1 1/2 Tablespoons butter
    Combine in a Dutch oven and bring to a boil.

Part II
2 Cups flour
1/4 Cup sugar
1/2 teaspoon salt
1 egg
3 1/2 teaspoons baking powder
milk to make stiff dough

    Sift the dry ingredients together. Stir in beaten egg and enough milk to make a stiff batter.
    Drop the dumpling batter, a spoonful at a time, into the boiling mixture. Cover tightly with lid and cook for 15 to 20 minutes. We used to eat this with thick cream poured over it, but it is delicious with ice cream or whipped cream, or just plain.

    Sharing does not drain our resources, but provides a space for us to refill. Think about it!

Chapter 100 — Your Future

How do you gaze into your future? Think about it!

We never really KNOW what is in store for us in the future, or even as far as tomorrow, but we always look forward to good things happening. It is best that we don't really know, because if we did we would lose hope. We can always dream of a bright future with no problems or setbacks.

When we do have disappointments, deaths, or illness, then we deal with them, but we cannot know exactly how we will handle those situations until we are faced with them.

Somewhere along the line I have clipped out of something the following thoughts of the "Ten Commandments for Facing the Future". They are not original with me but whoever wrote them is brilliant, and gave them a lot of thought.

Ten Commandments for Facing the Future

1. Thou shalt not worry, for worry is the most unproductive of all human activities.
2. Thou shalt not be fearful, for most of the things we fear never happen.
3. Thou shalt not cross bridges before you get to them, for no one yet has succeeded in accomplishing this.
4. Thou shalt face each problem as it comes. You can handle only one at a time anyway.
5. Thou shalt not take problems to bed with you, for they make very poor bed fellows.
6. Thou shalt not borrow other people's problems. They can take better care of them than you can.
7. Thou shalt not try to relive yesterday for good or ill; it is gone, concentrate on what is happening in your life today.
8. Thou shalt count thy blessings, never overlooking the small ones, for a lot of small blessings add up to big ones.
9. Thou shall be a good listener, for only when you listen do you hear ideas different from your own. It is very hard to learn something new when you are talking.
10. Thou shalt not become bogged down by frustration, for 90 percent of it is rooted in self-pity and it will only interfere with positive action.

I would like to shake the hand of the person who composed this gem of wisdom. If we would live this way, wouldn't life be wonderful. It seems to boil down to the thought that we should not fret or sweat or regret, but enjoy the NOW.

One way to enjoy NOW is to look around you for someone worse off than you are, and reach out and touch their life. It will change you and make you appreciate what you are and have.

Leave the pity party behind. Look at the bright side of things, of which there are many. Don't let yourself fall into the trap of being glum and down in the dumps.

One good way to enjoy now is to cook up a big batch of stuffed shells, toss a huge salad, heat some French bread, make a gallon of sun tea, and have some hungry people over.

Stuffed Shells

1 1/4 pound hamburger
1 small onion, minced
2 teaspoon parsley flakes
1 teaspoon garlic salt
16 oz. grated mozzarella cheese
26 1/2 oz. Traditional spaghetti sauce
36 large pasta shells

Cook hamburger, add onion, parsley, garlic salt, and 1/2 the cheese. Allow to cool to handling temperature.

Boil shells in salted water until nearly tender (do not overcook, as they continue to cook in the oven, and will tear if they are too soft.) Drain, rinse in cold water, and drain well.

Squeeze handful of meat mixture and place in shell. Place close together, with open sides up, in baking dish. Pour spaghetti sauce over all. Sprinkle with other half of cheese. Bake in 350 degree oven until cheese and sauce are bubbly.

It is more important to gaze into you soul for the meaning of life, than to gaze into your future. The future we cannot control. Think about it!

Chapter 101 — Retirement

Are you retired? If not, what will you retire to? Think about it!

We had planned to retire to our little ranch and raise a few cattle and be gentlemen farmers. Then Jim broke his back and we were forced to go to plan B. Consequently, we sold the cattle and even "Chief Crazy Horse" and resigned ourselves to living here in Enid and doing other things.

Even with retirement, Jim is busier than I am with two jobs and keeping a household in order. Jim clowns and visits the hospitals, etc. He has coffee most mornings with his buddies to solve the problems of the world. Then he gets busy and does his things. I am so happy that he stays busy. I don't know how I would react if he just sat around and did nothing.

It is better to wear out than rust out. My father in his 90's is testimony to that. He still manages a quite large ranch, although he has great help with the physical chores. He probably would not last long if all his life's work were taken away from him and he couldn't run the ranch. He would be very unhappy, and so would we. It is important to him and to us that he stays busy and keeps his mind alert and does what he is able to do.

If you are going to retire to travel, then travel. Don't wait too long. It is always sad when people plan all their lives to travel when they retire or when their ship comes in, or some other reason. Then one of them is quite ill or dies, and traveling is not fun unless you have someone to share the joys of the scenery and excitement. Why wait? Do it now. Go on a journey of discovery!

For those retired or just slowing down, there are wonderful classes to take in almost every subject. What fun it is to associate with people who are seeking wisdom just like you are and in the same field. And you meet somebody new to tell about your grandchildren. Of course, you have to give them equal time, but that is fun too.

Volunteer. There are so many places where you can be of service: the hospitals, schools, many organizations and institutions. Most of these can use an extra pair of hands or a mind to help plan things. There is something that you can do if you will just look around you. Age has nothing to do with your ability to serve. If anything, age is an advantage. You already know how to handle young people and those who are ill. Put that knowledge to good use.

We get our greatest dignity, our courage, our joy in work because of the accomplishment and the goals that we set for ourselves. Service is a way we can get involved in the whole world. In every one of us there is an infinite and restless drive and desire to stay in the life of the community. If we find a place where we can be of use, we are hitched to a star and move with it. When we try to serve the world, we touch what is divine.

Life is still before you. You can sink in the mire, or you can climb to the mountaintops in service. You can look up in service or look down in selfishness and despair. You can just say you are too old and do nothing or you can enrich your remaining years with excitement and enjoyment. Which is it going to be?

We have come to the time of life when we enjoy simple foods and simple living without all the frills. We may not be to the "mush stage" yet, but we like things like cornbread and milk or sardines and crackers. These are better to us than caviar or croissants.

For a finish to a simple casserole meal, try this elegant/easy dessert:

Tropical Topper

2 ripe bananas, sliced thin
1 small can crushed pineapple
1 stick butter
1/2 Cup honey
1/4 teaspoon cinnamon
1/4 Cup chopped pecans

In skillet, combine pineapple juice, butter, nuts and honey. Cook until bubbly and reduced about 1/4. Add cinnamon, bananas, and pineapple. Bring to boil. Cool slightly. Serve on ice cream. (We like it best when it is served still warm over the ice cream, but it is good served chilled also).

When you retire...don't retreat! Retread and keep on trucking! Think about it!

Chapter 102 — America's Freedoms

Aren't you proud to be an American? Think about it!

With the extensive D-Day coverage, it has become apparent that we again cherish our heritage of winning wars and waving our flag to show our patriotism. We are not ashamed to hail Old Glory. For awhile allegiance was becoming a lost art. I was afraid we had lost sight of the fact that many brave service men had fought so that we might have the freedoms we take for granted and use every single day.

During World War II, every house "advertised" that it had a representative in the service by placing a star, or in many cases several stars, in the window. Again, we are unashamed to fly a flag or wear a flag on our lapel to show our love for our country. Everyone was involved then, and everyone did something for the war effort. We all saved, and rationed things, and gathered scrap iron and other metals to sell to be recycled. No, recycling is not a brand new concept. It has been around for generations.

July 4 was a great time to reassess our feelings for our country. In the olden days (when I was younger) no matter how busy one was on the Fourth of July, the day was celebrated. We were usually in wheat thrashing season and very busy, but we always closed down that day and went to town and celebrated all day and into the night.

There were parades, picnics, turtle races, three-legged races, horse shoe games for the men, pie eating contests, and other fun things to do. We saw all our neighbors and friends there and lots of people we had never seen before. But all had a great time together. There was usually a parade or if not that, at least a band played from the band stand. It seems there was music all day.

We all wore red, white, and blue. We carried flags. There were banners strung up all over downtown.

People sat in lawn chairs or on the ground on lovely old quilts and had picnics, sharing with everyone. No one was embarrassed that they had a lump in their throat with the playing of the National Anthem.

We never hesitated to hold our hand over our heart when we saw our flag. It received a reverence due a banner for our country.

It seems like some of that respect is returning. Every Independence Day, there is a glorious program on the mall of our nation's capitol. We have fireworks in nearly all small and large towns. The kids play with sparklers. The older kids shoot off fireworks. It is happy noise and pretty lights...a celebration of our country's independence. We are independent, yet some think that they can be dependent on this country, that the government will always take care of them. It should be the other way around. We must take care of our government and remember that this country was founded for freedoms.

Anytime is a great time to be patriotic. We need to hold our flags high for all to see. We need to hold the symbolism close to our hearts for the freedoms we have. Much blood was shed and lives were lost so that we could enjoy these freedoms. Many veterans said they were fighting for "America, the flag, Mother, and apple pie." Those pies were worth fighting for.

Sour Cream Apple Pie

2 C. peeled, chopped raw apples (I use Jonathan apples)
2 T. flour
1 egg
3/4 C. sugar
1 C. sour cream
1 t. vanilla
1/4 t. salt

Mix all but apples, beat until smooth. Add apples, pour in unbaked 9" pie shell. Bake one hour at 350 degrees. Remove from oven. Sprinkle on topping:

1/3 C. sugar
1/2 C. flour
1 t. cinnamon
1/4 C. butter

Mix all this together and sprinkle on pie. Bake for ten minutes more.

Exercise your PRIVILEGE of patriotism. Enjoy your "fought for freedoms". God Bless America. Think about it!

Chapter 103 — Remembering Names

Have you ever goofed on someone's name? Think about it!

Have you called someone by the wrong name and later realized your error? Or completely forgotten someone's name? Or ran up to someone on the street and hugged them and thought they were a long-lost friend and they looked at you like you were some kind of kook? Well, I have...and felt so foolish.

I have talked to a person for some time and couldn't recall their name for anything. I was too embarrassed to ask them, since I had talked to them for some time and knew all about them...except their name. I ought to know...and do know...I just can't think of the name until two hours later. Then it is perfectly clear to me.

More and more Jim and I "fill in the blanks" in a conversation with others. He, or I, will be telling a story and come to a pause and look over at the other one to help with a name or place or a date. Everyone does...or will have that problem as they get older. Either our minds GO or our minds are so crowded with other things...

It seems to me that it is more important to remember <u>about</u> the person and forget the name, than to remember the name and know nothing about the person. It is easier to remember a face than it is to remember the name that goes with that face.

Dale Carnegie suggests remembering names by associating the name with a product or something bazaar. Consequently, I have called been Michelin, Dayton, Firestone, and other names. But they tried!

Have you ever asked a friend about their parents, for instance, and found out they died two years ago? Then you felt terrible and wished you could take the question back. But is it better, and kinder, to ask and find out than not to inquire at all?

I have a friend who seemingly knows everyone. I asked her one day how she remembered all their names. She said that she really didn't but she makes them think she does. She called them "Lady Bug" or "Pretty Lady" or a pet name. They all just love it and feel special. Isn't that the key...to make someone feel special? It is alright to forget names. It does no harm to anyone except maybe their ego when their name escapes us.

Mistakes happen...take for instance this cake. I thought they had named the wrong ingredient when they said creamed corn, but that is right...and it is great. I bet it started out as an error. Someone opened the wrong can or something...isn't that the way recipes are born?

Mistake Cake

1 (17 oz.) can creamed corn
3/4 C. packed brown sugar
3/4 C. sugar
3 eggs
1 C. oil
2 1/4 C. Flour
1 T. baking powder
1 t. salt, soda, and cinnamon
1/2 C. chopped nuts
1/2 C. raisins (I use golden raisins)

Mix all thoroughly by hand. Bake in 13" x 9" greased/floured pan. Bake 30 to 35 minutes in 350 Degree oven. Cool before icing.

Icing

Bring to boil 4 T. oleo
1/2 C. packed brown sugar
Remove from heat and add 1/4 C. milk
2 or 3 Cups powdered sugar to desired constancy

The only people who don't make mistakes are those who do nothing. Forget your errors. Clear your mind of guilt. It is the PERSON that is important...not just their name. Think about it.

Chapter 104 — Communication

Do you communicate well? Think about it!

Communication is connecting. It takes two...one to send and one to receive. It takes talking AND listening. It is best to not be thinking of your reply while you are listening, and don't interrupt.

During disagreements, it is very easy to get irritated, even angry, and be turned off to what the other person is saying or trying to explain. Frustration follows, and more quarreling.

It is much more convincing, and kinder, to organize one's thoughts and present a slide without thought of rebuttal. There is plenty of time for thought after the other person finishes what he/she is saying.

I believe that the key to a good marriage is total communication. I almost know what causes a disagreement in our home and try with all my might to avoid it. But then, so does Jim, so it makes for good communication and total understanding.

Friends understand friends and the feelings they wish to convey, many times without any words said. It is not what is SAID to someone in the loss of a loved one, it is just that they came, and cared. Sometimes words are lost...but the communication is there just the same.

And boy, can I remember some communication when I misbehaved in church or somewhere. A simple glance my way told me that I had better stop, and now! I knew what it was I was to stop and I knew when I was to stop it...no one needed words to tell me.

A glance, a wink, a touch, a pat on the back, a smile, a frown, a scowl, a blank stare all convey messages of one kind or other, and the receiver picks up that important message. It does not have to contain words to express clearly what is meant.

Being on the same wave length is what is important. Being of like mind says a lot and saves lots of idle talk. Sometimes I have asked Jim "Did you see...?" and he'll reply, "Yes". How did he KNOW what I was thinking...but he did. This happens many many times. And I am sure it happens to other couples who have been married for several years. It is a comfortable feeling that the other person knows what is in your mind. When two souls really communicate, there is something so beautiful, radiant, stimulating, and mysterious, that even poets have failed to find sufficient words for it.

Can we honestly say that we always communicate with friends and family? Do our parents turn to us for companionship? Do we just turn to our folks as the family pay check? Does anyone ever say to you, "If you don't know what I mean, ask so and so, they always understand what I am trying to say?". Kinda scary that we don't understand or are misunderstood.

Many people are endowed with great messages for mankind with the gift of writing. Others have gifts of music that "speak" to us. Or pictures they paint that stir within us a feeling or wish to be within that scene. There are many ways to communicate besides verbally.

In our family, food is a way to communicate love. If I served Jamie peas, she'd think I detested her, or beets to Jim would bring the same reaction...but make a pie, and they all think I love them, and they me! Certain foods, like hot bread, just have a way of saying "welcome" or cookies say "you did a good job". One can convey a lot by delivering a cake to a bereaved family. Or a neighbor who brings in fresh picked strawberries conveys a message of friendship. All little gifts give off a BIG message of love and friendship. The size of the gift is unimportant...the love is very important.

This dessert is heavenly...thus the name Heavenly Hash. It is sinfully simple to make and will communicate caring for your family and/or friends.

Heavenly Hash

Thoroughly mix:
one can (8 3/4 oz.) pineapple tidbits, drained
2 C. thawed Cool Whip
1 C. angel flake coconut
1 C. miniature marshmallows
1/2 C. chopped maraschino cherries (optional)
1/2 C. nuts, chopped (optional)

Chill about one hour. Make 6 servings.

Communication is important in family, work, play or anytime. It reflects our very existence in the world. Think about it!

Chapter 105 — Sleep

Isn't sleep a blessing? Think about it!

I don't really think about it being a blessing so much until someone speaks of having insomnia. It must be terrible to not be able to relax in sleep. I have never had that problem. I usually just die when my head hits that pillow. My eyes just snap shut and I am gone.

Sleep feels so wonderful on a rainy Saturday morning when you know you don't have to get around for work, and the rest of the chores for the weekend can just wait. Of course...ANY Saturday morning is pretty tempting, not just the rainy ones.

When one is ill, isn't it great to drift off into sleep and be free of fever, chills, and pain? That rest is a great healer.

Naps can do almost as much good as a full night's sleep sometimes. I can come home from a full day's work and take a ten minute nap and be up and going strong again. My husband can "rest with his eyes closed" in his chair and have a quiet nap and STILL know what happened on T.V. or what I have said to him. I don't see how he can, but he does. He says he relaxes better reclined in his chair than he does in bed sometimes.

Now sleeping in church is another matter. Why is it we get relaxed, and quiet and no matter how interesting, enjoyable, or challenging the sermon is, we sometimes feel ourselves slipping away? Praying?? Meditating?? My dad, who is in his nineties, yet young, says that he doesn't really sleep in church, that he is just real relaxed in the presence of God. Maybe he has the right idea. Who can argue with that logic?!

Naps are wonderful. Sleep is wonderful. BUT there is a saying that my friend has as a sampler on her dining room wall that says, "When your goal in life is to take a nap, something is wrong." There is more to life than sleeping all the time. Sleep was meant to refresh and rejuvinate and get us ready to LIVE.

After a full night's rest, it is good to get up to a big breakfast on Saturday morning. The other mornings are pretty regimented getting ready for work and the day's activities, so they are usually toast and cereal days. But on Saturdays...here is a simple, but great breakfast:

Grandma's "Stick to your Ribs" Breakfast

six slices bacon (or four if they are the thick kind) cut in 1" chunks
2 or 3 potatoes, sliced and peeled
1/4 onion, chopped (optional)
salt to taste
pepper to taste
six eggs, slightly beaten
about 4 oz. sharp grated cheese

Cook bacon until crisp. Remove from skillet. Drain off all but about 2 T. bacon drippings. And potatoes, onions, and season with salt and pepper. Fry until tender. Pour eggs over potato mixture, sprinkle bacon on top. Cover and let cook gently until the eggs are set. Sprinkle cheese on top. Replace lid and let cheese melt but do not cook further. Serve with Picante sauce. Serve with hot biscuits or muffins, fruit juice, and coffee or milk, and it will make your Saturday memorable.

Just a simple night's rest is so refreshing. At dawn everything is fresh, light, and simple. Every new morning is a new contact with existence. Go to bed with a problem to solve or a dilemma and with the dawn comes a fresh new outlook and possibly a solution. Think about it.

Chapter 106 — Pioneer Spirit

Do you have a pioneer spirit? Think about it!

I think back to my grandparents who staked claims in this great land. My grandma was thirteen years old when she drove a team hitched to a hack, to Indian Territory. That is only one year older than our youngest granddaughter. What a responsibility!

They were sturdy stock with great endurance and fortitude. They gambled everything they had to settle this country. They left their native states, never knowing if they would ever see their families again.

They had no modern conveniences as we do. Nothing was easy. The mere struggle to stay alive was a challenge. There were no extras. Yet these pioneers were happy people and accepted setbacks as challenges.

My ancestors would be the first to say that we are all still pioneers in our own way. Walking on the moon and space travel, airplanes, and automobiles were all pioneer undertakings.

And what about computers...now THERE is a new field of challenge, one that many older people have not mastered. But ask any youngster and they are completely unintimidated by computers or VCR's or anything mechanical.

The pioneering spirit is essential to ALL progress. The satisfactions of our present life are the gift of adventurous souls of the past.

Being a pioneer demands the leadership of men and women of courage and daring; people possessed with the spirit of adventure.

The desire to explore new territory, to think new thoughts, to discover new truths, to enjoy new experiences in every realm of living...is inherent in youth. It is a gift. Without the pioneer spirit life would become static and civilization decadent.

We are ALL pioneers in our quest for beauty, in our quest for knowledge, in our quest for service. It is not necessary to "stake a claim" as our forefathers did to be a pioneer. So long as we accept challenge and continue to look for new horizons, we are pioneers and have that spirit.

And we are made of sturdier stuff than we think we are. When we are faced with a challenge or a setback, we WILL come through it and grow because of those hardships. We will ride out the storm and be stronger for it. Even without labor saving devices or time saving devices, so long as we keep on keeping on we have the pioneer spirit.

Turnips, Turnips. Turnips. Grandma told of eating so many of them the first fall in the new territory because it was their first crop. They probably didn't really like them morning, noon, and night, but it was FOOD and survival was the name of the game. They made do with what they had. We could do that too if we had to.

We still serve turnips each Thanksgiving to remind ourselves of the hardships of our ancestors in this early statehood. I like turnips cooked or raw but lots of people don't, so I will spare you a recipe for turnip kraut or something. Instead, I will share another old timey recipe for "Corn Oysters". I don't know where they got the name oysters, unless it is because of the size they turn out when they are cooked. They are rather like fritters, but Grandma called them "Corn Oysters", and that's good enough for me.

Corn Oysters

1 can (12 oz.) whole kernel corn, drained well
2 egg yolks, beaten
1 t. salt
dash pepper
1/4 C. flour
2 egg whites, beaten stiff
1/4 C. shortening

Place corn in bowl. Stir in egg yolks, salt, pepper and flour. Mix well. Fold egg whites gently into mixture. Heat shortening in skillet. Drop teaspoons of corn mixture into fat. Cook on both sides until golden brown. Drain well.

You ARE a pioneer so long as you are making the way easier for those who follow after you. Think about it!

Chapter 107 — Accomplishments

Have you ever accomplished something against great odds? Think about it!

There isn't a one of us who hasn't surprised a member of our family or a friend by winning a race, or graduating with high honors, or gotten a job, or launched a career, or written a book, or married someone special, or accomplished something grand. Isn't it great to be able to look them in the eye and say, "I knew I could do it."

I am sure that many pioneers who left home for the "wild west" made it in spite of what their "stay-at-home" friends and family members thought. Thank goodness, they had the spirit and courage to continue west over those wagon trails with the unknown risks, not knowing what was around the next bend or over the hill. I am so proud of my ancestors for the fearless attitude they exuded to come to this new territory. It certainly was against all odds!

Every new undertaking requires a certain amount of boldness and bravery. It is easier to sit back and not try new things or stay in a rut, but it is better, sometimes, to try something that you really WANT to do.

There never was a book written by an author who believed at first that it would be published. There never was a dress sewn that the seamstress thought would be worthy of a dress-up occasion, when she started making it. There never was a song composed that didn't have a little apprehension involved at the start. There is always a little trepidation with any new venture.

I guess I am a "late bloomer" in many things I have done in my life. It took me thirty-five years to graduate from college. Now, mind you, I did not go all those years, but from start to finish it was that long a span. When I graduated, someone told my husband that she hoped it didn't take her all those years to get out of college, like I was the dumbest thing that ever came down the pike. But along the way, I have had a good time!

Nearly everyone does something every day that when you look back you wonder how you did it, and wonder if you could do it again. We all remember a ball game when the underdog won by a great margin and flabbergasted the favored team. I tell my granddaughters all the time that if we already KNEW who was going to win a game, that there would be no need to play it. There are often surprises, one way or the other, against all odds.

Wars have been won, marriages survived, health regained, races won, goals attained, miracles achieved, elections won, feats accomplished, all against some unfavorable odds. Yet we are somehow spurred to accomplish them. We are almost driven to complete those things that mean so much to us. And isn't the feeling good, when we can settle back and look at a job well done.

A simple recipe that turns out delicious against all odds is Fun-yun Onion Burgers. When I first heard the recipe from my Creative Writing teacher, Johnny Quarles, I thought, "Yeah, Sure, Yuk!", but I tried the recipe and it is delicious...better than it sounded. Now when I want a hurry-up meal that is good for a crowd, I make this ahead and heat it up, toast the buns, put them on a picnic plate and call supper. Everybody loves them.

Fun-yun Onion Burgers

One pound lean hamburger
2 T. flour
1 can (10 1/2 oz.) French onion soup, undiluted
1 T. Worcestershire sauce

Brown the hamburger. Do not drain. Sprinkle flour over the meat and stir until flour is absorbed. Stir in the soup and worcestershire sauce. Cook until thickened. Serve on toasted hamburger buns with Mayonnaise (not mustard) and a pickle, with potato chips and baked beans. Enjoy!

You have it within yourself to accomplish something against all odds. You can do whatever you WANT to do. Think about it!

Chapter 108 — Priorities

What is your top priority? Think about it!

As one gets older and older, their ideas change and one of the great lessons we discover is what is number one in our life. When we KNOW what that is, then all things revolve around it, focusing on it. It is different for every person and no one can decide for another what that priority is. It may change from time to time to education, job, home, family, security, health, or something else. But there is always a number one...or should be.

Remember a time when you had special guests and wanted the meal to be just perfect, but the oven went on the blink so you served a microwaved T.V. dinner or cheese and crackers. Everyone had a great time and you DID survive and even laughed about it later and it became a memorable experience and one of the best times of your life. See...it was no biggie! You rose above the situation and decided what was really important...friends and family over food and failure.

Have you ever noticed that after a terrible tornado, or fire, or other disaster, that when the T.V. cameras show the survivors and they are interviewed, that most of them are so positive and when asked how they feel about things, will reply, "Things could be worse. We will be alright. Our family is alive. I can't believe how wonderful people can be". Or they pick out a few rags of belongings and are thankful for the things that were spared. THIS is showing what has the top priority in their lives. Suddenly all the material things have little value. The important things are family and friends...and LIFE.

To a person who is very ill, their health is important. To a drowning person, air is important. To a saddened person, peace is important. The busy work-a-day world is a challenge to triumph over one's environment and to really strive for what is significant.

Remember the lines of the poem we learned in grade school: "Had I two loaves, I'd sell one and buy me hyacinths...for hyacinths would feed my soul." This is another way of saying that man does not live by bread alone. We need something to feed our minds and thoughts, and soul. Our determination to enter upon such a quest should bring sympathetic regard from others for our goals. They will learn to respect our search for our objectives.

We don't see many movies, but one we saw (and even bought) was "City Slickers". In this movie, runs the thread of a lesson that what we feel is our top priority, or number one desire of life, is what we should strive for at all times at all costs. We have to search for that priority sometimes, but when we discover what it really is, then all things revolve around it and all efforts point to the fulfillment of that priority.

My family means a great deal to me and is a high priority. When I was twelve years old, my little brother came into my life. He was, and is, a joy to me and I admire his honesty, his work ethic, and his basic beliefs. When they invite us over to their ranch for supper, we always hint for Judy's special noodle meal. Her recipe is wonderful and easy to fix and can be made ahead of time to allow plenty of time for visiting. Here is her recipe:

Spanish Noodles

8 ounces dry noodles
1 pound hamburger
1 large onion (chopped)
one can creamed corn
one can tomato soup
one can tomato juice (16 oz. or less)
1/2 t. garlic salt
1/2 pound Velveeta cheese (cut into chunks)
3 T. Chili seasoning
Salt to taste

Cook noodles in salted water, drain well. Brown hamburger and onion. Add all other ingredients. Bake in 350 degree oven until bubbly (or cover with foil and keep warm in the oven for as long as an hour). She serves this with a special dessert but just fruit salad and crispy French bread would make a tasty dinner.

Keep your priorities straight...and everything else will fit into proper place. Think about it!

Chapter 109 — Fun

What do you do for fun? Think about it!

Abundant living demands that our program of life shall include both work and play. Work of even the most satisfying nature requires concentration and nervous energy that exhaust our mental and physical reserve. That old saying, "All work and no play, makes Jack a dull boy," is psychologically correct. The person who does not at times feel the need of throwing himself freely and joyously into some form of wholesome recreation and is not refreshed and revitalized by it, should be concerned about his future. Fun helps us meet and conquer the irritations and disappointments of life.

There are some "amusements" in life that seem to allow one to throw away every vestige of reserve and dignity. Some of the most difficult and perplexing problems that confront us today center around the recreational life...in the name of FUN. One of the best tests of the quality of a civilization is what its people do with their leisure. One can tell much about a person by noting the pastimes turned to for joy and fun. We should get up the next morning after a social experience, refreshed, with new strength and courage, new hopes and ideals, a better disposition, and more ambition for our work.

For every person that needs vocational training, there are many who also need training for leisure and fun. Some of us have never really learned to be kids at heart, enjoying the simple things. How long has it been since you went wading, or splatted in mud? Or laughed until you cried at something that was really funny, but nothing...and the next day it didn't even sound amusing? We feel self-conscious to be seen making a fool of ourselves doing something kid-like.

Sometimes I think fun is why grandchildren come in so handy. We can ride on a merry-go-round with them, or sing silly songs, or skip down the street, all in the name of doing it with the grand-children, when in reality we are experiencing again the joys of our own childhood.

A "fun-food" is: Mud Pies

Mix:
1 1/2 C. flour
2 t. sugar
1/2 C. oil
3 T. milk

Pat in 9 " pie plate, on the bottom and sides. Bake 10 minutes in 350 degree oven. Remove from oven (it will not be done)
Meanwhile make filling of:
2 eggs
1 C. sugar
1/2 C. butter (or oleo)
1/2 C. flour
1/3 C. cocoa
1/4 t. salt
1 t. vanilla
1/2 C. Semi-sweet chocolate chips
1/2 C. Peanut butter chips
1/2 C. chopped nuts

Beat eggs, sugar and butter. Stir in flour, cocoa and salt (that have been sifted together). Stir in vanilla, chips and nuts. Pour into partially cooked pie shell. Return to oven. Bake an additional 30 minutes. (Pie filling will not test done in center). Serve plain or with ice cream and chocolate syrup drizzled on top.

Put a little fun in your life. Relax and enjoy. You only go around once. Think about it!

Chapter 110 — Friends

What kind of friend are you? Think about it!

I am sure I am not the kind of friend I should be or want to be but I have friends that are wonderful. There are friends who accept you just as you are, through good moods and bad. Through loss and failures. Through thick and thin...and diets. These friends are not just "fair weather friends", but stick by you through all kinds of foul weather too.

We can all look back to a friend who had helped us though a crisis that we thought we could not endure. Maybe we don't have to look back that far...maybe we are in the midst of one now. And if so, aren't friends a comfort?

Friends won't let friends suffer alone. They are there beside you and behind you all the way. They sometimes let you make silly mistakes and refrain from saying, "I told you so". They help pick up the pieces after you have broken all the rules of common sense. They KNEW all along you would pull through and come back to your good senses. They let you be yourself and make you own mistakes.

Friends share our joys, our jokes (sometimes the same ones over and over), and our journeys. They share our grouchiness, our griefs, and our gripes.

It is impossible to keep a ledger balanced with friends. They always seem to give more than you can give back to them. At least, that is the case with our friends. It seems I am always owing letters to them or favors to them. I just can't get ahead!

Montaigne said something like, "If anyone should ask me to give a reason why I loved my friend, there could be only one answer: 'Because he was he, and because I was I.'"

I have a dear friend who used to live in the same home town. We often got together to play 500 Rummy. We laughed and cried together and her daughter minded me just like she did her mother. We don't see each other much anymore, sad to say, but I think of her often and if we were to get together, we would play Rummy and pick up just where we left off. It is awful that we call each other, it seems, only when there has been a death in the family or some other tragedy. Other news seems to wait until Christmas card time. What a pity!

Arthur Benson expressed friendship:

Life is a sweeter, stronger, fuller, more gracious thing for the friend's existance, whether he be near or far. If the friend is close at hand, that is best, but if he is far away he is still there to think of, to wonder about, to hear from, to write to, to share life and experience with, to serve, to honor, to admire, to love."

I have a dear friend who recently moved from Enid. This town will never be the same with her absent. She left a big hole when she moved. Friends miss you when you are away or if they are gone. When she left she gave me three quilt tops and other treasures to remember her by. I do not need those reminders to think of her but they are truly appreciated and a lovely part of herself she left behind with me. She also gave me the recipe for these pickles and a jar of them already made to show me how good they are. They are extremely easy to make but delicious. They are called Cheat/Sweet Pickles.

Buy the cheapest jar of dill hamburger sliced pickles (40 oz.) you can find. Drain very well. Bring to boil:

1 C. white vinegar
2 C. sugar

Cook to dissolve sugar, bring to rolling boil and boil one minute. Pour over drained dill slices in jar. Let set 24 hours. Drain juice into pan. Add one more cup sugar. Bring to boil and boil hard one minute. Pour back over pickles in jar. Let set 24 more hours. Repeat this, adding one more cup sugar. Pour over pickles. Refrigerate. They are ready to eat. These are a crispy sweet pickle and so easy to make. I'll never mess with making them the old way again.

You cannot put a price on friendship. It is priceless. Think about it!

Chapter 111 — Discovering

Have you ever watched the excitement of a child who discovered something for the first time? Think about it!

When a child first discovers his toes and fingers, or his tongue and tries to talk. Or when he really recognizes you as a person. It is an exciting time for both parent and child.

But beyond being a baby, it is fun to watch a child's eyes light up when something is discovered that you have known all along and see all the time. Teachers have this great joy of seeing a little light bulb come on over a student's head when he/she finally figures something out that has been explained and demonstrated over and over. When that light comes on, all the pieces of that puzzling problem fit into place. Then the teacher can move on to a more difficult, indepth study.

I had the privilege of conducting two classes at our city library on fossils for kids. I have quite a collection of Oklahoma shell fossils that I enjoy sharing with others. Well, these kids first made an impression in play dough to discover how the process works. Then they were turned on by having a fossil of their own to identify by a chart I had made. I was surprised and thrilled by the way some of these kids took to this interesting study. They wanted to know where and when we could go fossil hunting. Oklahoma is full of fossils since we were once a sea bed. Just look around and you'll find them. The class did as much for me as it did the kids...it brought back the joy of excitement of seeing something for the first time.

We took our youngest granddaughter to Omniplex in Oklahoma City to see all the things. She was as fascinated by watching little chickens hatch as she was all the other stuff to see and do. She kept going back to that display to see how things were developing. I can still remember how excited I used to be when our chickens hatched in the incubator. Suddenly it just bursts with excitement and LIFE. I can still remember the smell of that coal oil incubator that we kept in a cellar. I still remember how we transported the tiny chicks to the brooder house. Shelby's seeing those chicks hatch at the Omniplex brought back a flood of memories for me and helped me again see things through the eyes of a child.

Kids like to see beans sprout or pumpkin vines grow. One can almost see them grow inch by inch, hour by hour, they grow so fast.

It is a joy to see when kids discover that it is as blessed to give as receive. For a few years it is questionable as they usually just WANT, but suddenly they begin to shop for presents for parents and grandparents and cousins and see how much joy they BRING to the other person and they are transformed from a taker to a giver.

Kids like to bake cookies or otherwise help in the kitchen. I think it is because they are doing something themselves that is creative and they are discovering a fun thing to do...and it tastes good too! Just brag a lot on them and they have a sense of accomplishment and satisfaction at doing something themselves.

A simple, yet good thing kids can make is Rice Crispy Treats. They may need a little overseeing with the hot butter, but they can at least help with the mixing...and the eating!

Marshmallow Crispy Bars

1/2 C. butter
5 C. miniature (or 40 large) marshmallows
1/2 t. salt
5 C. crispy rice cereal
1 C. peanuts (optional)

Melt butter in 8X8 inch microwave-safe dish in microwave. Stir in marshmallows and salt. Microwave until soft and melted, stirring often. Stir until smooth before adding cereal 1/3 at a time. Add peanuts. Stir until all cereal is coated. Press into dish with fork. Cool, cut into squares.

Adults need to see things sometimes through the eyes of a child. Simplicity makes one appreciate things again...Maybe even more when re-discovered. Think about it!

Chapter 112 — Autumn

Isn't autumn beautiful? Think about it!

Or summer, or winter or spring too for that matter. But fall is my personal favorite. I am ready for the beauty of fall. By autumn, I am tired of HOT, sweltering weather and sweating, and yard work, and bugs, and hot cars.

It is time for a change of pace, cooler days and evenings, fall showers (that always come during the Fair or the first weeks of school), football games, cooking chili, and getting ready for winter.

It is time to check the wood pile, cover outdoor furniture and patio things. It is time to let the plants die down and/or bring them in to save for next year. It is time the lawns had a good rest (and the mower too!). It is time to have the chimney sweeps come for their yearly duty.

It is time to curl up on the sofa and read or write. It is time to take another class in creative writing or something of interest to get the mind back in gear and to stimulate thinking and/or writing skills.

It is time to clean closets and drawers to cull out all that stuff that we don't (or can't) wear.

What a beautiful time of year to go on a little fall vacation to see this gorgeous countryside. I am ready to go over to our ranch and rustle in the leaves and stomp the dried ones and hear them snap. I want to gather pecans and eat wild persimmons. I am ready to spend a day hunting Oklahoma fossils to see if I can find an interesting, different one for my collection.

As soon as it is cool enough that the chiggers go away wherever it is they go, I am ready to go on one last fishing spree and see if I can catch a nice bass. And isn't it time to go on a cook out and roast marshmallows and "weenies", or better yet, fry up a pan of fried potatoes and onions and bacon over a campfire.

I am ready to start cooking. When the weather turns cool, it feels good to have the oven going and something baking that smells good and inviting. Something like Bierox:

1 lb. Ground beef
1/2 C. chopped onion
2 C. cabbage, shredded
1 t. salt
1/4 t. pepper
1/4 t. allspice
1 T. flour

Fry onion and beef in heavy skillet until meat is not pink. Add cabbage. Stir and simmer about 20 minutes. The last five minutes of simmering add seasoning and flour. Stir frequently to keep it from scorching. (If it appears too dry, add a couple tablespoons of water, but you don't want it soupy).

Remove from fire and cool slightly.

For the crust, you can use your favorite bread dough or (like I sometimes do) use canned crescent rolls. Separate dough and form into four inch squares. Spoon about 1/2 C. cabbage mixture on one end of square. Fold over into triangle shapes and press edges together to seal.

Bake at 375 degrees for 12 to 18 minutes until golden brown. Serve hot. Makes about eight.

Sure, it is time to do a LOT of things...but we may not get around to ALL of them. I'll bet you have just as many activities and "must-dos" that you look forward to doing when your favorite season comes around. Every season has its own beauty and blessings to enjoy. Think about it!

Cahpter 113 — Special Skills

Do you have a special skill? Think about it!

Of course you do. Everybody has at least one...and most people have several or many. I'll never be able to quilt like Margaret Sunderland, or write like Johnny Quarles, or sing like Rick Hill, but I do have a few skills that I truly enjoy.

My mother had a skill, an art really, of conversation. She always thought she was too shy and could not talk out to people, but she was a wonderful listener and everyone liked to talk to her. She knew just the right leading questions to ask to get them started on their favorite subjects and away they went. Then she didn't have to do much beside nod and listen and ask another question now and then. Consequently, because she listened...truly listened, she knew a lot about a lot of subjects from football to music to different countries and locations.

I dabble in many things like tatting, fossils, writing, music, quilting, cooking, painting, and antique collecting. But none of these things am I really what one would call "good" at. I'm not real adept at any of them...but they bring me a great deal of joy.

Maybe the trick to learning a skill is doing what you can, where you are, with what you have. My ancestors had very little in the way of material things, but Grandma made a beautiful quilt from scraps and lovingly put them together for something that has been handed down like an expensive heirloom. It means more to me than something she would have purchased at the fanciest store. This is because of the skill involved and because she made do with what she had and took advantage of her time in making something useful and beautiful and lasting.

Some skills take no money. Skills like calling on the sick, or helping the bereaved. This is a gift and an art that they develop over the years...the art of making people feel better. The art of showing love and caring to their fellow-men.

Some people are great hostesses putting on elaborate dinner parties with just the right crystal, china, and table appointments. There are those who are equally wonderful hostesses that serve bread and butter and sugar sandwiches with a hot cup of coffee, served with delightful conversation and you just can't wait to be invited to their house. Some of these great hostesses seem thrilled when you just drop by unannounced. I'll have to work on this one. I still think about my house first when the doorbell rings...not that it would matter that much, I probably wouldn't clean even if I KNEW someone was coming...but it is just the fact that we are being surprised and I am not prepared for entertaining. Of course, we have many friends who are so sweet that they expect nothing special and just their very presence makes every occasion a party. That is the kind of true friends to develop and cultivate.

I have been blessed with the guidance of gentle grandmotherly types who have had the patience to sit and help me learn to tat. Or a creative writing teacher with endless positive remarks and critique. Or teachers at school who quietly looked at my coffee can full of rocks to help identify great fossils I have found. This help in itself is a skill that they pass on to me and others. A recipe that takes no skill is Easy Chili Rellenos

Vegetable cooking spray
1 can (4 oz.) whole green chilies
6 oz. shredded Monteray Jack cheese
1 C. low-fat sour cream
3 eggs
2 T. chopped jalapenos (Or we like none, or less than 2 T. Use your own judgement and family preference for amount to use.)
 salt and pepper to taste

Preheat oven to 350 degrees. Lightly spray 9" X 9" baking dish. Rinse, drain, and cut chilies into strips. Arrange in dish. Top with cheese. Blend sour cream, eggs, jalapenos, salt and pepper. Pour over casserole. Bake until custard is firm, about 20 to 30 minutes. Serve with Salsa. This makes four servings.

If you have a skill, share it. If you don't have one...get one. Think about it!

Chapter 114 — Normal Routine

Isn't a normal routine comforting? Think about it!

As much as I love Thanksgiving Day, the Christmas Season, and New Year's Day, with birthday and wedding anniversary all within that two month span, it just feels kinda' good to be back in a routine again.

We had so much sweet stuff and rich foods and late night and early morning activities, parties, and programs that plain food and an easier schedule is real welcome.

The house is back to normal (whatever that is!), the good dishes are put away and we're back to using those less fragile and precious. The regular pots and pans are in use again instead of the pudding molds and food grinders and candy thermometer. Even the apple butter kettle has been put to rest along with the other canning equipment. For a few months things will be calm and quiet.

The decorations are back up in the attic. The poinsettias have shed their leaves. The fruits in the center pieces have all been eaten.

We are in a comfortable routine. We have a set system to getting around in the morning. It just feels good to relax over a good cup of coffee.

Our bodies are glad we've quit overeating and those same bodies are glad to be in bed at a decent hour. We know where we are supposed to be when, without looking at a calendar or date book. And doesn't just a plain old hamburger sound good?

I guess some people feel real let-down after the busy holidays. They have a feeling of "Is that all there is?". Maybe it is the way I was brought up, or maybe it is because I enjoy the calm after the storm but January and February are enjoyable times to me. There is time to relax and think, explore new territories, discover new truths, experience new feelings. It is a time of serenity, of semi-solitude, a time to sit back and reflect on the happenings of the past.

It is too early to spring house clean. It is too early to do much in the yard. It is too early to drag out the summer stuff. It is too unpredictable to travel much. So, we enjoy the comforts of home. It is a time to play games that were received for Christmas, to fill the freezer with baked goodies for summer, to try new recipes, to start an exercise routine...many things. It is a time to write the all-American novel, to practice the piano, to sit down and write letters to friends and family beyond the notes that we enclose in the Christmas cards. There are all kinds of things to do for yourself and others at this calm, relaxed time of year. Time seems like such a terrible thing to waste...Even the winter months when one is more-or-less confined to the house.

During this time, we may seek new worlds, new knowledge, new treasures, new ideas. Within this search we may find something extraordinary about ourselves that we didn't even know before. It is OK to take time for yourself, to take inventory of self. It is not a time to be restless, but relaxed. If we are so unacquainted with ourselves that when alone we feel as if we are with a stranger, our lives are sadly empty and resourceless. Then we are left with poor company. Do something about "self". Be your own best friend.

It's time to make a simpler meal. Time for Fish Cakes:

1 can (6 1/8 oz.) tuna, crab, or salmon
1 egg
1 t. Cajon seasoning
1/4 C. finely chopped onion
about 20 soda crackers, rolled fine

Drain fish well. Add other ingredients. Form into cakes about 2 1/2 to 3 inches in diameter. Spray skillet with spray oil. Cook covered until brown on both sides and onion is clear. This makes 6 to 7 cakes. We like it with creamed peas and baked potatoes.

It doesn't take very long and we are off to a granddaughter's basketball game or a quiet evening at home, where peace and quiet are appreciated. Doesn't it feel good? Think about it!

Chapter 115 — Habits

Is there a habit you need to make or break? Think about it!

I am not proud of the fact but a long time ago I used to smoke. I wanted to quit and finally I just said to myself, " Self, do it now!". I quit cold turkey. When I quit I still kept a pack in the tea towel drawer so I knew it was me that actually quit and not just because I was out of supplies. I never smoked again...and never will. I am so very glad I quit. I cannot imagine how I'd feel if my precious, beautiful granddaughters smoked because they saw Grandma do it and think it was OK. That picture in my mind keeps me from ever smoking again...ever. See, I WANTED to break the habit.

You or I or anyone will never quit a habit until we want to. Whether it be smoking or interrupting, or being tardy, or overeating or nail biting, or what ever. We've got to WANT it to WILL it. Lots of people have quit bad habits and will admit it takes a desire to quit and fortitude to stay with it! One can't lay the blame on anybody or anything else. A bad habit never disappears miraculously. It is an undo it yourself project.

Jim is very punctual. That is a good habit I learned from him. FEAR changed that habit. I was afraid if I wasn't ready on time he'd go off and leave me. It becomes a habit to always be late to work, or church, or wherever, and always have an excuse...the car wouldn't start, a button popped off, there was a wreck and they rerouted traffic, etc, etc. Yet others have the same alloted 24 hours each day and manage to be on time. Could this also be habit? It is inconsiderate that some people keep others waiting. This isn't to say that occasionally one could run late, but if it happens more than once a week, it is a habit...a bad habit!

Borrowing can become a habit. Funny those same borrowers don't have the habit of returning. It becomes embarrassing to have to ask for your own possessions back yet the owner shouldn't be the one to be embarrassed. It should be the habitual borrower/keeper.

And non-payment of little debts can become habitual. It is easy to forget to pay your part of a gift when several have planned to share the cost. Reminders don't always bring results. It finally becomes awkward and embarrassing to ask for payment. Many friendships have been strained over this very thing.

Snacking is a habit. So is overindulgence. Eating is not a habit...it's a necessity. However, eating chocolate cake instead of healthy food IS habit (now I have stopped preaching...and gone to meddling. Ha!)

Some good habits to make are flossing your teeth, putting the laundry in the hamper, making your bed, leaving things like you found them, smiling, being kind, consideration of others, writing thank you letters, writing any letters, remembering birthdays (not the years, only the days), courteous/ defensive driving, cleanliness, temperence in all things...the list goes on and on. There are as many good things we NEED to do as there are bad things we don't need to do. You know yourself better than anybody!

After the holidays with mounds of cakes, cookies, candies, and other confections, doesn't it feel good to give the taste buds a rest and eat something like Scotch Supper.

8 oz. elbow macaroni
1 can corned beef, chopped
1/4 pound sharp cheese, diced
1/2 C. milk
1 can condensed cream of mushroom soup, undiluted
1/4 C. chopped onion
dash of garlic salt

Cook macaroni in salted water until it is tender. Drain well. Add other ingredients. Pour into casserole and top with a little grated cheese or bread crumbs. Bake in a 350 degree oven about 20 to 30 minutes until slightly brown on top and cheese melted. Great served with green beans and a tossed salad.

You can turn over a new leaf anytime and begin a good habit or end an old one but the first of the new year is as good a time as any to tell yourself, "Now's the time". You'll be glad you wanted to change. Think about it!

Chapter 116 — Christmas Spirit

Do you feel the spirit of Christmas? Think about it!

It is sad to say that many many people will be glad when the holiday season is over. Trying to overspend, overshop, overeat, overgo, or overtax oneself may be the reason. But in this excessive hustle and bustle are they not missing the real meaning of the season?

Times were when we all went caroling to the neighbors' houses. Everyone invited us inside but we went on our way because we had lots of homes to visit. It was cold as blue blazes and our noses and fingers were frozen, but we sang on, even if we woke the next morning with a sore throat. It was still worth it to see all the happy people.

Maybe it would be best if we could go back to simpler times when most gifts were homemade and planned all year and secretly sewed or painted after the kids had gone to bed or the grownups were busy elsewhere. THEN more emphasis was placed on giving instead of getting. Maybe I have just forgotten in my old age, but I can not remember making want lists as some people do now. I have to ASK my family if they have a preference of gifts. Whatever we get or make for them is just what they wanted. They always say, "Oh, Grandma, thank you, thank you, thank you." They are just as happy with a little as a lot. Those kinds are fun to buy for or make for.

One of my favorite gifts of all times was a dolly quilt that my grandma made me when I turned five. She died just one day before my birthday, but the quilt was already made and I got it for the following Christmas. I still have it and it is as cherished now as it was then...maybe more so.

Jim remembers his best Christmas was when he got his first bicycle. That was a BIG present in those days. He rode it every day to school and all over town on Saturdays and Sundays. He literally wore it out.

The best Christmas we both together had was when we got our belated Christmas present on December 30, and our first granddaughter was born. I know how Mother Mary must have felt in loving anticipation. She wanted the world to know the good news. I still feel that way about Jamie, our great news. Our world has never been the same since that day.

The first year we were married, we had just gotten into our first house and most of the evergreen trees in town were sold. All but one. We finally found a dinky little tree that was sadly bare of needles and had a bent top. We bought it anyway and it was the nicest tree we have ever had. I can't remember if we had any presents under it. All I remember was that delightful tree that spread such cheer to our first house that Christmas.

It seems to me that the REAL meaning of the season is the spirit of love that is within the stores and with our families. It is not just the shopping, but the wrapping, the planning, the cooking, the songs, the happy secrets, the cards and hearing from old friends and family, the programs and services of the nativity; the entire atmosphere is different somehow. The world is different.

Your life is not complete until you make a steamed pudding for Christmas. It really is not so difficult and looks so pretty on a cake stand.

Steamed Carrot Pudding

1/2 C. fat
1 C. brown sugar
1 C. grated raw carrots
1 C. chopped apple
1 C. golden raisins
1 1/2 C. flour
1/2 t. salt
1 t. cinnamon
1/2 t. allspice
1/2 t. nutmeg
2 t. baking powder

Cream fat and sugar. Add carrots, apples, and raisins. Sift dry ingredients together and add to shortening/sugar mixture. Mix well. Pour into one large, well oiled mold filling 2/3 full. Steam about 3 hours. This makes 10 to 12 servings. Serve with hard sauce made with 4 T. butter, 1 C. powdered sugar, and a little lemon juice mixed together until smooth.

The way to steam a pudding is to cover tightly with an oiled lid, or cover with foil and tie securely. Place on rack with boiling water to cover mold up to 2/3 its depth. Close kettle tightly.

Honor Christmas in your heart this year, and like Charles Dickens, try to keep it all the year. Think about it!

Chapter 117 — Plan "B"

Do you have a plan "B"? Think about it!

Disappointments and discouragements will come to everyone who attempts to achieve something worthwhile. The heartbreak of failure has been experienced by even the most successful men and women. Every person has high hopes that are never realized. It takes courage to rebuild the castle of our dreams that has been wrecked by circumstances. The path to achievement is one of struggle, courage, and sometimes turning to plan "B".

Sometimes the second choice turns out to be the best way to achieve something. And many careers have taken a sharp turn when the first plan did not work out. Then, it is usually better than expected. How many people do you know that are trained for one profession yet accept another as plan "B" and are very successful and even happier in the second plan?

The real test of character is one's ability to make a satisfactory adjustment to new and different situations. The possibility and the probability that such demands may someday be made upon us, challenges each of us to build into the fiber of our being resources that may be drawn upon in the hours of our supreme need.

I remember when we planned the fiftieth anniversary for Mama and Daddy. We could not plan on how many people would be there so we planned for lots of friends and family. The one thing we did not plan for was one of the worst snow/ice storms that had ever hit Pawnee in February. Call after call came in saying that they would love to come but they were afraid of the weather conditions. Well, we all had four-wheel drive vehicles so we just went to gathering up those people and took them to the church where the reception was held. What resulted was a wonderful party where everyone came and stayed and stayed instead of just a quick greeting, a sip of punch, and then leaving. It was a memorable occasion and one of the best days the folks had ever had...plan "B"!

There is not a one of us who has not had to make a change of plans because of Oklahoma weather. But doesn't it keep life exciting to not be in a rut that one cannot change.

In one split second a life can change forever. Then there really is a change of plan. Poor health can change plans quickly and forever.

When you planted those tomatoes last spring, you thought of all the fresh vine-ripened tomatoes you would eat all summer sliced, in salads, etc. Then frost threatened and you were left with vines and vines of green ones that would never ripen. Time for plan "B". Make Chow-Chow. There are many ways to make it. Some use cabbage in theirs. Others use hot peppers. I am sure you probably have a favorite that you have always enjoyed. One that I try to make every year or so is this one:

Chow-Chow Sweet Relish

20 to 24 average size green tomatoes
2 average size green bell peppers
2 average size red sweet peppers
6 to 8 onions
Grind and drain well.

    Add:
3 C. sugar
3 C. white vinegar
1 T. mustard seed
1 T. celery seed
1 t. tumeric
1 t. allspice
1 T. salt

Bring to boil and boil 15 minutes. Can in sterilized jars. Shelby and I made it this year and we got seven pints plus a little bit more from this recipe. It is great on hotdogs or with a pot of beans and a slice of onion.

Helen Keller said, "We cannot choose what life will bring us of joy or pain, but what our souls bring to meet the challenge, this is in our power." Think about it!

Chapter 118 — Marriage

Isn't marriage wonderful? Think about it!

We recently had the pleasure of "standing up" with friends when they renewed their marriage vows after forty-four years. The minister who performed this beautiful ceremony noted the vast difference between a wedding and a marriage. A wedding does not a marriage make. It takes lots of patience and work and time to make a real marriage. Some weddings NEVER "take". Theirs did!

These same friends returned the favor by attending us at the renewal of the twenty-fifth anniversary of our marriage. The ceremonies were nothing alike, yet each had the same theme, that a marriage endures, not because of an elaborate wedding, but because of a special magic and love that it has.

We have always said that there is nothing better than a good marriage and nothing worse than a bad one. That is certainly no reflection on a person. One can take two absolutely wonderful people and put them together and things are not always so wonderful.

I have had good teachers of what makes a happy marriage. My grandparents and parents adored each other. They couldn't hide that love from the world. One could tell in their glances, and the sincere caring, and in the way they kidded each other. It announced to everyone that they had a special love that remained to the death of a spouse. My grandma died in November. Then Grandpa died the following February. I was real young but I can remember people saying that Grandpa was not really sick, that he just grieved himself to death. I guess he just could not go on without Grandma after their many, many years of marriage and raising eleven children in hard times.

Those hard times can strengthen a close marriage, as can a serious illness. Yet we have all seen marriages that simply crumbled under the strain of an illness of a child or one of the mates. Or they didn't pull together in a hardship and one or both of them wanted to break the team. Luckily, most of the time a set-back gives a marriage added strength. There is a sense of appreciation of having someone share that hardship in understanding and love.

It seems to me that it helps to share the same basic beliefs and cultures and interests. But we have all seen unions that flourished on those differences. One thing is clear, one cannot choose another's life partner. Sometimes the most "unlikely" couples have the most successful marriages. Who can tell?

Marriage takes a lot of patience and forgiving, and sharing. We both love the theater, western movies, concerts, ball games, vacations, shopping, museums, visiting and friends. We share the same beliefs in religion, and political parties and most everything. We both think it is good to both like the same food, and house furnishings, and modes of spending and saving. It helps if both share the same priority of health and dental care, and taking care of oneself. I would think it could destroy a marriage if one was messy and the other was real neat, or if one was clean and the other not so fastidious.

Sometimes when I come home from work the house smells wonderfully inviting, and I know that Jim has been in the kitchen cooking up supper. One of the favorite things on a cold winter night is his Bean Chowder.

Bean Chowder

one mediun onion, chopped and steamed until transparent

To this add:
1/2 pound all beef wieners, sliced about 1/2 inch thick
2 cans (16 oz. each) butter beans (one drained but one not)
1 can (15 oz.) Cajun stewed tomatoes
1 can (8 oz.) tomato sauce

Season to taste with salt or other seasoning. Bring to boil. Make a skillet of corn bread. Simmer chowder until cornbread bakes. This is a feast!

In the letter that I wrote to Jim on our anniversary, I said, "Let us live and love, so that when one of us is left alone, we will have no regrets for the things said or unsaid, done or undone." Think about it!

Chapter 119 — Assets

Do you assess your assets? Think about it!

To mind comes the words of the song that goes, "You've gotta accentuate the positive, eliminate the negative, latch on to the affirmative." How nice it is to see the good of things and not just the bad, to see the positive side of things and not just the negative.

It is rewarding to be proud of what we HAVE, not pining for what we don't have. If we don't have good health, then maybe we have a good mind. If we don't live in a mansion, then maybe we at least have enough to eat and a warm place to sleep. We have the ability to read and write. We are hopefully able to hear, and see, and feel, or at least some of these.

We live in a free country where we can talk of our political leaders without fear of death. We are able to vote for the candidate we truly believe will do the best job in helping our country, and state, and country.

We are not locked into a profession or particular class just because we were born into a certain family. We can be what we WANT to be. It may take extra effort, but we CAN do it!

Most everyone has things they really don't count as blessings until they are taken away. We really do take things for granted. It is not the qualities we have; it's the qualities we recognize we have that will make the difference. We need to recognize these good traits in ourselves. We need to assess the positives and turn them into assets.

Remember back in the "olden days" when we were happy with an orange, an apple, some nuts, and maybe some ribbon candy in our stocking at Christmas-time. I don't know what little boys got for presents, but we girls got a new doll dress for the doll we already had. Funny, how Santa knew just what color our special dress was and made the doll's dress from the same material. I don't recall that we ever whined or complained that we didn't get more. We assessed our assets and counted our blessings. If we got anything else, it was a simple toy or something we needed, like underwear or socks. But we had wonderful Christmases! Those were happy times. We were happy with what we had and didn't ask for everything in sight.

Something we always had for holiday dinners was mincemeat pie. It smelled sooooooooo good when it was cooking. It used the scraps of things, so nothing was wasted. I still love mincemeat pie.

Mincemeat for two large pies

1 C. cooked and coarsely ground meat (lean pork and beef of either)
1/4 C. beef suet, ground (for richness)
1 C. dark raisins
1/2 C. golden raisins
4 to 6 cups raw tart apples, diced
1 C. dried apricots, coarsely ground or diced
4 t. grated orange peel
juice of one orange
1 T. lemon juice or vinegar
1 C. sugar
2 t. cinnamon
3/4 t. allspice
3/4 t. cloves
1/2 t. nutmeg
1/4 t. salt

Combine in kettle. Add liquid, meat broth, fruit juice (cherry or apple or grape) or water to just cover. Cook, stirring often, until raisins plump and apples and apricots are tender. However, cooking in the oven eliminates much of the stirring (and scorching). This makes about ten cups of mincemeat. If it seems too thin, use Minute Tapico for thickening. If it seems too thick add a little juice. Bake in two-crust pies.

Assess your assets. They are many. Think about it!

Chapter 120 — Fears

What do you fear most? Think about it!

For Jim it is a debilitating, crippling disease or condition. For me, it would have to be being left alone, a widow.

I heard a speaker once say to a group of women that in this day and time with the law of averages, when most women outlive their husbands, that it is not a matter of "IF" you will be left a widow, but "WHEN". I have thought about that lots of times. I'll bet you could ask any person and no matter how much they have planned, they are never ready to be left alone. I don't mean to sound like gloom and doom, but it is just a fact of life.

There are many people handicapped, who never dreamed they would be in that situation. In one split second their life took a drastic change. They weren't prepared for that either.

For us, growing old is not a worry. It sure beats the alternative. Death is not a fear. I had someone tell me once that they didn't mind dying, they weren't afraid of that, they just didn't want to be dead. Life is too precious to want to give it up.

Some people fear poverty. I guess that equates with hunger but when we were poor during the depression we were never hungry because we lived on a farm and had chickens, eggs, meat, milk, and home-grown veggies and fruits so we never really knew what hunger was. We didn't even know we were poor because everyone seemed in the same situation. Maybe poverty is a state of mind.

One of the saddest fears of some people is rejection. The fear of being left out of a group, whether real or not, motivates people to live beyond their means financially in able to "keep up with the Jones." It is rejection or peer pressure that causes some kids to get into drugs or gangs or crime. They just want to be accepted and wanted. Recognition is very important to some.

Public speaking makes some people terrified. They just break out in hives or lose their voice and their knees knock and they get actually sick. Others accept it and it doesn't bother them at all.

Driving, especially in the big city streets or highways, can be a real fear to some people. It is not only their own driving, but watching out for the others that can be fearful.

Many of us fear failure, of one kind or another. In fact, we each define failure our own way. For some it is not having a professional job, for others, it is social position. For others, it is the botching of a performance of singing, speaking, etc. Whatever that "failure" means to each of us, we each think about what it would be if that circumstance came our way, and in our own way we dread the thought of it happening to us. It is such a blow to our ego, that something might be less than our expectations.

I've had people tell me that they are "afraid" to cook. Well, there is nothing to it. Especially in this day and time with so many helps in the grocery store, on the shelves and in the frozen food section. It is simply a matter of following simple directions and serving it with a smile. Most of the mixing and measuring has already been done for you. Don't be afraid to whip up something. Your friends will love you for it. It isn't so much what we eat as how we enjoy it that makes a meal memorable and satisfying. Keep recipes and menus simple to begin with. Don't start with sauces that curdle, or a standing rib roast, or a flan, or a cheese cake. Start with pineapple sauce. It is delicious served on pancakes, waffles, French toast or biscuits. It is wonderful served on ice cream, vanilla pudding, simple baked custard, angel food cake, or pound cake. It is equally scrumptious served on baked ham or pork chops. Your meal will come alive with it.

Pineapple Sauce

1 small can crushed pineapple
1/2 C. pancake syrup (I like maple, but any will do)

Bring to boil. Let cool to lukewarm and serve. That is all there is to it. What could be simpler or less fearful?

Fear is our own worst enemy. Think about it!

Chapter 121 — Personal Growth

Are you growing as a person? Think about it!

I am always so thrilled when I read in the paper or hear of older people who have gone back to school to learn something of interest. They set an example for young people that says it is never too late to learn. We never get too old to learn something new and exciting.

There are many people who begin an entirely new career at middle age. They always seem so happy and successful. They are doing something they really want to do. They are stretching themselves, using their minds and physiques to do something interesting and profitable.

We have heard it said that a mind is a terrible thing to waste. Usually we think of it in reference to young people but it applies to every age group.

One of the joys of my life was going back to school after many years and getting a college degree. Whether or not I use it in my work is really not so important. It is just the satisfaction of the going to school and having done something for myself that is important to me. I don't even care if anyone else knows it or not, I did this for me. No one can take education away from me. It is mine to keep and I earned it.

Many churches and organizations have winter classes or summer classes or short courses that people can take to renew an interest or start a new project. There are many varied classes available that would delight every age, interest, and physical or mental ability. The costs are usually very minimal or even free for the asking.

It is fun and challenging to take on new projects and interests and goals. I know retired people who have recently taken up computers to master. Many writers just discovered this interest and talent in later years after their kids are grown and away from home when they have time (and money) to pursue their own interests and try new ventures. The same can be said for other fields of endeavor, like music or painting.

Every time I talk to my remarkable old dad, I learn something else interesting that he has learned or thought about. His mind is so sharp. What a blessing! And he never lets it go to waste. He uses it.

Remember the story of "Boil, Pot, Boil," when the rice, I think it was, continued to expand and expand and there was no stopping it. The mind is kind of like that...it just continues to expand and grow until we choose to turn it off, which I hope is never!

Speaking of rice...let's make Baked Rice Pudding:

2 large eggs
1/2 C. sugar
1/4 t. salt
2 C. milk
1/4 t. nutmeg
2 C. cooked rice
1/2 C. seedless raisins (optional, but we like them)

Mix all together and pour into 1 quart casserole and set in pan of water (1" deep). Bake at 350 degrees about 1 hour and 15 minutes. Serve warm. Makes about six servings.

Grandma used to make it with uncooked rice but it seems to take forever to cook and has to be stirred ever so often as it bakes for hours, so I do it the lazy-man's way and it tastes just as good.

Never be afraid to try something new to help your mind grow. In moments of exaltation and vision we see ourselves free from lazy mental habits that prevent us from reaching intellectual attainment. At our very best we determine to free ourselves from harmful physical habits and excesses that rob us of the energies required for vigorous living. We are challenged when we read of the great men and women of the past. We see elements in their lives and in the character of great men and women of our own time that we long to possess, that we may share in their greatness.

These dreams may all come true. With purpose, determination, and patience, they shall come true. Think about it!

Chapter 122 — Homesickness

Have you ever been homesick? Think about it!

I remember as a kid, when I went to camp for the first time, and as I remember it, the first time I was away from home for any length of time with someone other than relatives, I was dreadfully homesick. About Tuesday evening many of us campers began to long for home. The special counselors anticipated this so kept us extra busy with activities. It worked and before long it was over. Then when the end of the week came, we dreaded leaving our new friends and going home to routine things. We wanted the camp experience to last a lifetime.

When Shelby was about six, she spent a few days with us while her parents went on a trip. While they were gone, when we tucked her into bed, she became sad and told us that she missed her momma. The poor little thing was just homesick. Instead of yelling at her or talking her out of it, I just sat on the edge of her bed and explained that it is a very normal reaction, that I miss my own mother, too, and she has been gone for many years. One never gets too old to miss having their mommas with them. Shelby and I talked and talked and soon she was asleep. Missing your parents is a form of homesickness, and it is very real at any age or stage.

Jamie is attending college away from home. She has done very well adjusting to changes of lifestyle that college presents and she has matured a great deal. However, one of her friends has already dropped out of school because she has been so homesick. I almost know that if she could have just toughed it out, that she would be fine by the end of the semester.

Age doesn't have a great deal to do with homesickness. After I have been away from my own home for about one week, I begin to miss my bed, and my house, and my shower, and my dog. I just want to be HOME with familiar surroundings and the things I love. I am this way even when Jim is with me. He misses the comforts of home also. We are always delighted when we drive in our driveway. Coffee just tastes better at home too.

And our dog is overjoyed to see us. He is elated each time we leave and return whether it is one hour or one month. He greets us warmly and is a great welcome committee.

Author Arthur Benson said it better than I could when he wrote: "Perhaps for most people, the best results of travel are that they return with a sense of grateful security to the familiar scene. The monotonous current of life has been enlivened. The old relationships have gained a new value. The old talk is taken up with a comfortable zest. The old rooms are the best, after all. The homey language is better than the strange tongue. It is a comfort to be done with cramming the trunk. It is good to be home."

Yes, Home...ah, home...where we can truly be ourselves, with no pretense and no masks, and no interruptions unless we want them. When I feel a little melancholy and yes, when I miss my dear Momma, I get busy and cook. I use the old dishes and use Momma's old black pan she made cornbread in. I make a big batch of Sausage Chowder and maybe an apple pie and I feel all better. I hope it helps you too.

Sausage Chowder

one pound sausage
1/2 onion, chopped
1 large stalk of celery
1/4 cup green pepper, chopped
1 can Ranch Style beans
1 can whole kernel corn, drained
1 can tomatoes
1 (5.5 oz.) can V-8 juice
1 Tablespoon Picante Sauce
1 teaspoon garlic salt

Brown sausage and drain. Combine all ingredients in a heavy kettle. Simmer, covered, for one hour.

It is impossible to explain how comforting and happy one feels to be enfolded in the arms of home. Think about it!

Chapter 123 — Pain of Sadness
(Written in May, 1995)

How do you bear sadness, loss, and pain? Think about it!

For the past few weeks, which seems like months, we have been glued to our TV sets because of the terrible bombing in the Heartland of our nation, Oklahoma City, on April 19. This is so close to home that every life has been touched in some way by this tragedy. We can't watch it, or we can't NOT watch it. We are literally glued to our sets to know what the next move will be. In all this we have experienced many emotions: fear, anger, loss, hurt, devastation, sorrow, sympathy, and others, depending on how we have been touched. We all have mixed emotions, elation at one moment as the rescuers do their appreciated job, and then sadness when we learn that all those involved did not live.

Our hearts go out to these families, to the children, to the many workers whose jobs are affected, to the rescuers. Our hearts are heavy for all the families and friends involved.

It seems nearly everyone in his/her own way has contributed to overcoming this tragedy. Even many people from out-of-state have felt moved to do something. All want to help, but what do you do? What can you do? Many wear ribbons. Many donate food, clothing, or money, or offer their services. No list can be made of all the people who have poured out sympathy and caring in such a generous way.

Many people find it difficult to talk about such a calamity. Others cannot stop talking about it. Everyone handles it in his/her own way. The people of America have shown their true colors in responding to the bombing. It is too bad that it takes an incident like that to bring out the best of people. The helpfulness was there all the time. It just needed a route out, a reason to manifest itself.

Isn't it that way most of the time? It takes a sadness like a severe illness or funeral to bring some families or communities together. Then it is under such strained circumstances. The weight on one's shoulders becomes loving concern. We all have within us unrealized possibilities of things we can do. Opportunity has just never been challenged to such proportion. We grow from ordinary to true greatness.

Death and severe illness or injury seems to make us stand back and take a look at ourselves and count our blessings. In our appreciation and caring we want to do something for someone else. We turn to heroic tasks. Even little kids in school have made cards and written poems and sent notes of love. We have all turned to acts of kindness that we can do for others.

When you need a break from worry and sorrow, or if you need to sit with a friend to discuss the worry and sorrow, serve this:

Fruit Finale

1 (6 oz.) can frozen orange juice concentrate
1 (6 oz.) can frozen lemonade concentrate
1 Cup sugar
two (10 oz.) boxes frozen strawberries, thawed
4 to 5 large bananas, mashed
one Number 2 can crushed pineapple (with juice)
1 (16 oz.) bottle 7-Up

Mix orange juice, lemonade, and sugar (do not dilute juices). Add strawberries, bananas, pineapple, and 7-Up. Mix well and freeze in 9 x 13 inch pan 24 hours or longer. Thaw a short time before serving. Keeps well for two months in freezer. You may substitute any kind of fruit you wish. Also you can pour in paper cups to freeze, then when you want dessert or a refreshment you just take one out at a time.

We have all felt a great sadness, loss, and pain. Time will ease it some-what. We can meet any challenge. Think about it!

Chapter 124 — Hidey Hole

Do you have a "hidey hole?" Think about it!

When I was young and lived in the country, everybody had a cellar for their canned fruit, vegetables, and meat, along with things like lard and eggs, milk, butter, and the like. It was always cool in the cellar in the summer and in the winter it seemed warm by comparison. That was such a cozy place to be and one was always surrounded by wonderful smells of food.

There was also a long bench down there and when it would storm, which is quite often in Oklahoma, we would each get up out of bed, take our flashlights and a folded blanket and go to the cellar. I cannot remember that we were ever afraid or hysterical, as so many people are today when the news even hints there will be a "thunder storm." This was before we had the T.V.'s to warn us of storms and had to rely on how the sky looked or how the air felt.

There are other places we go to protect ourselves from the storms of life. Most of us have a special place we can retreat to when we want to get away from something or spend time alone. My special place is our "back office" where I do most of my writing and typing. It is really nothing special, except to me. I feel comfortable and cozy there and can do my best thinking.

When I go home to Pawnee and see Daddy, I can sit on the footstool by his chair and feel all secure and almost like a little girl again. He even seems to think I'm a kid. We have some of the best talks with this arrangement. I don't recommend trying to escape into being a little child, usually, but this is nice occasionally. For a moment I can flee from a world of pressures, stress, decisions, and concerns.

Our hidey hole can be anywhere, any time we retreat from real life and its daily activities. We can feel safe and secure and relaxed and unhurried. It can be in the car on our way to or from work. It can be work. It can be home.

Most of our homes are our place of security. We are surrounded by things we love and enjoy. We can be what we truly are, with no pretense. We can answer the phone or door only if we feel like the intrusion. Other times it may be a welcome sound.

It is just fine to have a hiding place so long as we do not live in a world of make-believe where all is a fairy story with pretend people and fabricated, fantasy lives. We must face reality at some point and get our head out of the sand. We have to come to grips with our fears and withdrawals. And most of all we cannot hide from ourselves. We are our best company, or should be. If we are not, then we need to do some work on it. We can hide behind a facade, or a mask to others, but we cannot hide our real feelings from ourselves.

No need to hide! If peace is in your heart the wildest winter storm is full of solemn beauty, the midnight lightning flash but shows the path of duty. May serenity be in our lives so we don't have to hunt a hidey hole.

It won't be long before we will need to be making salads and things for holiday meals. This is a simple salad but one of our favorites. Make it in a jiffy, and then go on to something else you need to do, or retreat to a special place and wrap presents or send cards, or read a good book.

Cranberry Salad

1 small package Red Jello
1 Cup boiling water
1 can whole cranberry sauce
10 ice cubes
1/2 large delicious apple, chopped fine
1 can (11 ounces) mandarin oranges, drained and rinsed
1/2 cup chopped pecans

Dissolve Jello in water. Stir to dissolve. Stir in cranberry sauce and mix well. Add ice cubes and stir occasionally. As cubes dissolve the Jello will begin to set up. Chill until almost set and stir in apple, oranges, and nuts. Pour into a pretty crystal bowl. Cover with plastic wrap. It is ready to cool until time to serve. Don't forget and leave it in the refrigerator, as I have been known to do, when dinner time is at hand.

No need to hide. Within yourself is a great unexplored kingdom where you can live in peace. Enjoy! Think about it!

Chapter 125 — Looking Back

Can you travel back in time? Think about it?

We just attended two Scottish Festivals, one in Tulsa and the other in McPherson, Kansas. We do this in memory of Jim's mother who came from Scotland and died when Jim was a tiny baby. Therefore, we know very little about Jim's heritage. But it is fun to go to these festivals and clan gatherings because each time we learn something more about his family history. We can go back in time by listening to the stories of the old country and talking to people about those old times.

Close your eyes and listen to music of your youth and you can certainly return to old times. Nothing (unless it is food) reminds us of the fun we had and the romance of being young like the music of yesteryear. Each era had its own particular likes and dislikes, and favorite tunes.

Mother had packets of old letters from relatives and friends that were very revealing about times gone by. We used to sit and read them and go back in time to the years of the Civil War in some of those letters. She also had school notes from Daddy. These are precious. So are old valentines and post cards that told of travels and interesting events taking place. As much as I use the telephone, the sad thing about their use is that we have nothing down for history. It is all for the moment...and then gone.

Things can take us back in time. Our house is FULL of stuff that is old and full of history. It may not be earth-shattering history, as some know it, but each thing in our house has a story to tell. Many of the things are gifts from our granddaughters and family. Many are old things that belonged to my parents and grandparents. Each has a story and a message of love, that certainly evokes emotions.

High school reunions or any reunions will take us back to good times. We remember names we have not thought of in years. We remember incidents that we thought were long forgotten. We can have those same memories just seeing friends or talking to them.

Those cultural events like the Scottish Games richly merit the time and attention we devote to them. Preservation of our heritage is important. Scotland is a rich country. Its nationwide respect for learning, the honesty and morality of its character, and the honor of its soldiers are assets that no Scotsman would exchange for any material blessing. We have our shields, our crests, and tartans to remind us of these traits.

It is truly marvelous that our ancestors were able to create out of very limited raw materials such a broad, tasteful, and filling cuisine. Their recipes, or from any country, are a tribute to the ingenuity of people, as are the contributions of science, literature, and philosophy. Food is a wonderful way to go back in time. These old country recipes bring the past to the future as we experience those same flavors.

Gingerbread Waffles

1 1/2 Cups flour
1 1/2 teaspoons baking powder
1/2 teaspoon soda
1 teaspoon cinnamon
3/4 teaspoon ginger
1/2 teaspoon salt
2 eggs
1/3 Cup sugar
3/4 Cup buttermilk
1/2 Cup molasses
1/4 Cup melted butter

Combine the dry ingredients. Sift into a bowl and set aside. Beat eggs and sugar until thick and foamy. Stir in buttermilk and molasses. Add to dry ingredients and stir until dry ingredients are moistened. Stir in butter. For each waffle pour 3/4 cup batter onto preheated, greased waffle iron. Bake. Serve with sliced bananas or peaches and whipped cream.

Enjoy your trips back in time, for the past mirrors the future and people change little. Think about it!

Chapter 126 — Growing Old

Are you growing old gracefully? Think about it!

I guess first one should define old. It is a state of mind. Middle age seems to get later and later and later. It will continue to do that as long as we feel young and necessary. We are as old as we feel.

My dad is 94 years old (young) yet he doesn't seem old since he is in relatively good health, can eat anything he wants, can still work circles around most younger people, and still cares for himself and has a sharp mind. He says he doesn't feel old until he thinks about the fact that almost all of his life long friends are no longer around. He has gillions of young friends but it is just not the same. He keeps active and has just started a new hobby, raising buffaloes. He just had two new calves born this summer and is so excited about them.

Our granddaughters tell me I look like a grandma, whatever that is. I take it as a compliment as I don't pretend to be young. I have earned all these gray hairs and wrinkles. Grandmas don't have to dress frumpy, but neither do they have to wear little short shirts or sleazy outfits either. There is a certain dignity to age, in actions and appearance. Gracefully accepting age is important, by keeping active and interested in things.

We admire people who continue to take college courses and try new activities. They will never grow old. Even with more birthdays, people need to look ahead and not just be content with where they have been or where they are now.

I was so lucky to have grandmas and parents who were fun. I have wonderfully happy memories of cooking, playing games, making things, fishing, exploring nature, and just being with them. From all of them I learned to be industrious and interested. Even if we may not be so nimble we are still active and curious.

Being around young people creates a youthful spirit. Just watching their activities is a joy. Hearing their music educates our eardrums. Doing things with them helps both generations learn from each other and appreciate the differences and similarities. If we close our eyes and ears and senses to the things of today, we have admitted that we are too old to learn new ways.

For my last birthday, my family gave me a clock. It has a picture of two little girls and their "fluffy" grandma. One of the girls has dark hair and one has blond hair, just like our Jamie and Shelby. Above the picture is inscribed, "Grandmas are just antique little girls." I look at it a hundred times a day and am reminded how very true that is.

Old recipes, like old people, still have a great deal of worth and flavor and relevance. Take for instance this recipe for Strawberry Bread:

3 Cups flour
1 teaspoon salt
1 teaspoon baking soda
2 Cups sugar
3 eggs, well beaten
2 pints fresh strawberries, sliced (or two ten oz. packages frozen strawberries, thawed)
1 1/4 Cups vegetable oil
1 Cup broken pecans

Sift dry ingredients together in a large mixing bowl, making a well in the center. Mix remaining ingredients and pour into the well. Stir enough to dampen all the ingredients. Pour into two well greased regular loaf pans. Bake at 350 degrees for one hour. Cool ten minutes before turning out.

When we close our lives to new experiences and vitality, we are old. Think about it!

Chapter 127 — Listening

Are you listening? Think about it!

How many times, when you were a kid, did your mother ask you those very words? And you always answered, "yeah." We were listening, we thought, but were we really hearing what was being said or meant?

When we go to the ranch at Pawnee, we hear only the still quiet of the night. It is so quiet, compared to the noises of the city, we can hardly sleep. Daddy, who lives in the country, hears many sounds that we can't detect. He hears the pump of the oil wells. He says they say, "Nickel, Nickel." He hears coyotes howling in the distance. He hears cattle if they are moving about. I think he hears these sounds because he is listening for them. We hear them only if they are called to our attention.

Many cars go down the street with "music" so loud it is impossible to hear the tune or words because it is simply a boom-boom. I wonder if the listener really knows what he is listening to, or is it just noise for the sake of noise? Some background music is just that, a noise to drown out any other noise or conversation. Eventually we fail to hear the music and it becomes den. In my office the copy machine makes a kind of buzzing, high pitched noise. I fail to hear it but one of my co-workers is distracted by the constant sound. I find a radio during working hours the same distracting racket. Others probably don't hear it at all. It all depends on how much we listen and for what.

Mothers can be sound asleep and still detect a faint cry from her child, or can hear the baby roll over in the crib. In our house I cannot hear trucks driving down the street, but if our puppy scratches the least little bit, I hear it. We can all remember a time that a different noise awoke us from a sound sleep.

When I was a kid, in Pawnee County, we could put our ears to the ground on summer evenings and hear the distant drums of the Pawnee Indians. It was a musical sound to me. I don't know what this has to do with this article, but I guess it is just that it taught us to listen in different ways. I loved it!

Do we sometimes hear but not heed? Some teenagers, and other too, say things to us and we really don't listen for the hidden meanings within their words. Sometimes they are trying to tell us something that they, themselves, cannot put into words and terms. They are wanting us to hear a hidden, deeper meaning and we are not on the same wave length. We do not hear their cry for help.

Many times in my writings I hear my parents or grandparents speaking. Their words come through my typewriter. I can sometimes hear myself in Jamie and Shelby now, too. Does it pass down through generations?

I always have an ear open for a new, unusual recipe. One I heard just recently is great and perfect for those cold evenings we will have soon.

Traylor's Texas Beef Stew

1 1/4 pound beef stew meat, cut in 1 inch pieces
1 Tablespoon cooking oil
1/4 Cup chopped onion
1 1/2 teaspoon garlic powder
1/4 teaspoon pepper
1 can (16 ounces) tomatoes with liquid, cut up
1 Tablespoon ground cumin
1 teaspoon salt

In a large kettle, brown beef in oil. Drain. Add other ingredients. Simmer for 45 minutes or until meat is tender. Serve with rice. If there is any left over, Olive says it is better the next day with a can of Ranch Style Beans added.

Stop, look, and LISTEN. A life may depend on it. Think about it!

Chapter 128 — Your Disposition

What is your disposition? Think about it!

When describing oneself or a friend or someone else, it seems we say it in one word, and that word usually describes their manner more than their looks. In reality, one's behavior is much more important than whether he/she is tall or short, blond or brunette. A person's demeanor is more memorable than any physical attribute.

There is a joke about someone who has an even disposition...always mad. The same can be said for any person who is always angry or whatever.

We all know happy people who are like a ray of sunshine and who always take things in stride and look for the positive side of things. These people are a joy to be around. They are kind, loyal, sweet, and bubbly.

On the other extreme are those people who are always angry. They have a sour disposition and a glum outlook on life in general. They are impatient, whiney, and negative. We stay clear of them because we don't want their actions to rub off on us.

Some sadness is natural. Anyone who is grieving or has had experienced a terrible loss, whether it be job, family, or financial, has every right to be sad. But when the sadness hangs on for years, then it is time to make a change in some aspect of our lives.

Some people are depressed, "gloomy and doomey", and often have an inferior feeling. They think everyone and everything is against them. They look down at the sidewalk rather than look up to the sky. Their mouth is always drawn.

Life is great! Why shouldn't we celebrate it and be happy? One is miserable if they go through life in a dower mood all the time. It isn't natural to always be jolly either. People who never show a change have no feelings. They cannot see the pain around them or the need of people.

If the scales tip to the negative all the time, it is time to take a look within yourself and see if there is not some ray of hope in every situation.

I am very fortunate to have been raised in a family that is positive and laughs a lot. My dad, at age 94, still has a sunny outlook on life. He does not complain and usually has a quick, funny response to any question about his health or life in general. This does not mean that he has not had his share of illness and sorrow in his life. My parents raised our big family in lean times but never complained. We were taught to be thankful for what we had, and during those lean years we did have much more than many families because we had the right, positive attitude and worked hard for what we had. In fact, it was only after I was grown that I realized just how poor we were in material things, because we were so rich in other areas...the areas that really matter in life.

Grandma always said, "What you are at 40, you will be twice that at 80." If you are happy at 40 you will be twice as happy at 80. But if you are down at 40, you will really be a downer at 80. I would take that a step further and say what you are at 20, you will be twice that at 40, etc. The time to change your attitude is now if you are not what you want to be all your life.

Look for balance in the things you cook too. A one dish meal sure speeds preparation and is just as good for you. Try this recipe for a skillet meal. Add an easy salad, fruit for dessert and all you have to do is set the table.

Frontier Meal in A Skillet

1 1/4 Cup yellow cornmeal
3/4 Cup flour
4 teaspoons baking powder
1 teaspoon salt
2 eggs, well beaten
1 Cup milk
4 Tablespoons shortening (I use bacon drippings)
1 can whole kernel corn (well drained)
1 pound lean ground beef
1 onion, chopped
1 pound cheddar cheese, grated

Brown beef and onion. Combine cornmeal and other dry ingredients. Stir in shortening, milk, corn, and eggs. Pour 1/2 batter into well greased 9 inch iron skillet. Pour meat/onion mixture over this. Pour on the other half of the batter. Sprinkle with grated cheddar cheese. Bake in 350 degree oven about 1 hour or until brown on top and tests done.

How will you be at twice your present age? Do you need to change? Think about it!

Chapter 129 — Important Things

Do you have time for important things? Think about it!

Why is it we can find time to sit down and send twenty-five to one hundred Christmas cards with messages at this special time of year, and hardly find time the rest of the year to send one greeting card to someone.

Or bake: We find time to bake all kinds of goodies now when the rest of the year we use mixes or frozen stuff. It is such a joy to bring out all those old recipe cards and dog-eared cookbooks to labor over a hot stove fixing the things that Grandma made for Thanksgiving or Christmas. The food just tastes better that have wonderful aromas and memories.

Or decorate: We adorn everything with finery when the rest of the year we are so exhausted we do well to pick up and straighten the house or water the thirsty plants. We decorate not only the interiors of our homes but also the yards and housetops. We don't want to look like Bah, Humbug! When our neighbors do such a beautiful, artistic job of lighting up the plains. We feel we have to decorate to get into the real spirit of the season.

Or shopping: We see men who would never set foot in a grocery store if they were starving, go into malls and shops and stores, laden with packages and getting into the spirit of the season shopping. They may not be really enjoying it but they are doing it anyway. And it makes their families and friends happy.

Or wrapping: We hide and seek and wrap until the very eve of giving. We tie bows and tag packages and make each an original work of art. We hide them again, hoping we can find them when the time comes to deliver them.

With all this preparation we must not lose sight of the true meaning of the holidays, whether it be Thanksgiving, Easter, Veteran's Day, President's Day, or Christmas. We often fail to remember WHY we have those holidays. We think of them as three day weekends or time off from work without deeper thought of the real reason for the celebration. We need to take time to remember.

Anna Brown Lindsay wrote some prose that says a great deal about time and the use of it. She says: "It is worth while to be wise in the use of time. In the eternal life there is no waste of the years. It is with time that we purchase everything that life has of good. The most reckless spend-thrift in the world is the one who squanders time. Money lost may be regained, friendships broken may be renewed, houses and lands may be sold or buried or burned, but may be bought or gained or built again. But what power can restore the moment that has passed, the day whose sun has set, the year that has been numbered with the ages gone?"

We need to find time all the year for the things that we usually reserve for special times of years. We need to write notes of love and friendship, bake special things for family and friends, shop and wrap and surprise someone unexpectedly. We need to make our surroundings pleasing and enjoyable.

Take the time to make this a special time for yourself and someone else. Fix these treats and serve with a cup of coffee and enjoy.

Magic Moments

1 Cup all-purpose flour
2 Tablespoons cornstarch
1/2 Cup powdered sugar
1 Cup butter
1 3/4 Cups Angel Flake Coconut

Mix flour, sugar, and cornstarch in bowl. Blend in butter until a soft dough is formed. (If dough is too soft to handle, cover and chill.) Shape into 3/4 inch balls. Roll in coconut. Place 1 1/2 inch apart on baking sheet. Bake at 300 degrees about 20 to 25 minutes, until lightly browned.

Take time for important things. Unless a person undertakes more than he can possibly do, he will never do all he can do. Think about it!

Chapter 130 — Ready for Christmas

Are you ready for Christmas? Think about it!

This seems to be the question everyone is asking now, and really expecting no answer. Sort of like, "How are you?" Then not waiting for a detailed response. The inquiry begins before Thanksgiving and will last up to Christmas Eve.

I feel so sorry for little kids who don't have the same concept of time that big people have. The displays begin in September, and Santa Claus is on the T.V. so early, that the little kids think Santa will be here tomorrow, and tomorrow never gets here. They begin to think the big day will never arrive.

I feel the same way sometimes. There is so much that must be done, and so much we want to do, and so many demands put on us with school programs, and church programs, and parties. No matter how well organized one is, there is usually some slip-up or some unplanned meeting to attend.

There is the house to get ready, and the decorations to put up, inside and out. There are all those Christmas cards to mail. And all those letters that we write only once a year. Most of all there are all the cookies, and goodies and food to prepare for gifts and for company and for ourselves.

Are we making Christmas preparations just too complicated for our own good? I know back when, that Mother and my grandmas were real busy but I cannot remember Christmas being so complex. We never asked for anything for Christmas but we always got something. Maybe it was doll clothes and underwear, but we always got something. I cannot recall that we were ever disappointed with what we got. We were happy to get anything. In our socks, that we hung on Christmas Eve, we would get an orange, an apple, a peppermint stick, and perhaps some nuts. Nothing like the lavish gifts today that have become the norm.

I'm not too sure that the old way wasn't best. Most, if not all, gifts were hand made lovingly. There was none of this last minute rush to shop so that the receiver didn't get a duplicate of what they already had. There were no such things as duplicates. If so, they were still appreciated.

One of my favorite Christmas gifts is the doll quilt I got when I was four years old. My grandma died the night before my fourth birthday, but she had already completed a doll quilt for me. So when Christmastime came, I got the little quilt, lovingly made with her gnarled hands. It is still a treasure to me. It represents the true meaning of Christmas, that of a gift of self.

We used to put the tree up on Christmas Eve or only a few days before Christmas. Now they are lighted in windows at Halloween in some places. It seems to me that it loses some of the magic by being up so soon. Then we wonder why we are so eager to remove all signs of Christmas the very next day. We are sick of the hassle, and things out of place, etc. What a shame that we have allowed the most wonderful holiday of the year to change our real spirit of Christmas.

Here is a recipe that will help you be prepared for your busy days. It is an old recipe I found in Grandma's things. It can be used as a breakfast fruit, with lunch, or on ice cream or custard for dinner. It was made with the dried fruits that she would have on hand in the winter, as fresh fruits were not available.

Visions of Sugarplums

1 Cup pitted prunes, cut in fourths
1 Cup dried apricots, cut in bite sized pieces
1 Cup dried apple slices, cut in bite sized pieces
1 Cup dried cranberries
1 Cup dried cherries
1 Cup golden raisins
1 Cup honey
1 Cup brandy (I use Apricot Brandy, or orange juice)
2 Cups water
1 teaspoon cinnamon
1/4 teaspoon ground cloves

Combine honey, brandy, water, and spices in a saucepan. Bring to boil over medium heat until dissolved together. Pour over mixed fruits, stirring gently. Store in airtight container in refrigerator or cool place, at least two days before serving, stirring gently each day. Will keep for several weeks.

May you find the true meaning of Christmas and keep it all the year. Think about it!

Chapter 131 — Peace

Are you at peace with yourself? Think about it!

At this time of year we hear a great deal about peace. We hear "Peace on earth, good will toward men." We hear "Let there be peace on earth, and let it begin in me." We hear, "May the peace of Christmas be with you." and we pass it on.

But sometimes we are warring within ourselves. We act angry at people because we fail to have an inner peace in our own lives. We lash out at others when we don't know how to address the anger within ourselves. Ask any psychiatrist, many people have to delve far back in their minds to find the source of a deep-seated anger. They carry this anger with them all the time until they find the source of it and either resolve it or let it go.

Sometimes we are warring with our family. These family riffs can be caused by something so insignificant that it is difficult to remember the real cause. The only thing remembered is the way we felt at the time. These arguments can go on for years. So can the disregard for the rest of the family. Usually when they are finally brought to light by an unbiased observer, they are easily solved and great reunions occur.

Sometimes disputes between neighbors cause hard feelings for years. Usually, they too, are caused by simple disagreements over a tree or a dog or noise. Simply discussing the problem will usually solve it and make for much more pleasant living.

Even disagreements between co-workers are usually caused by a simple misunderstanding. Everyone is entitled to a bad day now and then and sometimes the least little thing can cause hurt feelings. It is always best to find a quiet time away from the other workers and apologize and sort out the feelings and what was said...and what was meant.

With the stress of the holidays and the stress of over worked check books and demands on shopping, there can even be misunderstandings between couples who truly love each other. It is so easy to misinterpret what was said. It is just as easy to talk it out and find the real cause of any problem. The holidays are not the time to have friction within a team.

Marriage is the most serious venture in life. A business can dissolve without serious or permanent damage to either party. Marriage cannot. Marriage is not all songs and roses and laughter. Major adjustments have to be made by both parties. Health problems, financial problems, other problems may come into being, but a marriage team must have the peace and love to withstand anything and everything.

We hear of the wars in other countries. We feel we must take a stand on one side or the other. We feel compelled to get involved. We truly want peace on earth. About the best we can do is find peace within ourselves. And from that peace and strength do what we can to help others find peace.

Don't let the sun go down on an argument. Take a plate of these cookies as a peace offering and go to that neighbor, or friend, or co-worker, or family member and seek forgiveness and understanding.

Shared Sugar Cookies

1 2/3 Cup sugar
1 Cup oleo
2 eggs, beaten
1 Cup oil
4 1/2 Cups flour
1 Tablespoon vanilla
1 teaspoon salt
1 teaspoon cream of tartar
1 teaspoon baking soda

Cream together the sugar and oleo. Beat in eggs, flavoring and oil. Combine dry ingredients. Gradually add to mixture. Refrigerate overnight. Form into small balls about 1 inch diameter. Place on ungreased cookie sheet. Dip fork in water and flatten cookies, crisscross. Bake in 350 degree oven for 12 minutes or until lightly brown. Makes more than six dozen. The dough keeps in refrigerator over a week if covered well. We add 1/2 Cup nuts or chocolate chips for variety. These freeze nicely.

May you find inner peace and the joys of the season. Think about it!

Chapter 132 — Speaking the Truth

Do you say what you believe or what people want to hear? Think about it!

We all are aware that there are times when we cannot say what we really want to say. That isn't to condone white lies but we are sometimes compelled to agree for the sake of peace within a family or office, etc. Then there are those times with we best keep our mouths shut, not agreeing nor disagreeing. You know those times!

It is sometimes easier to be a "yes-man" than it is to buck the system and always voice our opinion. If this affects the way you live and you find it upsets you, then it may be time you changed jobs. If, on the other hand, it does not bother you to always have to agree, even when you truly don't, then that is your business and I wouldn't try to change you.

There are those people who voice objections no matter what is proposed. They just rebel against ANY change. After all, we have NEVER done it that way. Never mind that it isn't working, or why, it is just that we balk against any change. We like things the way they are.

There are just as many people who never object to anything no matter how much they disagree on its being done. They don't care what course of action is taken so long as they, themselves, don't have to act. If they say something often enough and long enough, they begin to believe what they do and say is okay.

People, in general, want to avoid an argument if possible. We all hate discord and we all dislike friction. We will go to almost any lengths to avoid confrontation. Therefore, we just sit back and nod our heads or shake our heads, whichever is appropriate at the time. Thus we avoid any conflict. And we think that will make us more popular. Well, it just doesn't work that way. Popular is not necessarily the most liked. Eventually the others discover we are wishy-washy and non-committal.

One can disagree without being disagreeable. If you are against some-thing, then it is perfectly alright to say you disagree, but then give a workable solution to the problem. Too many people just are against something but have no other course to suggest. This is what cooperation is all about.

All of the world's great achievements are a result of faith. Doubt always limits. Most insisted that the earth was flat but Columbus believed it was round and the history of civilization was changed because of his theory. Our space travels are a venture in what was believed beyond many obstacles. They stood up for what they believed could be done and should be done and did not go along with the masses. It takes real courage to launch out sometimes, but to grow and like ourselves, we have to stand up for our convictions and what we believe to be right for the good of all.

We are indebted to the daring souls who have burst the bonds of the status quo and have led us out into the future by having a vision and not just nodding their heads and agreeing with "what is." To those of all ages who used the knowledge of their generation to point a step forward, we owe our gratitude. Where would we be if they had said only what others expected to hear?

After a great dessert, we expect people to cheer and give lavish compliments, but on this dish don't really expect it. It is great but is just another way to do corn.

Scolloped Corn

1 beaten egg
1 can cream-style corn
14 saltine crackers, crushed
3 Tablespoons milk
1 Tablespoon finely chopped onion
1/8 teaspoon pepper
1 Tablespoon butter, melted

Combine egg, corn, half of cracker crumbs, milk, onion, and pepper. Mix well. Place in casserole dish. Combine remaining cracker crumbs with melted butter and sprinkle on top of corn mixture. Bake in 350 degree oven for 30 minutes. Add one tablespoon Picante sauce to corn mixture if you like.

The only way to like yourself is to be true to yourself. And say what you believe. Think about it!

Chapter 133 — Wisdom

How wise are you? Think about it!

There is a vast difference between being wise and educated. There are people who have a high degree in education yet who are not wise. And there are those who are very wise and have little education.

My grandpa received only a fourth grade education, yet he was a wise man. He was self educated. He farmed and owned lots of land and cattle and stayed busy mentally and physically all his life. He was constantly aware of the things around him and was curious about everything. He read a lot, and a lot of different things from the classics to the daily newspapers and was well informed of world affairs and literature. I always thought he was such an intelligent person. I always wanted to be like that when I grew up.

You have known people, and so have I, who have a lot of book learning but cannot carry on a simple conversation because their high-tech knowledge interferes with their communication skills. I feel real sorry for these people because they don't know how to use their education to good use.

And some of those same educated people have absolutely no common sense. They cannot think beyond what the books have taught them. Jim used to work with a gentleman like that. He had a high I.Q., but he could not figure out how to stack a bunch of boxes so they would stay. It was just beyond him. Kids can be taught how to have common sense. It is simply a system of thinking and reasoning and planning ahead. Our granddaughters have a lot of common sense. Once when Shelby was stood up by her ride from the mall to her home after a movie, she had the good sense to call us for a ride. That doesn't sound like much, but some kids would have stayed there all night...waiting. Not Shelby, she knew it was time to act and did. We are glad she did. We'd much rather she called a thousand times and not need us than to not call and need us. It takes "gumption" to know what to do.

Wisdom takes a gift of imagination, wherein lies the genius of all creative artists and thinkers. Wise people see with their minds as well as their eyes. And they make things happen. They transform the commonplace things of life into realities that are inspiring and challenging. They make dreams come true. They are not afraid to dream.

I am certainly not putting down education. Our daughter is a teacher and I am sure a great one. My father was a teacher and I have a teaching degree, although I don't teach now. I have many teachers in my family and I am proud of the profession. But education does not always take the place of acquired wisdom. It is surprising how much you learn after you think you know it all. Experience is a great teacher. The school of hard knocks can instruct you real quickly and have a lasting effect.

This time of year, as any time of year, it is wise to have something in the freezer to quickly serve to drop-in guests. This bread can be sliced, wrapped, and frozen for just such occasions. All you need to do when the doorbell rings, is remove slices from the freezer, top with a dollop of Cool Whip, make the coffee and you have a party.

Apricot Bread

1/2 Cup diced dried apricots
1 egg
1 Cup sugar
2 Tablespoons melted butter
2 Cups flour
1 Tablespoon baking powder
1/4 teaspoon soda
1/2 teaspoon salt
1/2 Cup orange juice
1/4 cup water
1 Cup chopped nuts

Dice apricots, cover with hot water. Let stand 2 1/2 hours. Drain, then puree in blender. In separate bowl beat egg. Stir in sugar and butter. Mix well. Add sifted dry ingredients. Mix with orange juice and water. Add apricots and nuts. Stir just until well mixed. Do not over stir. Bake in greased 9x5x3 loaf pan 1 1/2 hours at 350 degree.

A wise person knows: the more he knows, the more he knows he doesn't know. Think about it!

Chapter 134 — Disappointments

What is your greatest disappointment? Think about it!

I guess my greatest disappointment was not being able to have children of my own. But I have always said the good Lord knew what he was doing because I married a man who had a teen age daughter, who is now like my own child, and who has given us the two perfect, precious granddaughters. How lucky can one person be! The greatest disappointment turned out to be the best thing that could ever happen, because it eventually brought the best things to my life.

My sister had four sons. Each time she was expecting, she would wish for a girl. A girl to dress frilly, and to teach how to play the organ, and to enjoy cooking with, etc. Well, it didn't happen that way. She had four boys. She said many times later if she had had a girl it would just be in the way. Boys could wear hand-me-downs, and share rooms, and share hobbies and do many things together. The disappointment was short lived. She is the perfect mother for boys.

Daddy's disappointment was that not all of us seven kids got the college degrees that he had wished we would and that he had financially planned for us. All of us did but two and both of them have careers and positions that probably would not be furthered with more education. They are quiet self sufficient, and successful, and happy. Daddy's disappointment was soon over.

Many of us have been disappointed for awhile, and then found that things worked out better than we could possibly expect. Those disappointments turned into something very positive, and many times better than we could ever plan for ourselves.

A friend recently told of a lemon sponge cake that she had made for company. The cake was an absolute flop. She quickly dumped it in a bowl, thinking she would discard it later. The son of her company came into the kitchen and said, "Oh, lemon pudding, my very favorite". There was nothing Jan could do but go ahead and serve it for dessert. She played like it was lemon pudding all along. It was her little secret. Her disappointment became something grand for her guests.

If we cook at all, we have all had recipes that we were not satisfied with, and/or were inedible. We either order out, eat out, or throw out and start over. We call these learning experiences. I have told you of some of my dreadful failures that I tried to feed Jim. Most of those mistakes (except two that stand out in my mind) he ate and seemingly enjoyed.

Christmas or birthday lists include presents that are never received. But does the recipient remember that they were disappointed? In our household they are not. They are always grateful for what they receive and soon forget about the long wish list. They are too busy enjoying what they did receive to miss the things they did not receive. If there were disappointments, they were short-lived.

Sometimes we have had failures that have devastated us for some time. We think it is the end of the world and that we will never recover. But time heals all wounds, and out of many of those disappointments come a better life or solution. We just have to stay positive and look for the good from every situation that faces us. Out of every defeat comes hope, and out of every hope comes some good.

This is a recipe we are never disappointed with. It is easy, fast, and has good flavor. I sometimes make up a big batch, and freeze it, and then we thaw it in the Dutch Oven over the fireplace and feel like we have "cooked" back in olden times. It is great with corn bread. You'll have no room for dessert.

Sizzlin Soup

1 1/2 pounds lean ground beef
1 medium onion, chopped
1 can (16 ounce) whole kernel corn, well drained
1 can (16 ounce) Ranch Style pinto beans, undrained
1 can (16 ounce) tomatoes with chili seasoning
1 envelope taco seasoning
1 small can tomato soup

Brown meat and onion. Add other ingredients. Simmer to sizzling and it is ready to serve. What could be simpler or easier to serve?

Don't let disappointments get you down. When life hands you a lemon, make lemonade. Think about it!

Chapter 135 — Recycling

Do you recycle? Think about it!

When I was young, we recycled everything. We thought nothing of wearing hand-me-downs. Everyone did. When our clothes were beyond wearing, we cut the skirts off and had the softest tea towels. The rest of the garment was used for cleaning rags. We saved any buttons, snaps, or zippers.

Quilts were created out of the good scraps of fabric after a garment had been made. Nothing was wasted. Those quilts have been lovingly handed down for generations, and are works of art. I have an old pre-Civil war quilt that Grandma gave us. When she presented it, she said, "This is not much for beauty, but it still has a lot of warmth left in it. " It is not beautiful compared to most quilts but it is made of homespun wool and must have taken years to make. Part of the warmth comes from the fact that it has been lovingly preserved all these years. When she hovered under it on her trip to Indian Territory in the wagon that October I bet it felt pretty good.

It pleases me that the city has begun a recycling program in our neighborhood. It takes a little longer to put out the trash on Mondays but it seems like a worthwhile program to me.. it is surprising how quickly the stacks of newspapers and plastic milk jugs pile up. It is really not much trouble to sort the papers from the plastic, from the cans, from the glass, and in time it will all add up to saving our landfills and ultimately our beautiful countryside.

During the Depression years and war years we saved everything and used it again, passed it on to someone who could use it or recycled it in some way. No garden produce was ever wasted. No clothes were ever just thrown in the trash. Every thought was given to who could use it after we had outgrown it or were beyond its need. Books, games, puzzles, toys, clothes, household items, were all given away. I never heard of garage sales when I was a kid. We just gave things away when we were finished with them. And people appreciated things then. I remember loving to get hand-me-downs from cousins or friends. We did the same for them. It still doesn't bother me if someone offers me something they are through with. I love it when my younger sister cleans her closets and calls me to come to her "store." The clothes are NEW to me. She does the same with my discards.

We never wasted food either. Leftover bread was used in bread pudding, dressing, casserole toppings, or French toast. Roast was planned so you could get hash, barbecue sandwiches, or salad out of a large roast. Vegetables were saved for soups. Fruits were used in puddings. Stew and chili were better the second or third day. I have always saved corn bread to eat in milk or buttermilk, or use in dressings, until a dear friend recently told me about corn bread salad. It is surprisingly delicious. If you use left over corn bread, you may want to adjust the ingredients somewhat so it is not all vegetables and mayonnaise. It can be made ahead of time and chilled before serving. In fact it seems better that way.

Helen's Corn Bread Salad

1 package corn bread, baked, cooled and crumbled
1 bunch green onions, chopped fine
1 large red bell pepper, chopped fine
1 large green bell pepper, chopped fine
3/4 Cup mayonnaise

Mix all ingredients and moisten with mayonnaise.

Recycle. Reuse. Let the things you discard fill a need instead of a landfill. Think about it!

Chapter 136 — Darkest Hour

When was your darkest hour? Think about it!

Most of us don't even have to think about it to know when it was. It is still clear in our minds, and will always stay there. However, hopefully time will diminish some of the vivid details and hurts and hopelessness.

It is during those dark moments that we are unable to see even a flicker of light at the end of the tunnel. In fact, we cannot even see a tunnel. We feel that the world has closed in around us. All is black. There seems to be no way to turn. We feel desperate. We feel isolated. We feel like not going on.

It is always darkest before the dawn. Soon some tiny ray of light will appear far off in the distance. We see a tiny flicker, then a little more, and then some more. Eventually the flicker will become a light with enough brilliance to light our way. Either we are getting closer to the source of light or the light comes closer to us. In either case, the two come together.

Anyone who has ever had a dark, desolate moment will identify with the hopeless, heartbreaking feeling of loss of direction. If you have not had such a moment, then you will. Everyone does at some time in their life. It is a feeling shared by all, although not all moments are the same. No problems are the same, but the feeling and the outcome are very similar.

If you have gone through your experience, you are in a position to pass on to others the way of hope and repair. I have told you before about my older sister who lost two of her beautiful four sons. One died of cancer. The other was struck by lightening.

She has had several dark, dark moments in her life but has become stronger by those experiences. Now if anyone has the loss of a son in the family, she is the very first person on their doorstep with a word of encouragement. She KNOWS how they feel when they are faced with such a tragedy.

There are other dark moments in our lives besides loss of a loved one. There are job changes, transfers in jobs requiring moving to a strange, new location. There are changes in families beyond our control that greatly affects relations.

Many times when we look back on them in later years we find that those changes and dark moments were for the best and we grew from those situations. We find that it is true that every cloud has a silver lining. We just couldn't see things clearly at the time and we could not know what was in the future after those changes.

Truly strong people, and those who are a joy to be around have usually gone through many of these depressed incidents. They know how to appreciate what they now have and what they have survived and put behind them. They are a ray of sunshine themselves. They exude this hope and optimism. They are fortified and therefore bolster those around them.

When you have a dark day go to the kitchen and make something. Knead bread. Beat a batch of candy. Do anything that will require a lot of energy or concentration. Or better yet, make something relatively easy and call one of those fortified friends over to cheer you.

Almond Bar Pie

1/2 Cup milk
five (1 1/4 oz.) chocolate almond bars
15 large marshmallows
1/2 teaspoon vanilla
1 Cup heavy cream

In a heavy saucepan, or in microwave, heat the milk, almond bars and marshmallows until melted. Stir in vanilla and allow to cool. Meantime, whip cream to stiff peaks. Fold in chocolate mixture. Pour into prepared graham cracker crust. Allow to cool until set. Better if chilled overnight, but three hours is enough.

I. Panin said, "One furnace melts all hearts...love;
            One balm soothes all pain...patience;
            One medicine cures all ills...time;
            One light illumines all darkness...hope."
Think about it!

Chapter 137 — Weather

How's the weather? Think about it!

Isn't it funny that when it is cold and snowy and we are forced to stay in, we read gardening magazines and wish it were warm, and when it is hot summertime, we read skiing magazines and wish it were winter. We seem never to be satisfied with whatever the weather. Yet it is one of the things we can do absolutely nothing about. We have to accept what comes.

I remember hearing Grandpa tell about the deep snows they had back in the olden days, when the snow was so heavy they had to string a rope from the house to the barns so they could follow that rope to find the barns to feed the livestock. I know it also was no picnic to have to go out daily in that freezing weather to chop ice for the cattle to have drinking water. That is still done now. My brother, who has a ranch, still has that chore to do and the ice can get pretty thick when the temperature stays at sub-zero degrees. Wielding that ax can take the joy out of an otherwise beautiful day.

On those terribly cold days, the cattle and horses and other livestock need more attention than any other days. Those are the days when you really wish you were in some other line of work. But ask any rancher, it has many rewards and few would trade places with anyone.

I can remember only one snow when it was so deep we could not see the tops of the fence posts. The spillway of the pond was so full of snow that we could hardly tell where the pond was located.

Even with all the snow and ice and bad weather, I do not remember that school was ever cancelled. However, I quickly add that it was a time before school buses, and I would not want the responsibility of driving a bus of fifty kids on roads and perhaps end in a ditch turned over or worse. When it was frigid and icy Daddy would take us to school on the huge sled we used to take hay to the cattle. We hitched it behind a tractor or a team of horses.

It is wise to prepare for winter. We used to gather fire wood and have a great big pile stored up for bad weather. Now we have a rick or two and think it is enough, which it is, with only the fireplace using it. We don't depend on the fireplace to heat like we used to have the old stove in the dining room. It was so cozy right by the fire, but go into the next room and it was so cold, one could hang beef in there and know it would be refrigerated enough not to spoil.

Even with all the stories of how cold it used to be, I cannot remember being cold. Oh, the rooms were cold, but we dressed by the stove and make a B-line for the bed and warmed our feet on a heated brick wrapped in old towels. The bed was cozy. In the mornings, we jumped out of bed, grabbed our clothes, and hurried in by the stove to dress.

Now, I complain about the cold weather, even before it starts. You know why? Because my bones tell me when the weather is going to change. I wear coats, mufflers, gloves, and boots now but when I was a kid my folks had to make me put on the proper attire for inclement weather. I never really noticed that it was so cold. Of course, we did not have nice outdoor thermometers back then to tell us how cold it was. Now we look at them first thing in the mornings and then figure the wind chill and talk about the weather more.

One way to weather the weather is to cook something real hot and soothing for supper. Something like Snappy Stew.

Snappy Stew

2 pounds lean stew beef
1 large onion, cut in large chunks
3 carrots, cut in 3/4 inch pieces
3 to 4 medium potatoes, cut in 1 inch cubes
1 (16 oz.) can Snappy Tom tomato juice

Fry meat in shortening until brown. Drain well. Add other ingredients. Cover. Bake in 350 degree oven about 45 minutes until meat is tender and vegetables cooked.

Enjoy the weather, whatever the weather. There is nothing you can do about it, and as Will Rogers said, "If you don't like Oklahoma weather, wait a minute." Think about it!

Chapter 138 — Luck

Are you lucky? Think about it!

How lucky I am to have my background living in the country and growing up on a farm in the era I did. I was (am) so lucky to have had my special parents/grandparents. I was so lucky to have had a thrifty and sharing upbringing, with emphasis on thinking of others and not just self. I was so lucky to have received the education I did in a one-room school. In every way I can think of, I was lucky to be a kid when and where I was.

My adult life has been just as lucky. I am so glad Jim came into my life when he did, with a teen-age daughter, whom I adore. My luck continued with a great son-in-law and now two perfect granddaughters. How lucky can one person be?

How lucky I have been in my careers. I have had only four jobs in my entire lifetime and all four have been handed to me without my having to apply for them. I was just called up and asked to come to work. What a joy that is to know that I was wanted. I hope I have not let my employers down in any way. They have all been enjoyable, challenging jobs, with many rewards and few fiascoes. I have loved each and every job, and was sad when I had to move on.

Luck did not just happen. It is a matter of being at the right place at the right time. It is a matter of hard work and planning. Sometimes we are handed a poor hand but the secret to winning the game of life is not so much in holding a good hand, as it is playing a poor hand well. It is making the most of what we have in the circumstances we are placed. We can't just sit around waiting for good things to happen to us. We've got to keep our eyes open and be alert at all time for opportunities.

A few moments of reflection and thinking, will reveal to us our utter dependence on others in every satisfaction in life, whether it be the comforts, conveniences and jobs of life, or our food, our clothes, our homes, or our "things". Before we have been up one hour in the morning, others have served us. Can you think of one single thing that we possess and enjoy for which we are not indebted to someone? So luck is not all in what we do for ourselves; it depends upon others! We never want to let our abundance and comforts cause our gratitude to sink to the level of smug self-satisfaction, thinking that we did it all for ourselves.

The same thing can happen to two people and one will interpret it as good luck, while the other will think it is bad luck. It is all in how we view it. Each circumstance can be a learning experience or a set-back. If we stay positive and try to find something good in every condition, then we will have good luck. If we feel sorry for ourselves and look for the down-side of conditions, then it will surely be due to a "streak of bad luck."

We always hear of the luck of the Irish. Well, let me tell you, the Scots and Germans have had a lot of good luck as well. I am a smidgen Irish, but mostly German and I can attest to some of that good fortune. I have been blessed in many ways and I know everyone else has also, if they but look for that pot of gold at the end of the rainbow.

Here is a good, easy recipe that is Scottish in origin and is really great tasting. We like it with meat loaf.

Colcannon (Cabbage and Potatoes)

6 average potatoes
1/2 stick butter
1 teaspoon salt
1/2 teaspoon pepper
1 Cup heavy cream
1/4 Cup minced onions
About 1/2 head cabbage, shredded

Boil potatoes until done and mash, leaving a few lumps in them. Cook cabbage until done but still a little crisp. Add salt, pepper, cream, butter, onion, and well drained cabbage to potatoes. Adjust salt and pepper to taste.

I think it was Oprah Winfrey who said, "Luck is a matter of preparation meeting opportunity." You are lucky! Think about it!

Chapter 139 — Teamwork

Are you part of a team? Think about it!

When I was a youngster on the farm, we had a team of horses I remember well. Their names were Scott and Dan. When Daddy would open the barn door to hitch them to a wagon or farm machinery, they came out in a certain order and always, always got in the correct place with Scott on the left and Dan on the right. They had been trained that way and never varied from that pattern. They seemed to love to get out in cold weather and were frisky and raring to go.

Before Scott and Dan, we had a team of mules that Daddy worked. Both started out as black mules but in time Joe turned white. I guess Jude died or Daddy sold him, but when I was real young, we used Joe to work in the garden because Mother said he was so sure-footed and never stepped on the rows of the garden. How he knew where his feet were, I'll never know but that's what Mother said. I remember Grandpa telling a story of a wagon that came by his place that had lost one of its team of oxen. They bought a replacement from Grandpa, but the new team member knew nothing about pulling a wagon. When the people came back through the country several weeks later, that replacement was working just like the original ox. Working together made them operate like a real team. It was a skill that was learned.

I work in an office that has teamwork. Every person has their own specialty, but everyone works beyond their own job and if a phone is ringing they answer it, or if something needs doing, they do it. It sure makes for pleasant working conditions and good terms. There is no such thing as, "It isn't my job." I've worked in that office for fourteen years and it is just as pleasant now as it was the day I started. It is a joy to work in a situation like that.

One of the greatest team efforts is a marriage. It is the most serious venture in life. Nothing but true love can stand the test of married life. It is a team, so we must not enter into marriage thoughtlessly and hastily. If one loves truly and deeply, no sacrifice is too great. All the worries and set-backs and accomplishments and joys serve to create teamwork and bind two hearts closer together.

When kids think of teamwork, they refer to their basketball team or football team or other sports activity. Our Shelby did not feel well last week. Nevertheless, she played basketball. She did not want to let her team down. She has been taught that the team is depending on her, so she doesn't give a second thought to whether to miss a game or not. She goes. Most kids would feel the same way. That's teamwork. That is what wins games. That is what builds character. It prepares us for life and working in later years with other teammates.

A food that is more fun prepared as a team is raised doughnuts. The dough can be mixed by one, but when time comes to cook them, it is easier and more enjoyable to work as a team. Just do be careful of the hot grease and don't let but one person do the actual cooking. The others do the icing of the doughnuts.

Raised Doughnuts

1 1/2 Cup lukewarm milk
1/2 Cup sugar
2 teaspoons salt
2 packages yeast dissolved in 1/2 Cup lukewarm water
2 eggs
1/2 Cup soft shortening
7 to 7 1/2 Cups flour

Mix milk, sugar, and salt. Stir in dissolved yeast. Beat in eggs and shortening. Add 1/2 the flour and mix well. Stir in remainder of flour. Knead about 5 minutes until smooth. Place in greased bowl and let double in size. Press out to about 1/3 inch thick. Cut with floured 3" doughnut cutter. Leave uncovered so a crust will form on the dough. Drop into deep hot fat (about 375 degrees). Turn to brown on both sides. Drain on paper towels. Ice or turn in sugar/cinnamon mixture. Glaze is: 1 Cup boiling water and 1 Cup confectioners sugar.

If you are not pulling as a team, you are pulling against each other. Think about it!

Chapter 140 — Good Old Days

How well do you remember the good old days? Think about it!

I dearly love to hear stories of when Daddy was a little boy or when Grandpa and Grandma settled in this wonderful new land. Those stories could go on and on and I'd never tire of them. Mother, too, told wonderful anecdotes of when she was growing up.

I love to tell stories of when I was a kid going to that one room school house. I love to talk about the weather back then and what we did for play. Even the work was fun in those days. Growing up on the farm was so different, I am sure, than life in the city. We made an enjoyable adventure out of the work that had to be done, like gathering cattle, making hay, thrashing, etc.

I was mostly in on the cooking for the thrashing crews, but my sisters and I also got to be "water monkeys" and take fresh water to the crews working with wagons and teams gathering the shocks of wheat for the thrashing machine. We just loved doing it. I cannot remember that it was hot and dirty and sweaty. All I remember is the enjoyment of riding our little cow pony and taking water in big jugs to the crew.

In the winter we took feed to the cattle in deep snow and it was terribly cold outside. But I scarcely remember the weather, and all I reminisce about is the fun we had and how cozy it was playing in the big barns.

Even school was fun with few stresses and long recesses. Opening rituals, and the baseball games with other schools and the spelling bees, and the ciphering matches, and the huge stove in the back of the classroom, and the water cooler and individually marked cups that hung by the cooler, and the cloak room and cloak room duty, and riding to school on horse back, and cutting through the pasture to get to school on time, and seeing jack rabbits when we did; these memories go on and on and are etched in my mind.

We remember music lessons in the summer and how we hated to practice, but we liked going to town on Saturday for the lessons themselves. The summers were always fun. We did a lot of work but we had a lot of fun along the way. We picked blackberries and plums and helped in the garden and painted gates and barn doors and everything that needed that annual coat. We waded in the creeks and played house and picked flowers and played outdoors in the evenings when it was cool until it was too dark to see at all, and Mother would call us in.

As I get older, I think we have forgotten the bad things and just remember the good things of our childhood. The special ingredient that made life fun when we were kids, is that we were YOUNG. We were carefree and worry free and let our parents do all the worrying about everything. We were not concerned about tomorrow and concentrated on the fun we were having, with few boundaries and few restrictions. However, out in the country where was there to go, or what mischief could we get ourselves into?

Food always tasted good back in those old days. We were just as happy with a big thick slice or hot home made bread with butter and sugar, as we would be a fancy dessert now. The more I think about it, I'd still just as soon have that sugar/bread treat. Food and life were simpler then. We didn't expect as much and we enjoyed what we were doing and shared what we had with others. It was a calmer, more peaceful time back then.

If we wanted something to snack on, we'd stir up a quick crazy cake. Then cool off while it cooked and have a little refreshing party with the cake, spread while hot with butter.

Crazy Cake

1 1/2 Cups flour
1/2 teaspoon salt
1 Cup sugar
1 teaspoon soda
1 teaspoon baking powder
4 tablespoons cocoa
5 tablespoons melted shortening
1 tablespoon vinegar
1 teaspoon vanilla
1 Cup water

Beat all together for a few minutes. Pour into greased square pan and bake about 35 minutes in 350 degree oven.

Ah, the good old days! The nice thing about memories is that they don't spoil, no matter how long you keep them. Think about it!

Chapter 141 — Wise Choices

Do you make wise choices? Think about it!

Standing at the threshold of a day, we greet life in a number of ways. We face decisions about business and money, about time, about activities, about artistic endeavors and about daily living like meals and housekeeping, etc.

No matter what is our business or career or job, we must ask ourselves with every move if it is profitable, reputable, and feasible. We are guided by our life long morals and business sense. Where we ever got an idea that work is a curse is beyond me. Work can be just as enjoyable as our play. In fact, we need to find a life's work that we enjoy doing so we won't even feel like we have been laboring. It will be pure joy just doing a day's task. Our powers develop and our personality grows as we give ourselves to our work. One of our first choices of business is to make the right choice of a career or job. Then the day-to-day choices are easier to solve.

Probably the hardest decisions we make have to do with how we spend our time, whether working or playing. There never seems to be hours enough in our days to do all the things we want to do and need to do. We have friends that we feel we are almost neglecting because we don't have an evening free to spend with them in relaxed conversation. We never have enough time to spend with family members. We never have time to do the hobbies we truly enjoy doing. And it is not because we waste time. There are just so many fun things in life, we can hardly get around to all of them.

Every action we choose has to do with our honesty and moral fiber. It must fit within our own set of standards of behavior. What is right for me and mine might not be the right decision for you and your family. We simply cannot go against the way we basically believe, and live with those decisions. The only wise choice is to be unswerving and true to oneself.

We each have our own work ethic and standard of excellence that we must abide by. If we go against those basic instincts we are not happy with any choice we make about any element of our life.

A wise choice must include pleasure and feeling useful and helpful. If we are doing something just for the sake of doing it, it brings us little satisfaction or joy. When life is before you, two voices are calling: one from the swamps of selfishness while the other calls from the hilltops of justice and progress, where even failure brings glory and joy. It is not too hard to make some choices. We need only to decide if we want power or contentment.

All of us have made some excellent choices in our lifetime. We all have made some pretty dreadful choices too. We have to just live with some of those mistakes, while others we can correct or overlook. So we are human! Move on!

An easy choice of what to prepare for dessert is this rice pudding with apricot/pineapple topping. It takes a few extra minutes to prepare but it is well worth the time.

Rice Custard with Apricot/Pineapple Sauce

3/4 Cup uncooked rice
2 Cups milk
1/2 Cup sugar
1/4 teaspoon salt
2 eggs, slightly beaten
1 teaspoon vanilla

Cook rice as directed on package. (I bake it for 30 minutes in the oven.) Stir in milk, sugar, and salt. Bring to a boil. Add a small amount to eggs. Stir egg mixture back into larger kettle of rice mixture. Bring to boil. Reduce heat to low and continue cooking while stirring, for about 5 minutes or until custard gets thick. Remove from heat and add vanilla. Top with the sauce made like this:

One 15 ounce can crushed pineapple, undrained
1/3 Cup chopped dried apricots
1/3 Cup packed brown sugar
2 Tablespoons lemon juice

Bring apricots and pineapple to boil. Add brown sugar and stir until it dissolves. Cook slowly until apricots are cooked and absorb some of the juice. Cool slightly and serve over warm rice custard. Good cold or hot or in between.

The greatest power that a person possesses is the power to choose. Think about it!

Chapter 142 — "My-Writis"

Do you have a case of "my-writis"? Think about it!

I guess I do, since I write about my, me, and mine all the time. I write about my Jim, my dad, my granddaughters, my family, my recipes, my country background, my philosophies of life, my thoughts.

We all seem to write about, or talk about that of which we know the most, mainly ourselves and our things. This does not mean that we are stuck on ourselves in any way; we are just prone to think about self, I mention my things only because they are my greatest blessings and I didn't have to be anything or do anything to have them. They are all beyond anything that I govern. It is not bragging because I feel so appreciative of those things I have been entrusted with. I speak of them only because I have been so fortunate to have had such a background and a reason for living.

The times it is dangerous to have "my-writis" is when we get so wrapped up in ourselves that we fail to hear anyone else or feel what they are feeling. I am always overjoyed when our friends have new grandchildren. I offer them equal time to show pictures and tell how great and cute and precious their babies are too.

The most popular and well liked people are those who do thoughtful things for others, little kindnesses that mean a great deal when sickness, sadness, or situations are in control of our lives. We are fortunate indeed to have many, many friends who fit into that category. They make every day pleasant.

I'm sure you have seen the bumper sticker that reads, "As me about my grandchildren." Now, any grandparent worth their salt can bring that into any conversation without being asked. Talk about the weather: "A good day for Jamie to drive to school." Talk about world affairs: "What kind of world for Shelby to grow up in?" Whatever the conversation, the girls fit in there somewhere, somehow. With practice YOU can do the same thing. People kind of expect a grandma or grandpa to boast about their wonderful offspring.

There is much to be said for solitariness. The great leaders of our times seek quiet places to see where they fit into the picture. They spend a lot of time in the secret garden of the soul, seeking answers to difficult questions and thinking of the future. The solitude of the wilderness is good for us and in no way makes us alone. Being about MY business, makes me a better person, if I realize where all those things originate and what they mean to me. I DO!

One of my favorite recipes is Refrigerator Rolls. I was taught at my mother's knee that hot rolls make any meal special. I believe it. The simplest fare with hot bread can be a banquet. This recipe can be made up anytime and will keep for at least a week in the refrigerator, but stir it down about every day until you make it into rolls.

Refrigerator Rolls

3/4 Cup lukewarm water
1 package yeast
3/4 Cup milk
4 Tablespoons shortening
6 Tablespoons sugar
1 1/2 teaspoon salt
About 3 1/2 Cups flour

In a large bowl dissolve yeast in warm water. Heat milk to lukewarm, adding shortening, sugar, and salt. Stir into the yeast mixture. Add 2 Cups flour and beat with whisk until smooth. Stir in rest of flour to make a workable, but stiff dough. Knead on board about 5 minutes until smooth. Place in a greased, covered bowl until dough is double in bulk. At this point, mix down. Make into rolls and place in refrigerator covered tightly, or cover bowl and place in refrigerator. Use rolls within a day or two, but dough in bowl will keep up to a week if you mix it down daily. To serve rolls, remove from refrigerator and allow to rise at room temperature about 2 1/2 hours before baking at 350 degrees about 25 to 30 minutes. Make rolls from bulk dough as you need it, allowing ample time to rise before cooking.

It is okay to have "my-writis". It is in your heart that you carry your life. It is through your heart that you have your greatest visions. From your heart comes your truest words and deeds. Think about it!

Chapter 143 — Dependability

How dependable are you? Think about it!

When you say you will do something for someone, do you? Most of us think we are dependable yet we have to be reminded that we said we would do something at a particular time. Being dependable means that we remember our obligations and promises. We not only say we will do it but do it on time.

There are people who are so dependable that one could set a watch by their promptness. They are not only on time, they are ahead of schedule. They are tuned into anything that might arise to cause a setback. They get up early and do their services so no one will have to wait on them for anything. I admire those people. They are a joy to work around and do projects with. They don't have to be asked twice if they have everything prepared. You always KNOW they have all preparations made and ready.

Then there are those people who are dependable in another way. One can always depend on their being late and holding up every schedule. They march to their own drummer, who by the way is usually a slow drummer. The drummer is missing about every other beat. Those people are selfish, thoughtless, self-centered individuals with little regard for the feelings of others. Thank goodness there are not many of them around. It only seems like there are a lot of them for a little of that bad habit goes a long way.

We are fortunate to have a child and granddaughters who are very dependable. If they are even going to be ten minutes late, they have the respect and decency to call and let someone know that they have been delayed. It sure saves a lot of worry on our part and proves how dependable, thoughtful, and mature they are. If they can be trusted to let family know of a detainment, they are certainly trustworthy in other ways too. It indicates just how reliable they are, and sets everyone's mind at ease.

One can almost evaluate character assets on the basis of how dependable a person is. If a person is dependable and reliable in one situation, the chances are pretty great that it will carry over into other areas of truthfulness. Their word is as good as their work, and their work is as good as their word. They go hand in hand.

Determination begets dependability. We can become dependable if we are determined to change our sluggish habits and simply do as we say we are going to do. This will land you all kinds of jobs on committees, boards, and offices. The world is begging for people who do what they say they will in the time allotted.

When we were kids "back then," we had many chores to do before we went to school. Each child had a specific job to do, whether it was bringing in wood or feeding an animal. Before we even ate breakfast that chore had to be done. We all ate breakfast together too. There was none of this "short-order cook" business for breakfast back then. All chores were completed and we were partially ready for school before we all sat down to a big morning meal. I think those chores we were required to accomplish taught us to be dependable and be on time. Without a lot of nagging, we just did what we knew we had to do. And by the way, our rooms had to be straightened and our beds made too before breakfast.

It is much easier to learn those habits of dependability when one is young. It is a difficult habit to break and can only be changed if one really wants to be more reliable. Jim helped me develop habits of promptness by explaining how tardiness was rudeness to others. He is right! 7:00 to him means 6:50, at least. Seldom does anyone have to wait on him. It is the old Marine training, I guess.

When you have run out of ideas of what to cook, you can usually rely on some old standby that you know your family likes that is a dependable recipe and easy to prepare.

Pork Chops Ole

6 to 8 boneless pork loin chops about 1/3 to 1/2 inch thick
1 tablespoon olive oil
1 16 ounce jar salsa
salt to taste

Brown chops in oil until brown. Drain off all oil. Pour salsa over chops. Cover skillet and bake in 350 degree oven at least 30 minutes. Remove lid last ten minutes of baking time. Great served with oven fried potatoes.

Be dependable. Always give people more than they expect to get. Think about it!

Chapter 144 — History

Isn't history interesting? Think about it!

In the one-room, one-teacher, eight-grades country school I attended through the eighth grade, I thought history was only dates, fact, and things that were completely irrelevant. Now, I know that that school system was a PART of history. That school went by the wayside like the great depression, World War II, segregation, and many other things. We can tell where we are going sometimes by looking where we have been.

However, history often repeats itself. It seems like we often do not learn, and repeat those same mistakes again and again. We try to protect the new generation from making the same mistakes we made but each generation must learn for themselves and make their own mistakes and discoveries.

I can remember Grandma saying that after they settled this new, great state that they thought everything would be smooth sailing for each new generation to come, but each era has its own set of problems and challenges.

One thing I can say for my forefathers though is that my life is much richer and tranquil because of the sacrifices and hardships they went through to come to America and settle this country. The harshness of their lives must have been unbearable at times, yet they continued on for their cause. This, too, is a part of history.

When our worlds turn topsy-turvy, we can look to history, and know that in past generations these same things have happened, and the world did go on as usual. From these back-sets come growth and appreciation of what we have.

Daddy is in his 90's and knows the rocks and hills and land of Pawnee County, Oklahoma, like the back of his hand. All my life he has pointed out things of interest to us kids. Things like where stage coach stops were located, where the wagon trails were, where the great springs were (are) where the cattle watered when the dry spells came, where the Indian encampments were, where certain homesteads were, where out-laws holed up in hiding, and many other fascinating things. At the time they were just blah to me, but as I get older they have become terribly interesting and I wish I had paid more attention when he was talking and telling us of these things from first-hand knowledge. I can pick his brain for hours now, wanting to know all that he knows. I am sure after he leaves this wonderful world that I will think of a gillion things I wish I had asked him, or that he told me about and I failed to get enough details.

He knows more history from simply being a part of it than most people can ever read about. He has seen the automobile come into common usage. He has seen the invention of the airplane. He has seen so many many medical and scientific breakthroughs. He has seen lives that used to terminate in their 40's and 50's be extended to an active life in the 90's and up, all because of medical science. He has seen great strides in education. Few people went to college when he was young (although he did, which was rare) but now almost every young person has this opportunity. As he would say, "Times are changing". What a part of history he is. His life reflects it.

Even though we were basically "beef people" (ranchers), we raised hogs too and every winter butchered for pork. That was great pork and hams and bacon. The best part of butchering was tender loin. Now, we just eat pork chops, but it is never quite the same with the bone around the loin. Here is how to cook pork chops:

Use six pork chops 1/2 inch thick. Combine about 2/3 C. flour, 1/2 teaspoon salt. Dip pork chops in one beaten egg and 2 tablespoons milk. Dredge chops in egg mixture, then in flour mixture. Heat about 1/4 cup oil in a skilled. Add chops and brown on both sides. Add 1/4 Cup water. Cover and cook over low heat one hour until done. Serve with this some fried apples made like this:

Core and slice eight Jonathan apples (but don't peel). In a large iron skillet, fry over medium heat in about 1/4 Cup butter or oleo, until apples are translucent, stirring occasionally. Sprinkle with 1 cup sugar and 1 teaspoon cinnamon. Mix well. Serve warm.

When older ancestors or friends tell about our early history, pay attention. Someday you will be glad you did. Think about it!

Chapter 145 — Appreciation

How do you express appreciation? Think about it!

On April 2, 1997, my world came to a standstill. Jim had a heart attack. All my life I have stood and watched as others faced such a crisis but never have I personally walked in their shoes. Until NOW!

First, you dial 911. Before I finished the call, I heard the sirens of help on the way. By the time I turned on the front porch light and unlocked the door, and went back in the kitchen to get a damp towel for Jim's face, the firemen were at our house.

The firemen with their life saving equipment went to work on Jim, giving him oxygen, an IV, and medication under his tongue. Within seconds the ambulance arrived and began injections for pain and moved him to the hospital. I rode in the ambulance to the hospital and the firemen secured our house and turned off the lights. Those rescue people certainly acted efficiently and knowledgeably. Within a few minutes Jim was in the hospital E.R. We are so very grateful that we live in Enid, America, where people are so kind and helpful, and prompt and go above and beyond the call of duty to save a life and help the family.

The personnel at the hospital were equally helpful and skilled. Within a few hours, after our wonderful doctor had checked him and Jim had gotten some relief from the awful, undescribable pain, he was airlifted to a hospital in Oklahoma City.

We were treated equally kind and considerate there. The physician was waiting for us when Jim was brought in from the helicopter pad. They worked feverishly with him and then the doctor took the time to come and talk to me about his findings. I never knew before how a family waits for that word of encouragement from a doctor.

Jim was in the hospital there, undergoing tests and a heart procedure, for a little over a week. In all that time our friends and family were absolutely wonderful. We can hardly discuss it without tears welling up. One just has no idea what friends and family are until they are in need of help. Believe you me, when friends said, "Let us know if there is something we can do," I let them know! It is still amazing to us how wonderful and helpful friends and family are. I am sure we did not deserve all the attention and aid but there was always someone there for us. We will never be able to thank them enough.

We are happy to report that Jim is doing very well. He is an excellent, co-operative patient who does everything the doctor says to do and knows that if he doesn't follow orders he is not hurting anyone but himself. He has been a joy to cook for and do for and is so appreciative. My cup runneth over!

Everyone from the sweet lady who answered my 911 call, to the physicians, to neighbors, to friends, to family, to my co-workers have gone out of their way to be generous and kind to us. People have brought in lovely meals, sent numerous cards, called many many times, been by to visit Jim, sent flowers, and other gifts, the favors just go on and on. We will NEVER be able to repay all these people. The only way I know of is to pass it on to the next person in crisis.

With all the lovely food that has been brought in to us I have almost forgotten how to cook. Somewhere from the recesses of my mind comes this little poem that goes somewhat like this:

Count your garden by the flowers,
Never by the leaves that fall.
Count your days by golden hours,
Don't remember clouds at all.
Count your nights by stars, not shadows,
Count your life by smiles, not tears,
And with joy on every birthday...
Count your age by friends, not years.

Even thought we feel like we have aged twenty years with this experience, we are blessed with so much and will never forget the love that has been poured out to us.

We would hope that everyone would be so fortunate when they are faced with a crisis similar to ours. We also hope that others will never have to experience it but if they do I hope we can in some way repay our debt to our friends. We are reminded that the service given to our fellowmen is the rent we pay for the right to life. Think about it!

Chapter 146 — Inner Strength

Do you have inner strength? Think about it!

You may not really know if you do have an inner strength until you are put to the test. I had no idea I had toughness and power until Jim broke his back ten years ago. We were at Keystone Lake when he had a freak accident on a three-wheeler and we knew by the symptoms he was in trouble. With help he was loaded into the car and I drove him back to Enid for care and treatment. On the way home I prayed for a State Trooper but didn't see a one. That was a long trip home. Jim was in such pain and all the way I was surveying my resources of how I would take care of this big guy if he was paralyzed, and how would I make the living, and how would I have what was necessary to keep him from being terribly depressed in his recovery time. During that one afternoon I learned a great deal about life and about myself.

With the best care in the world and a husband who was, and is, cooperative with doctor's orders, he recovered and with few exceptions, is as good as new.

But the lesson I learned will always be with me. I know that when the chips are down I can carry on. Oh, not as well as with things as they were, but I can carry on. I have that inner strength to do what has to be done. And you can too! Everyone can.

People who have gone through a traumatic divorce, especially where there are children involved, know the strength it takes to do what is right and to keep on keeping on. Eventually the fog lifts and one can see the sunshine, but for a while, it takes a special inner strength.

I would think the loneliness and grief would be almost unbearable after the loss of a spouse of many years that have been shared in loving devotion. I have never experienced it (luckily) but I have seen those who have and I ache for them. The strength to endure such loss must come in small doses, sometimes only minutes at a time, or an hour, or just a day. If they can just survive for one moment, they can carry on. And it takes time to recover grief and each in his/her own way. Saying to them, "This too shall pass," seems empty and hopeless. What can we know who have not experienced such a devastating event. These people eventually develop an inner strength that withstands everything.

There is a lesson to be learned from these people. Strength comes only when it is needed. We can't build up a reserve of it. We can plan for a reserve, but it is like manna from heaven, it only comes in small doses when it is greatly needed for survival. The best we can do is to think of our strengths and always plan ahead of what we MIGHT do in a situation.

I am sure everyone has gone through a trauma with a small child who was ill. When they are so sick, we do what we have to do. It must be done, whether it is watching them receive I.V.'s or giving them medicine they don't want to take. We must make them go through with it.

There is NO food that will give super-natural power and strength but if there were such a dish, this would come close.

Super Spinach

2 pkg frozen chopped spinach
4 Tablespoons butter
2 Tablespoons flour
2 Tablespoons chopped onion
1/2 Cup milk
1/2 C. vegetable liquid
1/2 teaspoon black pepper
3/4 teaspoon celery salt
3/4 teaspoon garlic salt
1/2 teaspoon salt
1 block Velveeta hot cheese (6 oz.)
1 teaspoon Worcestershire sauce

Cook spinach. Drain into bowl.

Melt butter, add flour, blend until smooth. Add onion until soft but not brown. Add milk, vegetable liquid and Worcestershire sauce. Stir until smooth and thick. Add spices and cheese until melted. Stir in spinach. Serve warm.

We are never afraid of what we know, then we can face anything with strength and courage. You do have an inner strength. Think about it!

Chapter 147 — Discouragement

Do you get discouraged? Think about it!

Thank goodness we who live in Oklahoma, are at home on the range, where never is heard a discouraging word. Right? Wrong! We hear them all the time. But luckily for most of us in this great land we have the background of pioneer spirits who braved many adventures and hardships to settle this once barren countryside.

I can look back at my grandparents' remarkable courage in coming to Indian Territory before statehood, and remember their stories of setbacks and misfortunes but they never seemed to complain or feel sorry for themselves. They had made up their minds they were going to love this land and they did! I recall the wonderful stories of when Grandma came in October there were no crops, so consequently no food supply except what was brought with them. That fall they planted a crop of turnips. They ate turnips raw and boiled and mashed and in turnip kraut. That was their existence. Yet they were thankful for those turnips and were grateful for what they DID have instead of getting discouraged and looking back to what they had left behind. Now I like turnips, but I am not so sure I am made out of that kind of substance and would eat them three meals a day without at least one discouraging word. It takes a lot of determination to stay enthusiastic and positive when all one is eating is turnips, turnips, turnips!

There are days when we take one step forward and fall back two. There are days when we wonder if we shouldn't just stay home or completely change courses. On those days, it is easy to get discouraged. It is easy to think that the whole world is against us. It is difficult to see good things coming from all those trials and tribulations. But take heart. There are better times ahead. "This too shall pass." Discouragements don't usually last a real long time before the road takes a different, brighter turn.

To be perky and grinning all the time sometimes seems a little artificial. No one can be in perfect harmony with the world about them ALL the time. We have to have a few dark hours to appreciate the sunshine. But if all days seem dark and dreary, better check into things. It could be a trend and could become a habit of resisting happy thoughts, so one wouldn't see the forest for the trees.

Encouragement and courage furnish the drive and energy and inspiration and challenge for our achievements. It takes strength and stability to accomplish our dreams and ambitions. We need a special encouragement in times of trials. It is then that we need to be less discouraged and more assured. We need to face life happily and unafraid. We need to look ahead into the unfolding future with hope and expectancy even though we don't know what that future is going to bring.

I feel so blessed to have such abundance compared to my ancestors. I can remember when my folks had few supplies in the house but Mother always seemed to come up with a delicious meal. She would make biscuits and gravy, or corn bread and milk, or boiled wheat that we ate like cereal with cream and sugar, or otherwise create a meal from seemingly nothing, and those meals always tasted so great.

When your cupboard is as bare as Ole Mother Hubbard's, and you have had a rotten day and don't want to stop by the store but you want to have something to eat, look into your sparse larder and come up with this enjoyable meal. Surely you have some dry bread slices and some bottom-of-the-jar jelly on hand to make this Baked French Toast.

Baked French Toast

1 egg
1/4 Cup milk
dash of salt and pepper, or cinnamon
4 slices of dry bread
2 Tablespoons butter or oleo

Beat together the egg, milk, and seasoning. Dip bread on both sides and place in a greased baking pan. Drizzle with the melted butter. Bake at 500 degrees about 7 minutes per side until golden brown. Now mix that left-over jelly with some pancake syrup and heat it to serve with the toast. It is really good served with sausage, or bacon, or ham. We like this in the evening better than we do for breakfast.

Don't let discouragements get you down. When you lift others, you lift yourself up too. Think about it!

Chapter 148 — Annoying Habits

Do you have any annoying habits? Think about it!

I am sure you don't, and I certainly don't have any either. But look at those other people around us. They certainly have more than their share. Don't they? Isn't it strange and funny that we never know of our own irritating little practices. We would swear we don't do them. But if we are normal at all, and most of us are, we ALL have them.

Doesn't it drive you crazy when someone clicks a pen while he/she is talking. Or chews on a metal paper clip while conversing. Or clicks their fingernails. Or rattles keys or money. One of the worst is men handling change in their pockets. I am sure they are not aware of it but it is most distracting: in fact poor manners.

People who crack their knuckles can get on your nerves. Or people who kick the back of your theater seat or church pew. Or those who otherwise tap their feet so that it vibrates the row of seats.

Some people constantly snuff their noses. Now I don't mean those who have colds and cannot help it. I speak here of those with the habit of sniffing all the time. Another annoying habit are those who constantly play with their hair. That habit is just like picking your nose or handling any other part of the anatomy. It is just not done by people with class and good breeding.

In our conversations are hidden little habits, like saying "Ah" or "You know" before or after every sentence. We also have speech patterns of which we are not in the least aware. They become so routine that they are a part of us.

I love music as much as anyone else, but I am distracted by those who hum all the time and think they are on key. Akin to that are those who play the radio or television and don't even know it is on. It is just noise in the background.

There is precious little we can do about anyone who has an annoying habit that gets on our nerves. They are harmless. They have taken a lifetime to create, so why do we try to change them. We are much better off trying to accept that person with that clicking, snapping, pecking habit. We are far wiser to ignore them and hope they (the habits, not the people) go away.

It is much more productive to let our thoughts dwell on beautiful things rather than dwell on little irritants. If we look for good in people we will find it.

Jim is not crazy about carrots, but if I make them into carrot cake, he loves them, and so does everyone else it seems.

Carrot Cake

3 eggs
3/4 Cup vegetable oil
3/4 Cup buttermilk
2 Cups flour
2 Cups sugar
2 teaspoons baking soda
2 teaspoons cinnamon
1/2 teaspoon salt
2 teaspoons vanilla
2 Cups finely shredded raw carrots
1 Cup raisins (we like golden raisins best)
1 (8 oz.) can crushed pineapple, undrained
1 Cup chopped pecans
1 Cup flaked coconut

In large mixing bowl beat eggs, oil, and buttermilk. Combine dry ingredients. Add to egg mixture. Stir in vanilla and other ingredients, mixing well. Pour into greased 13" X 9" baking pan. Bake at 350 degrees for 50 minutes. Cool. Frost with:

8 oz. cream cheese, softened
4 cups confectioners sugar
1 to 2 tablespoons cream or milk
1 teaspoon vanilla.

Beat all ingredients in a mixing bowl until smooth. Frost cake.

Don't be too hung up on little annoyances. You don't get ulcers from what you eat, but from what's eating you. Think about it!

Chapter 149 — Standing Up For Yourself

Do you stand up for yourself? Think about it!

It is sad that in the world today there are those who are so down-trodden and dominated that they are actually abused and can see no way out of their situation. It is difficult for those of us who are self-sufficient to understand what they are going through. If only there were some way to make them understand that they do have self worth and value.

Many of us are timid about one thing or another, whether it be making a speech or trying something entirely new to us. We are a little hesitant to launch out and conquer that unforeseen territory.

When Jim was first in the Marine Corps, he was quite timid. He had never been out of this part of the country and EVERYTHING was new to him. He also was only sixteen years old at that time which is a difficult stage of life. He was fortunate to have a lovely old sergeant who called him in one day and explained to him that even with all the yelling going on, that his officers could not eat him, that he was going to have to stand up for himself and not be so timid and afraid. That was all the advice Jim needed. He became a leader just from that small bit of advice. He stood up for himself from then on. This does not mean that he dominates anyone or runs roughshod over them. In fact he is gentler and more understanding because of his self assurance.

None of us likes to have our position threatened. We are not crazy about being told to do something or how, but none of us knows everything about everything so can need guidance along the way. There is no need to become defensive when we are directed. That is not the same as being controlled. We can disagree without being disagreeable. There is a way that we can assert ourselves without compromising our position and still get a point across. We do need to listen and consider all sides of a situation before we put up a guard. There is room for improvement in all of us, and no one is planning to throw us to the lions.

One way to be sure of ourselves and not allow anyone to dominate us is to be like the one pig in the children's story of the "The Three Pigs." Don't build a house out of straw or sticks but make sure we build of something more substantial like the stones. Then no matter when the wolf comes to our door, he may huff and puff, but he will never blow our house, or us down. If we have a background of sturdy beliefs and adhere to them, then nothing can blow us down. We will withstand any huffing and puffing that comes our way. We have the power within us to stand up for ourselves.

Also make sure that we don't run someone else's life for them. Even teenagers need spece to develop their own personality. Little tiny kids show a certin direction early in their lives. We shouldn't dominate them to the point where they lose their own sense of self. Many otherwise great marriages have been destroyed by a domineering mother-in-law or someone else. We cannot run another's life for them.

Some people stand up and demand that they abhor broccoli. Here is a sneaky way to encourage them to like it. The same can be said for any other vegetable. Just doll it up a little and you will be surprised how much they will eat.

Broccoli/Cauliflower Salad

2 Cups broccoli florets
2 Cups cauliflowerets
1/2 Cup chopped celery
1/2 Cup chopped green pepper
1/2 Cup chopped onion
1/2 Cup grated carrot
1 Cup mayonnaise
3 Tablespoons sugar
6 strips bacon, cooked and crumbled
1 Cup sharp cheese cubes

Mix all vegetables. Combine mayonnaise and sugar. Pour over vegetables and toss lightly. Refrigerate. Just before serving toss with bacon and cheese.

Stand up for yourself. Look after Number One. Allowing your life to be taken over by another is like letting the waiter eat your dinner. Think about it!

Chapter 150 — Planning

How do you plan your time? Think about it!

How we spend our time and how we plan our time are usually two completely different things. We usually are better planners than we are spenders. I'd much rather have friends drop in than clean the pantry or oven. Wouldn't you?

Have some kind of plan of action, even if you don't get everything done. Make lists and check the items off as they are accomplished. What a great feeling that brings. First do what you know you have to do. Then go on to the things you need to do. Then consider the things you want to do, always doing at least one fun thing each day to add spice to life. There is never time to do all the things you want to do so prioritize.

It is true that if you want something done, ask a busy person to do it. They are planners and get lots of things accomplished with seemingly little effort. They work hard but they plan well too. They organize their work and their time and their fun activities. They don't waste time on trivia. As Mother used to say, "They don't lollygag around."

I am lucky to be from a family who were planners and doers. I can remember sitting around the supper table discussing what they were going to do tomorrow, or next week, or next year. There was always a plan and a goal. If people don't have goals, how do they know when they have accomplished what they ought to do? It is just smart business to know the map you are going to follow to get somewhere. Detours can happen along the way, but at least you know where your destination is.

You will never find time for anything...if you want time, you must make it! This goes for the unimportant as well as the important things. Things don't just happen. You have to go after your goal. Plan ahead!

Be flexible. Some of the best times we've ever had were unplanned and spontaneous. Things done on the spur of the moment can make great memories. Always allow time for guests to drop in or for that unexpected phone call from a friend. Time waits for no man!

It takes a little time to plan and do this dessert but it is well worth it. Great for spring and summer meals.

Lemon Buttercups

6 Tablespoons butter
1 Cup flour
1/2 Cup finely chopped pecans
8 ounces cream cheese, softened
1 1/2 Cup confectioners sugar
1 1/2 Cup whipped topping

Filling:
2 Cups sugar
1/3 Cup cornstarch
1/4 teaspoon salt
2 Cups water, divided
3 eggs
1/4 Cup vinegar
1/4 Cup lemon juice
1 tablespoon butter
1 teaspoon lemon extract

Cut butter into flour until crumbly. Stir in pecans. Press into the bottom of an ungreased 13" x 9" baking pan. (Or press into metal baking cups that fit in cup cake pans. Thus the name buttercup. However, it is easier to do it in one large baking dish.) Bake at 350 degrees for 15 minutes. Cool. Beat cream cheese with powdered sugar until fluffy. Fold in whipped topping. Spread over crust. Chill. In a saucepan combine sugar, cornstarch, and salt. Add 1/4 Cup water and stir until smooth. Add eggs and beat well. Add vinegar, lemon juice and remaining water. Stir until smooth. Bring to boil over medium heat, stirring constantly. Boil for one minute. Remove from heat and add butter and extract. Cool. Spread over cream cheese layer. Chill at least two hours, but better if chilled overnight. Serve with dollops of whipped topping if desired.

It is better to plan ahead and prepare than to look back with regrets. Think about it!

Chapter 151 — Flexibility

Are you flexible? Think about it!

It seems that the happiest people I know are those who can bend when they need to. Sometimes things beyond our control happen and we can either get frustrated and angry or we can go to plan "B" and become flexible.

When I was young we used to play in the barn when it rained. I looked forward to rainy days just so we could all play hide and seek in the hay. Now I know that we went to the barn so that Mother could go on with her housework. But when I was a kid, I thought it was just for us.

Good teachers always have some kind of trick up their sleeve when the kids get rowdy or there is a crisis. No sense in studying on those occasions. It is best to be flexible and do something else. One blustery, windy day when I was in school, our teacher took us out on the grounds and had us each pick a leaf off the ground. When we went back inside, she had us write a story about why we were like the leaf we picked up. Some of those stories were wonderfully creative. One was about being used and cast aside while another was about the veins in the leaf that represented the different directions of her life. The point of this is that we were much better off writing a story that day than getting involved in study when it was storming outside. That great teacher used every moment to be flexible. She used it to her, and our, advantage!

Everyone of us can name a time when we felt like we needed to be made of elastic. We needed to stretch as far as possible to include the things that we had to do and needed to do. You know those times about yourself better than anyone else. Our daily lives make us decide what our priorities are, and then stretch to do them or have a change of plan.

Haven't you known people who were such delightful hosts that they could always come up with something, or a way to stretch a meal to make enough for drop-in company? I really admire those people. My mother was one of those. She could make a meal out of seemingly nothing and everyone enjoyed her great hospitality and food. Somehow, that just did not rub off on me like I wish it had. My flexibility includes something I can pick up at a store or take-out food to make do.

Being flexible does not mean that one ever needs to compromise their beliefs and morals. We can be supple without sacrificing our principles. The flexibility I speak of is the kind that helps you adjust to an awkward situation or an unforeseen emergency or setback. Then be as bendable as possible to make yourself and others comfortable.

Sometimes one's entire life has to be changed because of a particular incident. One can have their heart set on something and then have to be flexible and accept something else. I am sure those with illnesses, family deaths, or other emergencies don't really plan for them to happen. But they have to be flexible and work around those tragedies. And I am sure it is not easy in many circumstances. But one has to do what one has to do.

These breakfast burritos are great for breakfast, but they can also be used for supper in a pinch, when you need to fix something quick and easy.

Breakfast or Anytime Burritos

1 pound bulk pork sausage
1 small onion, chopped
1/2 green pepper, chopped
fresh mushrooms, sliced (or use other vegetables)
6 eggs, beaten
1 Cup sharp cheese, shredded
8 large (about 7 inch) flour tortillas

Brown sausage. Drain. Add onion, peppers, and mushrooms (or other vegetables) and cook until tender. Add the eggs and stir until set. Spoon egg mixture on tortillas, sprinkle on the cheese, and wrap up quickly so cheese will melt into the egg mixture. Serve with salsa. This makes a pretty fair lunch or supper served with a small salad and some fruit.

When life throws you a curve, it is to teach you how to bend. Think about it!

Chapter 152 — Family Closeness

What knits a family group together? Think about it!

It is difficult to figure out just what it is that holds a family together but for many of us it is the one matriarch or patriarch that seems to be the glue that holds everyone in harmony. In my family, it is my father who is that great organizer and leader. With his sense of humor and wit he gives advice and guidance without being bossy. His counsel is given with a good mixture of how things were in the past, and his dream for our future.

It takes a lot of understanding and working and playing together to knit a family or group. Respecting the likenesses and differences makes us all fit into the group. If we all were alike, it would be terribly boring, and no family group that I know is boring. If anything, the cluster of members makes life very interesting. It is this sharing that makes the Scottish clans what they are. When we recently went to the Scottish Games, I was not sure if I would be included in the Brodie Clan. The leader said to me, "You married a Brodie, didn't you...Well, then, that makes you a Brodie, and therefore part of the clan". That sure helped me feel that I belonged. I can wear the tartan just like any member who is born into the family. It doesn't make one bit of difference. I belong!

Accepting viewpoints and opinions bonds a family or group into oneness. General respect for the differences makes us all grow mentally. Keeping an open mind helps us see every side of an issue. Usually there are more things alike than different in what we basically believe. The differences simply add seasoning to an otherwise bland flock.

Joys are not really joys unless they are shared with those we love. Neither are concerns. We just must share them too, with our families and work groups. Worries seem to diminish when we parcel out some of them to members of our family. Life is much easier when we share our burdens with those who love and understand us.

When I was a kid at home, mealtime was always happy time. We were not allowed to bring up unpleasant things while we were eating. No mention was ever made of a bad grade or a problem at school until another time. Usually it was resolved the second we got home from school. Then it was over and done with and we didn't have to dread it all evening. I am afraid mealtime for a busy family is becoming a thing of the past. Everyone has a different direction to go.

The planning of daily living combined with genuine concern with other family members seems to knit a brood into a caring, loving family. Being interested in their activities and directions and goals creates a great deal of coherence.

Recipes help remind me of my family and bring joy when I serve them. I even like to use the same pans that grandma or mother used to bake them in. It gives such a feeling of unity. We always like stuffed peppers.

Stuffed Peppers

1 pound lean ground beef
1 onion, chopped
3 Cups cooked rice
1 can tomato soup
1/2 Cup Picante sauce (or to taste)
3 to 4 large green bell peppers
3/4 Cup grated sharp cheese

Cook beef with onion until beef is brown. Add rice, soup, and Picante sauce. Cut peppers in half lengthwise, remove and discard seeds and stems. Immerse peppers in boiling water for three minutes. Drain. Spoon meat mixture into pepper halves. Place in 13" x 9" baking dish. If any meat is left over, spoon around peppers. Bake at 350 degrees for 15 to 20 minutes. During last few minutes of cooking, sprinkle with grated cheese. Allow to melt.

Enjoy the closeness of your family. A crumb shared is better than a banquet alone. Think about it!

Chapter 153 — Important Lessons

How do you learn the important lessons of life? Think about it!

When we were in school we learned a lot by repetition. The teacher would tell us what she was going to teach us. Then she would teach us. Then she would tell us what she taught us. That teacher used some repetition, but also threw in a lot of illustrations and demonstrations to help us absorb what she was trying to drill into our heads. Sometimes it "took" and we moved on to the next step. Then again, sometimes it didn't register and we had to go over a certain point for days, or leave it and come back to it at a better time.

We learned a lot by watching and listening to others. I always have been grateful for my schooling in that one room school house with one teacher for eight grades. Part of the time I was in a grade by myself and I know it must have been difficult for Miss Cunningham to plan lessons just for me alone. If I was a little behind in a subject, I could observe the grades lower than me to review and catch up. If I excelled in a subject and was no longer challenged by my grade level, then I could study with the older grades. This way I never felt that I had nothing to do or learn. It was all right there in front of me.

Just recently my brother found back in the heavy timber and old iron wedge, the kind used to split wood back in the days when we used wood for heating and cooking. He brought the wedge in to show it to Daddy. Daddy was surprised that he had found it as Grandpa and Daddy had looked for it for years and years. The story goes that when my Grandpa was a little boy, about nine, he came home from school one day and announced that he was as smart as he wanted to be and thought he would just quit school where he was, in third grade. Great-Grandpa said that was just fine with him, that Grandpa could just work with him the next day. Grandpa was elated that his father had accepted it so easily.

The next morning Great-Grandpa gave him an ax, a sledge hammer, that iron wedge, a dinner bucket with his lunch, and some water, and sent him to the timbers to cut and split posts all day. Surprisingly, the very next day, Grandpa thought better of his decision to quit school. He learned a valuable lesson by some great teaching. No words were ever spoken again about quitting school...or anything else.

Kids learn most by example. The trouble is, they don't know the difference in a good one and a bad one. So it is up to us to know right from wrong and be a good pattern to follow. They should be able to do as we do, not just as we say to do something. Kids observe and listen to more than we think they do.

I was fortunate to learn to cook at my mother's knee. She always had time for me to answer my jillions of questions and show me what and how to do something. Consequently I love to cook and love to pass on what I was lucky enough to absorb about cooking. One of the things we enjoyed making together was Chocolate Date Cake.

1/2 Cup chopped dates
1/2 teaspoon soda
1/2 Cup hot water
1 Cup flour
1/2 Cup sugar
1 Tablespoon cocoa
1/4 teaspoon salt
1/4 teaspoon soda
1/2 Cup butter, softened (or margarine)
1 teaspoon vanilla
1 egg
1/2 Cup semi-sweet chocolate chips

Topping for Chocolate Date Cake

1/2 Cup semi-sweet chocolate chips
1/4 Cup chopped pecans
2 Tablespoons sugar

Heat oven to 350 degrees. Grease and flour bottom only of 8 inch square pan. In large bowl combine dates, 1/2 teaspoon baking soda and hot water. Cool five minutes. Mix all dry ingredients. Add remaining ingredients (except chocolate chips). Blend, then stir in the chocolate chips. Pour into pan. Sprinkle with 1/2 Cup chocolate chips, nuts, and 2 Tablespoons sugar. Bake 25 to 35 minutes. Serve warm or cold. Wonderful topped with whipped cream.

We learn only from those we love. Think about it!

Chapter 154 — Crisis

How do you handle a crisis? Think about it!

Up until recently I had all the answers. I could have told you in several easy steps how to react during a crucial moment. But now I am a little more conservative about all that great advice. I would submit to you that no two people will react the same way because no two emergencies are the same.

It is best if you can keep your wits about you and try to control your head so that your senses will function. When I recently had to call 911 for our emergency, it was surprising how controlled I thought I was. I am sure the sweet operator might not agree but she did get the information she was seeking...and help was immediately on its way. How you keep your cool is up to you. I have no sage words of advice about that. Everyone is different. Just try to keep calm.

When the turning point comes in your life and you face a real tragedy, let your friends and family help you. Yes, LET. They want to help but sometimes they just don't know what to do or when to do it. If they offer, and they will, do call on them. Do not try to go it alone. Company at a time like this is so important. Being alone can be so lonely. It isn't that they say things so profound, it is just that they are there, ready and willing to be with you and help in any way they can.

There may be radical changes requiring many decisions in business deals. Find someone whose judgement you trust and listen to them. Often our minds wander and don't focus too well on the best thing to do. Jim and I have made a list of who to call for advice about our property, land, cattle, dishes, etc. etc. When the time comes that one of us is left alone, or worse yet our daughter has to straighten out our business we hope the list will be helpful. Do the list before a crisis hits.

Make all the arrangements you can before the decisive moment. It is surprising how many plans can be talked out when both partners are available to give input. It is hard enough just to keep on keeping on at a critical time, even if you have a lot of decisions made. It is much much more difficult if you have to determine and guess what the other would like when you have to make decisions alone.

Keep in mind that at any turning point you are going to feel confused and unsure of yourself. A speaker I heard once said that it is not a question of IF you will be left alone, but WHEN. It makes us think ahead to that time. It is going to be bad, no matter how well things are planned out. Expect to be sad and blue and give yourself time to mourn.

I make it sound like I am just speaking of the death of a loved one. But decision making can become acute even if one is ill, and not near death. One still has to be the stronger partner at a time of crisis.

When Jim was ill, a nurse in Intensive Care told me to be sure I took care of myself, eating right, sleeping right, and taking time for myself. It seemed harsh at the time, but she was right. We are no good to that ill partner if we are sick ourselves. I (and my friends) made sure I ate properly and did not overdo. One way was to eat salads and good meals and not just junk. A dear friend brought over a delicious salad that was like a meal by itself and so very good.

Bette's Broccoli Salad

One bunch broccoli
1/2 red onion, chopped
1 cup raisins
1/2 Cup coarsely chopped pecans
6 to 8 slices bacon, cooked crisp and crumbled
About one cup Miracle Whip or mayonnaise
1/4 to 1/2 Cup sugar
1 Tablespoon vinegar

Chop broccoli flowerettes and tender stems. Add onion. Mix Miracle Whip with sugar and vinegar. Pour over broccoli and onion. Refrigerate. Just before serving stir in the raisins, nuts, and bacon.

I know it is easier said than done during a crisis, but it isn't the load that weighs us down, it is the way that we carry it. Think about it!

Chapter 155 — Congeniality

Do you know the secret of getting along with people? Think about it!

If all of us did, wouldn't it be a better world? Those who seem to be best at it are the most natural, kindest, most concerned for their fellowmen. They seem to know when to say what and how to talk to people. What they have is tact. They are diplomatic in the way they deal with people.

One way to get along with people is to give them the benefit of the doubt. Don't assume anything about them. Let them speak for themselves. Then listen to them.

First of all in dealing with others is to understand yourself. Have self assurance. Respect yourself and then you can and will respect others. It makes a great difference in your actions and attitude.

Dale Carnegie, in his course and in his book, "How to Win Friends and Influence People", gives a simple, yet not so simple, formula for getting along with people and making people like you. If we could, and would just follow it....

Number one is: Use praise and honest appreciation. "Honest" is the key word here. It must be genuine and not fake feelings. Everyone can see though flattery and insincere or excessive praise. That really turns people off.

Number two is: Don't call attention to people's mistakes directly. What good does that do? They then become defensive and rightfully so. No one would like to have their errors pointed out without constructive critique and suggestions of how to make things easier and better.

Number three: Admit YOUR mistakes before criticizing others. It makes them feel better and admitting your faults and blunders is good for the soul. It then puts everyone in the same boat. None of us are without error, yet we all hate to have them pointed out to us with the attitude that we are the only ones who make any mistakes.

Ask, instead of giving direct orders, is Number four. My wise mother used this approach when she wanted us to do anything. It is surprising how much we WANTED to do things for her. It works!

Save the other person's face. Never embarrass a person in front of others. In fact, it is best to talk to a person about something in private and not bring an unpleasant subject up in front of others. This is true, whether it be co-workers or people in general that you deal with.

Number seven is: Give others a good reputation to live up to. This is especially true of teenagers. Both our granddaughters are such well behaved, sweet girls. But then we expect that of them. They would not disappoint us by being otherwise. Other people react the same way. They will live up to the reputation, good or bad, that is expected of them.

Encourage. Cheer people on at every opportunity. We all need a kind word now and then. Sometimes it means more to us than a raise in pay. A kind word goes a long way toward our well being.

Last but not least, is the rule to make other people happy and want to do your suggestions. Are people happy just being around you? Are you a happy person? If you are kind and not critical and truly have their best interest at heart, then people will want to be around you.

Most all of these suggestions boil down to one rule to live by and treat others by, and that is the Golden Rule, or doing to others like you would like to have them do to you. If we remember no other rule than that, then we will be happy and have happy families and co-workers and friends.

This recipe is easy and goes with soup or salad or a meal and pleases everybody.

Busy Bread

3 Cups self-rising flour
1/3 Cup butter
1 Cup milk

Cut butter into flour until crumbly. Add milk and mix together. Turn out and knead just until smoothed. Place round loaf on a greased cookie sheet. Slash an X in the top of the loaf about 3/4 inch deep. Spray with vegetable oil. Sprinkle with coarse salt. Bake in 400 degree oven about 30 minutes. Just tear off chunks to eat it as it is difficult to cut into slices.

Getting along with people is no secret. When hands reach out in friend-ship, hearts are touched with joy. Think about it!

Chapter 156 — Who You Are

Who are you now? Think about it!

No matter what or who you are now, you are not what you were nor what you will be. This can be a blessing, as we know we will not stay what we are right now. And we also know there is great hope for the future.

We are all a product of our pasts. I was fortunate to come from hardy stock who believed in hard work and doing for others. There is not a day that goes by that I am not reminded of something my parents or grandparents said or did that molded my life. Their concepts of honesty, endurance, beliefs, attitudes, sharing, caring, and perseverance all rubbed off on me. It is so ingrained in my spirit that it would be most difficult, if not impossible, to change those attributes.

However, I am not just a stereotype of my ancestors. I have added my own list of values to theirs to become what I am today. Even this generation has added to my life. I learn something from my granddaughters every time I am with them. They always come forth with something to make me think, or rethink my reactions. Probably I am learning as much, if not more, from them than they are from me.

Who we are today is different than we will be tomorrow. Our minds are always changing, and so are our bodies. We should be grateful that we do not actually know what the future has in store for us, whether it be good or bad. We have only today to live. Live it to the fullest and don't worry about tomorrow. Give everything to today's existence, but plan like we will live forever.

Our passport to life is issued to us by past experiences of past times. Each age and generation has created something great, lasting, and dignified and left it to add to the abundant life of those who come after. The love of beauty and truth of the Greeks, the high moral earnestness of the Hebrews, the sublime faith of the Middle Ages, the love of freedom from which was born the nation of which we are a part, the courage and fortitude of the pioneers who conquered the raw resources of a continent, all these are part of our rich inheritance of science and languages, our standards and our ideals, the things that make up our lives. We must be indebted to the daring souls who burst the bonds of the past and led us into the truths that make us free. We are indebted to those of all ages who used the knowledge of their generation to point us a step onward and upward. We have been brought out of a darkness of past ages into a marvelous light of these days, and have gleaned the best of what they gave us to incorporate into our own lives. What great gifts they gave us.

I wonder sometimes if we are passing on to the next generations the gift of appreciation of life that was given to us. I fear that life does not have the same deep meaning for some young people that it does for us and our ancestors. We fight every day for life and the pursuit of happiness while daily there are drive-by shootings, killings over the least little things, child abuse, and general decay of the things we hold dear. Their attitudes influence what we are today, and also what we will be later.

It is summertime. We are not in the mood to cook like we were during the cool months. Time to stir up something easy, yet refreshing. This is really a salad, but Jim and I like it best as a dessert. Pile it in your pretty dessert dishes and put a little whipped topping on it for a cooling dessert.

Fruit Salad

One large can (21 ounces) peach pie filling
3 firm bananas, sliced
2 Cups ripe strawberries, halved
1 cup seedless grapes, halved

Mix all together in a bowl. Refrigerate until serving.

May we be granted open minds and discerning hearts to quickly learn a lesson in everything and from everybody so that our lives may grow, and not be the same as yesterday or today. Think about it!

Chapter 157 — Being Remembered

How would you like to be remembered? Think about it!

When I think back fondly about my wonderful grandparents and mother, I am curious if they ever thought about how they would be remembered. They left such a legacy with all their offspring, of the pioneer spirit of hard work, optimism, and concern for their fellowmen. If there were a way that this attitude could live on, I would hope it would be because of something I passed on to succeeding generations.

Also important is how we want to be known now. Do we want people to think well of us or does it really not matter how the masses feel about our attitude? Somehow I feel that most of us do care how our peers perceive us. If we didn't care, we would not bathe so often, nor be so careful of what we say and how we say it. We would not be courteous nor care about others' feelings. We would live on an island alone some place and let the rest of the world go by.

How we are thought of at this time is not necessarily the way we will be remembered for posterity. My teachers were viewed as strict and overpowering when I was young. Now that I am grown, I think of them as caring and challenging. They made me buckle down and learn and in their way lit a fire of curiosity and admiration for life in general. They were more concerned about what and how they were teaching than they were worried about what we thought of them then, or now.

Being a parent is not a popularity contest either. It seems to me that some parents are more concerned about being a pal to their kids than they are being a guiding parent who starts them on the right paths of life. They seem afraid to speak up for fear their kids won't like them. So be it...isn't it a parent's responsibility to help their kids make wise choices in life and become trustworthy adults.

Bless these kids who don't give in to peer pressure. They may be called nerds or square now, but probably are envied because they do have a standard to live by. They will be remembered in later years as a person of principle and strength. Being popular isn't all it is cracked up to be. Sometimes the most popular are not the most well liked nor the most admired. It boils down to the fact that we have to be true to ourselves and be ourselves in every situation, without the primary thought being what others think of us at the time.

So many of the things we are remembered for are those attributes that we really don't even plan. They are character traits that have been handed down to us, like the wonderful, hardy pioneer spirit I spoke of earlier. These were gifts to me. I owe it to my parents and grandparents to keep these qualities alive for this generation and the next ones too. If it is to be it is up to me. I would hope I never let my ancestors down after what they have shared with me.

My mother had a great gift of making her guests feel at ease, even when they dropped in on her and she was in the middle of canning or cleaning. She always could put on the most scrumptious meals with seemingly little effort that her guests just loved. Here is one of those recipes that she whipped up in no time.

Baked Cherry Pudding

2 Cups flour
2 1/2 Cups sugar, divided
4 teaspoons baking powder
1 Cup milk
2 tablespoons butter, melted
1 quart (or two 16 oz. cans) pitted red cherries, drained

In bowl, combine flour, 1 Cup sugar, baking powder, milk, and melted butter. Pour into greased baking dish. Combine cherries with remaining sugar. Pour over batter. Bake at 375 degrees for about 45 minutes. Serve warm with cream, or ice cream.

One hundred years from now, it will not matter what kind of car we drove, what kind of house we lived in, how much money we made, or what our clothes looked like. But the world may be a little better, the universe a little brighter because we were important to a child. Think about it!

Chapter 158 — Emotions

Do your emotions bubble close to the surface? Think about it!

You don't have to ask my granddaughters if that is true about me, they will tell you right off that it is. We cry or laugh easily, and can cry at the most inopportune times, like when we have just received a present. The presents the girls give me are always so sweet. Just recently I received two darling signs to place in my potted plants. One says, "Love grows where it is planted ". The other says simply, "Welcome". Wouldn't that make any grandma cry with joy and emotion? The price of the gift doesn't matter at all; it is the thought behind the gift that matters.

Most of us think we are strong and usually are while there is crisis but just let that crisis end and we break down in tears of relief and joy.

Tears do not necessarily reflect sadness. When our family has tragedy, we joke and laugh just the same. It is our way of breaking tension. It does not indicate that we have less feelings than other people do. The way we express ourselves is not always an indication of how we feel on the inside. Don't be too quick to judge anyone of their true emotions.

We can be moved to tears by a simple childhood song or story that evokes a memory. We can be affected by the simplest expression of love and caring by those around us. Gratitude that is worthy of the name must find some kind of expression...crying seems to be the easiest to do!

When any turmoil strikes, we are often caught with our emotions showing. It is difficult to keep them in check when they are boiling so close to the surface. We are moved by our emotions more than we are any other drive.

Have you ever been in a solemn situation when all was supposed to be quiet and sedate and you broke out laughing and couldn't stop? This has happened, or will happen, to most of us at some embarrassing time. The more we try to get the giggling under control, the more we break out laughing. We feel so stupid, but it simply cannot be helped!

Loneliness, melancholy, joy, sadness, worry, stress, celebration, presents, family gatherings, meeting friends, reminiscing, holidays, picture albums, patriotism, our flag, songs, poems, or simply being with someone special are just a few of the things that can stir emotions and make a person weep. Some people can quietly wipe a few tears, while others have tears streaming down their face and start sobbing. There is little one can do about the way they express themselves.

Recipes can bring back happy times spent with family or friends. I can eat corn bread baked in Mother's old black pan and remember my youth. I can smell chocolate cookies and remember Grandma's kitchen. I share part of that memory with you in this favorite recipe for Brownie Cookies. These are so chewy and good.

Brownie Cookies

2/3 Cup shortening (Grandma used lard; I use Crisco)
1 1/2 Cup packed brown sugar
1 tablespoon water
1 teaspoon vanilla
2 eggs
1 1/2 Cups flour
1/3 Cup cocoa
1/2 teaspoon salt
1/4 teaspoon soda
2 Cups semisweet chocolate chips (12 ounces)
1/2 Cup chopped pecans (Grandma used black walnuts)

Cream shortening, sugar, water and vanilla. Beat in eggs. Combine dry ingredients. Stir into egg/sugar mixture. Stir in chocolate chips and nuts. Drop by rounded teaspoon on cookie sheet. Bake at 375 degrees for 7 to 9 minutes. Do not overbake. Cool a few minutes before removing from pan to cool. Makes about 3 dozen, depending on how much of the dough is consumed by grandchildren.

As a stream cannot rise above its source, so the soul cannot rise above the quality of its emotions and gratitude. Think about it!

Chapter 159 — Style

Do you have style? Think about it!

Dripping in diamonds or dangling in bracelets do not necessarily make one in style. Although there are those who wear then with flair and they are a style within themselves. They can be stylish if it is YOU. If is "put on" and not what you are comfortable with, then it is not style. Style is within the person wearing the fashion.

One can almost tell at a glance who is and who is not classy, with style. People with style and class do not throw trash out of a car window or leave trash behind them anywhere anytime. They clean up after themselves. We saw a lady at the hospital recently who took some candy or something out of her purse and looking around and not seeing anyone watching her, threw the wrapper under her chair, supposedly out of sight. That is not class. In fact it is trash!

People with class and style are thoughtful. Their speech and actions reflect it. They are self-assured and can forget about themselves in public and be attentive to others. They do not act better than anyone else, but they know they are just as good as the next person.

Style is not what you wear but how you wear it. My mother was always properly attired. If you weren't sure what to wear to a wedding or other social event, you could just look at her and know how to be correctly dressed. Back in the days of gloves and hats, you could always count on her to know when to wear what. On the other hand, my Dad was always dressed right for him. No matter where he went, whether it was to Washington, D.C., to meet the President of our United States (which he did) or to a community sale to buy or sell cattle, he always wore the same sort of outfit...jeans, boots, and a Stetson hat. People accepted him for just what he is. He was so sure of himself that he could forget about what he was wearing and concentrate on others.

One of the department stores here in town has the slogan, "Nothing is permanent but good taste". This is so true. Whether skirt lengths go up or down or whether coats are wrap-around or buttoned up, the clothes have to reflect the way you feel about yourself. We've got to take a good look at ourselves in the mirror, (for and aft) and then decide what is best for us. You'd be surprised how easy and comfortable you will feel when you find that correct style of dress for yourself. Wear what is appropriate for your age and stature, and then it doesn't matter what others are wearing, you know that what you have on is right for you. You cannot buy style. You buy something right for you with the colors that are attractive and lines that are correct, and you have style and flair. It shows in the way you carry yourself and the way you present yourself.

If you want to serve a dessert with little trouble but with lots of flair that it delicious, you must try this.

Crunch Sundaes

1/2 Gallon vanilla or chocolate ice cream
2 Cups chow mein noodles, slightly crushed
1 Cup chopped peanuts
6 ounces semi-sweet chocolate chips
2/3 Cup cream or evaporated milk
1/2 Cup peanut butter.

Scoop twelve ice cream balls of about 3/4 cup each, onto cold cookie sheet. Place in freezer. In large bowl, combine the crushed noodles and chopped peanuts. Roll ice cream balls in noodle mixture until well coated, returning to freezer as quickly as you can. Cover, store in freezer until serving time.

In microwave, heat chocolate chips with milk or cream until chips are melted. Mix until smooth. Stir in peanut butter until melted and smooth. Cool slightly. To serve, place an ice cream ball (or two) in sherbet glasses. Spoon the chocolate syrup over the ice cream. Whether this is served in your finest stem ware or a plastic bowl, the taste is the same, the style is different.

No matter what you wear, or what you do, your actions reflect the STYLE in you. Think about it!

Chapter 160 — Patriotism

Are you patriotic? Think about it!

It is well nigh impossible to live with an old World War II Marine and not be patriotic. Most everyone from that era that we know is almost fanatic and mushy about their love for this country.

Back in the olden days, we were taught in grade school to respect the flag and appreciate what it stands for. Every day, without fail, we stood and said the flag salute. We took turns leading it. We learned flag etiquette. It still amazes me how many people don't show respect when Old Glory is presented or the National Anthem is played. Perhaps they don't know. Perhaps they just don't care! Had they gone through what so many have experienced to keep our great country free, surely they would have a more respectful, nearly reverent attitude.

Many of us get all choked up just talking about America. The love we have for our country, and the things for which it stands, has nothing to do with politics or government programs. We may not always agree with what our country does but, right or wrong, she still is the best country in the world to live in and die in, and die for.

Why does it matter so much about the flag? After all it is just a piece of cloth, printed in red and white and blue. It is not because of its intrinsic value, which is only a few dollars. It is not really so pretty. It has no real function as a piece of cloth. It couldn't even shelter you from rain. But there is something about that piece of cloth that DOES matter. It matters a great deal! It matters, not because of what it is but for what it means. It matters because we matter...because every man, woman, and child in this country is precious. It is the symbol of its people. It matters because of you.

When we were in Washington, D. C., and stood looking at the Vietnam Memorial Wall, and the Tomb of the Unknown, and the Iwo Jima Memorial, we and umpteen hundred others were overcome by heartfelt emotions because of our devout patriotism. If one can be there and not feel like a true American there must be something sadly wrong with their allegiance to their country. The power is so overwhelming.

In America we differ in religion. We differ in politics. We engage in disputes over the meaning of the Constitution, and, and even challenge the wisdom of some of its laws, but within the folds of our flag is the representation of the intelligence of a Nation that rises above the wisdom of its parts and thus endures the future of the Republic.

Because of a near-tragedy within our own family, I have very mixed emotions about fire crackers and fireworks in the hands of kids. But the experts, who know what they are doing, put on magnificent displays for our enjoyment for July 4. Those fireworks, the ball games, three-legged races, watermelon feeds, lemonade stands, and picnics or cookouts help us express feelings for our country's independence and bring out our patriotism. Patriotism is characterized by baseball, Mom and apple pie.

A pie that is so good that you will just have to try it for the any occasion is: American Apple Pie

1 teaspoon cinnamon or apple pie spice
2 Tablespoons flour
1 1/2 Cup white sugar
pinch salt
3/4 Cup evaporated milk (or thick cream)
about 5 to 6 cups peeled, thinly sliced tart apples
(I always use Jonathon apples)

Prepare one pie crust according to your favorite recipe. Peel, core and thinly slice the apples into crust. Mix other ingredients and pour over the top of the apples. Bake at 350 degrees until apples are done, about one hour. Serve warm or cold.

The American's Creed ends with this quote," I, therefore, believe it is my duty to my country to love it; to support its Constitution; to obey its Laws; to respect its Flag; and to defend it against all enemies". That is true patriotism! Think about it!

Chapter 161 — Community Caring

How do you contribute to your community? Think about it!

We have heard it said that it takes a whole village to raise a child. We blame society for almost everything. If kids turn bad, we blame others. If kids turn out good, we take the credit for raising them. We all know that kids are influenced by those around them. Some towns are just tough towns, so sadly, the kids that are produced in that town turn out tough. They want to be "top dog" so to achieve that reputation, they do something "noteworthy" even if it is against the law or hedging on being mischievous, destroying property or defacing property, or otherwise pushing the laws to the limit. Could that be changed?

Others are from communities that are very youth oriented and the kids turn out caring for others, and themselves. Kids are certainly influenced by their home communities, whether good or bad.

We all owe it to ourselves and to others to do what we can to make this a better society. Some of us no longer have grandparents or aunts and uncles close as I did when I was growing up that took up slack when the parents were busy or gone. Many relatives live far away, so have no influence in the raising of a child. That is where volunteer work comes in by the community. Besides helping others, volunteering has its own rewards. You will feel so much better if you do something to help someone. There is a satisfaction in benevolence and the good feeling of seeing others made happy or fed or clothed. There is no salary that compares to the satisfaction of volunteering.

There is a job for everyone in community service for others. It has nothing to do with age or wealth or physical abilities. There is a need out there to suit your personality and your desire to help. What an inspiration to others that you took the time to do something for mankind.

I admire those who daily work in the kitchens to provide food for less fortunate people. They are "greatly to be praised". I admire their sacrifice. The same can be said for the tireless hospital volunteers who make something pleasant out of a time that is not so pleasant.

Many young people come from other states to work with Habitat for Humanity. What a great service they perform in making affordable homes for others. There is such joy in their carpentering and laboring. Others get involved too, by cooking meals or snacks for these young people. There is no end to the extent of contributions. All are essential and all are appreciated.

You might start volunteering in your own neighborhood. If you see a situation and you think "someone should do something about that", then DO IT. Branch out to organizations who need help. They ARE the community. Start small, the deed can be far-reaching and extend further than you might imagine.

Think of a shut-in in your community. What pleasure it would bring them for you to go see them and take a "care package" of your left-overs (which are new to them). Or bake a batch of these cookies to share.

Chewy Cookies

1/2 Cup butter
3/4 Cup brown sugar, firmly packed
1/4 Cup white sugar
1 egg
1 1/2 tablespoons milk
1 teaspoon vanilla
1 Cup flour
1/2 teaspoon baking soda
pinch salt
1 1/4 Cup rolled oats
1/2 Cup chopped pecans
6 ounces chocolate chips (optional, but wonderful!)

Cream butter and sugars. Add egg, milk, and vanilla and beat well. Combine dry ingredients and add to egg/sugar mixture. Stir in oats, nuts and chocolate chips. Drop by rounded tablespoons onto cookie sheet. Bake about ten minutes in 350 degree oven. Cool a few minutes. Remove from pan to finish cooling.

Albert Schweitzer said, "One thing I do know: The only ones among you who will be really happy are those who have sought and found how to serve". Happiness is revealed by giving more back to life than you get from life. Think about it!

Chapter 162 — Little Black Clouds

Does a little black cloud follow you around? Think about it!

It really probably does not, but there are times when we feel that a little dark cloud does become our shadow. We seem to have gloom and doom wherever we go, no matter what we attempt to do. Those times are usually when we are down and depressed. One thing leads to another. The cloud causes the depression and the depression causes the cloud. The thing we must try to do is break away from that little cloud of despair and hunt for some sunshine in our lives.

Remember when we used to lie out on the green grass in the hot summertime and look up at the clouds and see all kinds of shapes. Our imaginations went wild as we saw things like horses and fish and ice cream cones. We let the cares of the day pass by with those floating clouds. Now, when we look at the clouds it is usually because there is a storm brewing and we are concerned. We sometimes fail to just look up and observe the beautiful, harmless clouds. We wait for those black ones...hoping there is not a storm within.

We are back to that old lecture about attitude, but it seems that those who are always looking for the little black clouds will eventually find them. Those, on the other hand, who constantly look for the rays of sunshine that surround the clouds will find that too. It all depends on the way you look for things.

You have seen people who have had one tragedy after another. Yet they keep such sunny dispositions. They have learned to look for that silver lining. They find it. They dispel those dark clouds with their own ray of sunshine. These people have such great attitudes and are positive and cheerful most of the time. They radiate a posture that makes the dark clouds disappear.

I often think of my pioneer ancestors who settled this wonderful land in Oklahoma. They had so many set-backs. They were almost all "dirt-poor", as Grandma used to say, but they had their futures ahead of them with a new horizon to look forward to. They had such dreams of better times. They worked hard and had little time for worry. They were positive people. They didn't look for those little black clouds. They looked for rain clouds, but they welcomed the rains as life-giving charity from their Maker.

Most of us inherited that same positive attitude and hope for the future. The few who have down dispositions may have every reason to be sad, but it doesn't seem to solve anything. We have those problems whether we are sad or glad. We might just as well be glad and happy. Life is so much more pleasant when we make up our minds we will not give in to those dark clouds and gray skies.

When you do have a down day, do something you love to do until the day passes. Cook something that is a comfort food. Pamper yourself. Indulge yourself. Eventually that feeling passes and the cloud will go away. These muffins smell good and taste good and make you feel all better.

Peanut Butter Muffins

PART I
1/2 Cup brown sugar
1/2 Cup sifted flour
1/4 Cup peanut butter
2 Tablespoons butter, melted
1/2 teaspoon cinnamon

PART II
1/2 Cup peanut butter
1/3 Cup shortening
1 1/2 Cup brown sugar
2 eggs
2 Cups flour
2 teaspoons baking powder
1/2 teaspoon cinnamon
1/2 teaspoon salt
1 Cup milk

Combine all ingredients of Part I, until crumbly, and set aside. Cream peanut butter and shortening. Slowly beat in brown sugar. Add eggs, one at a time, beating until fluffy. Sift dry ingredients. Add alternately with milk, beating after each addition. Fill paper baking cups in muffin pans no more than 1/2 full. Top with crumbly mixture. Bake at 375 degrees for 18 to 20 minutes. Makes 24.

A life watered by tears and tragedy and suffering often becomes the most fertile soil for spiritual growth. Think about it!

Chapter 163 — Looking Back

Are you always looking in your rearview mirror? Think about it!

What fun it is to look back to our childhood, when we would go to Grandma's house and play hide and seek in her attic. We always seemed to bake cookies or something else equally delicious. My brother remembers working in Grandma's garden for a "banty hen" and a setting of eggs. I don't really know what good those little hens were, but they were such sweet mothers and had such precious chicks. They were another great memory of growing up.

We remember the good things of our childhood. It was HOT then, with no air conditioning. Even refrigeration was not like we know it now. A chunk of ice in water was a real treat. We were not so comfortable back then, but we really forget how hot or how cold or how tired we were. The things that stay in our memories are the wonderful care-free days of youth and all the fun we had. Forgotten are the chores, and getting out of bed on those frosty mornings and running (yes, running) to dress by the wood stove where warmth was produced.

We remember school as a wonderful experience. I am sure on test days we didn't feel that way. The walk to school each morning was no piece of cake either. But now we look back and think how fun it was to see the jack rabbits in the pasture and hunt rocks and flowers and turtles on our way to and from school.

It is so fun to sit in our easy chair and remember those "good old days" and tell our grandkids about them. We always leave out the part about the extreme heat or the cold that numbed your fingers. The important part is the accomplishments and the fun we had. Isn't that lapse of memory a blessing. It is so fun to peer into our rearview mirror of memories, and see only a misty haze of the things that were unpleasant.

Grandma used to say, "Never look back, except for inspiration". She was so wise. It is great to look back but we can't stay there forever. We do live in the present. The things that molded our lives back then are the things that make today pleasant. We need to mix those wonderful old memories with the thoughts of today.

I asked Grandma how she made gingerbread. Here is how she made it: "I take some flour, just enough for the cake I want to make. I mix it up with some clabber or buttermilk, just enough for the flour. Then I take some ginger, some like more, some like less. I put in a little salt and pearl ash, and then I tell one of the kids to pour in molasses until I tell him to stop. We build up a good fire and have gingerbread for supper." What a recipe! I have had to alter the ingredients and directions a little to update it but each time I stir up a batch, I remember Grandma and peer into my rearview mirror.

Heirloom Gingerbread

1 1/2 Cup flour
1 Cup sugar
1/2 teaspoon ginger
1 teaspoon cinnamon
1/2 Cup butter
1 egg
1/4 Cup dark molasses
1 teaspoon soda
pinch salt
1 Cup buttermilk

Combine flour, sugar, ginger, and cinnamon. Cut in the butter. Reserve 1/4 cup of this mixture for topping. Add egg to the remaining flour mixture. Stir in molasses. Dissolve soda and salt in buttermilk. Add to molasses mixture and pour into greased 8 inch square pan. Sprinkle the reserved topping over batter and bake at 350 degrees for about 45 minutes or until center is firm to touch. Serve hot.

We live in the present. We dream of the future. We learn eternal truths from the past. Look back and think about it!

Chapter 164 — Good Deeds

Do you accept good deeds and pass them on? Think about it!

There is a movement going on to do good deeds to others without that person knowing who did it. It has been discussed on television and radio and the media. Things like paying a toll for the car behind you at the turnpike gate, etc. The favor is done for someone whose name you may or may not even know. It is surprising how overjoyed the recipient feels. The idea is to pass that good deed on to another unsuspecting person and pleasing them.

This is a good idea. Kindness is always a better plan than trying to pass on something unpleasant that has happened to you. Too often if we have a bad day at work or while doing our shopping, we want to come home and kick the dog or take it out on someone or something. What good does that do? It only makes things worse. And then we feel terrible and sad because we have turned against someone we love.

It is difficult for some people to accept nice things that people do for them. They feel obligated to get even or outdo the first favor by returning something to the first giver. That is a never ending chore. You NEVER will be able to balance the ledger with your friends. They are always more giving than you feel that you are. Learn to accept things gracefully and appreciatively. Genuine gratitude goes a long, long way. You will WANT to reciprocate right then but wait a while before returning the favor or passing it on.

When I was in high school, I spent a weekend at Phillips University for a visitor's weekend. During that weekend, a terrible snow storm came through Enid. The buses were running way behind schedule but I knew the folks were looking for me home so I boarded the bus to arrive in Pawnee at about 9:00 at night. The snow was so drifted that the bus had to stop and wait until the highway was cleared before it could proceed. With all the delays the bus did not arrive in Pawnee until about 3:00 in the morning. All phone lines were down so I couldn't call out to my folks in the country. Everything in town was closed except for a little hotel that kept the lobby open all night. A gentleman was there who took me to the home of Miss Nellie, a sweet little lady who was a family friend and worked in the bank. I got her out of bed in the wee hours of the morning and she gave me shelter and a warm bed to sleep in until we could reach my folks, who by the way had long ago assumed that I had had sense enough not to start for home. Wrong!

Anyway, the more I thanked Miss Nellie, the more she acted like it was nothing...like she did that all the time, and was glad to run a boarding house. She was the one who impressed on me at that early age that one cannot pay back the person who does the deed...one can only pass it on to the next person who needs a helping hand. She taught a good lesson and one I will never forget.

By the way, we cannot repay our parents for their time and energy in rearing us. The only way we can pay back is in rearing their grand children. We appreciate the efforts of our own parents when we have children of our own.

I never knew what a job it was for my mother to cook for a large family. Now I make a big deal of cooking for two. She went to a lot of trouble to fix a big roast on Sunday, with gravy and all. Now it is so simple (and just as good) to slap a rump roast in a pan, sprinkle it with seasoned salt and a little garlic, then dump in a package of brown gravy mix, add one cup of water, put on the lid and bake in a 350 degree oven until the roast is tender and brown on top. No need to sear the roast and all that trouble. Just dump and bake and dinner is ready. This recipe was passed on to me as a good deed by a co-worker. Enjoy, and if you like it, pass it on!

Do a good deed with no expected return. One generation plants a tree, the next generation sits in the shade. Think about it!

Chapter 165 — Open Mindedness

Do you have an open mind? Think about it!

Some of us think we have an open mind when all we have is a mouth ajar. We are listening in awe but not really absorbing what is being said. Having an open mind means that we are truly listening and taking to heart what is said. That does not mean that we have to swallow everything said, but it does indicate that we are giving the other side a fair hearing.

There are usually two good sides to every argument or decision that has to be made. The wise thing to do is to give both sides equal time and then make a decision based on what is best for everyone. Often this involves compromise and not just one side or the other. Few things are clearly black or white; there is a gray area somewhere. This prevents hard feelings and is a mature way to solve arguments. Some people find it nearly impossible to make a decision they can, or will, live with. No matter what they decide, they regret the decision the day after. It is their way or none!

It seems that the happiest people are those who keep an open mind and make decisions based on the information they have at the time. It takes a lot of time and energy to make endless choices that we face every hour of every day. But the investment of time and energy can be greatly reduced if we have a clear and definite purpose, with every decision in harmony with our goals and morals. Within these boundaries, learning new ways is part of our education.

We keep an open mind but sometimes it is difficult to take suggestions from some people, especially if they don't know as much about a situation as we ourselves do. This is especially true in our careers and jobs. There are those who truly want things to run smoothly so they make wise suggestions about the way we perform our duties. We welcome their advice and counsel. Then there are those we wish would just stay out of our business! They know everything! And are extremely generous with their recommendations. Thank goodness, there were just a few of those people in the world, and even if they sometimes might give good suggestions, we have already turned a deaf ear to them and not kept an open mind.

In an old cook book I found this clipping about old recipes:

Keeping the Old

I clip them from old magazines,
And from newspapers too.
I gather them from neighbors and friends.

This is nothing new.
I take them down from radio
And file them all away...
From T.V. cooking schools I catch
New dishes day by day.
What fancy menus do I plan
From all the recipes
Oh, I'll bake this... or I'll cook that
My family I will please.
And yet somehow I find myself
Repeating, so it seems...
The same old meals I've done for years...
The rest are in my dreams!

Even though I really mean to keep an open mind about new recipes, the old ones still sound good so I cook the old familiar ones repeatedly for everyone. And they even seem to like them best. I could fix the same menu for every birthday celebration and my family would love it. They would never say a word, except of praise and appreciation.

This is one of those favorite salads I fall back on.

Helen's Salad

One pint carton cottage cheese, well drained
2 packages orange Jello (use dry, other flavors may be used)
1 twelve ounce carton Cool Whip
1 small can mandarin oranges, well drained.

Mix all together. Cool, preferably overnight. Serve as a salad or even as a dessert. It is delicious!

Malcolm Forbes said, "The purpose of education is to replace an empty mind with an open one." Think about it!

Chapter 166 — The "Bliss of the Blessed"

Do you have the "bliss of the blessed"? Think about it!

Since the first time I heard that expression by one of my dear friends, I have thought about what it means. We are all so blessed, yet do we have the bliss that should go with it or are we down in the mouth most of the time and worrying about things happening.

We needn't go into ecstasy about what we have but we should at least appreciate the joy that comes with being comfortable. Often I am reminded of the turnips that were the mainstay of my grandparents diet when they came into Indian Territory and staked a claim. Food was not just scarce, but nearly non-existent. Wild game was their meat, but vegetables were either wild or those fresh turnips from their first crop raised in the new land. Yet, my Grandpa and Grandma never complained. In years to come, they loved to tell the story and even still liked to eat turnips, although they had eaten them three times a day for months, prepared in every way imaginable.

Those turnips became part of our traditional celebration at Thanksgiving and Christmas. We were always reminded of the meagerness of that era, and the abundance of our present blessings were carefully listed and described in detail. Those "lectures" have helped me realize what could be...and what is.

Most of us are blessed with good health and healthy children. Most of us have ample food to eat and warm clothes and housing in the winter. Most of us have a place to go to stretch our legs and play outdoors. Most of us have friends in abundance who care for us and visit us. Most of us have medical attention available when we need it. We have all the freedoms afforded to us by our Constitution. Most of us have jobs to go to, or retirement, or other means of income. We have wonderful schools to attend.

Yet with all these blessings and "perks", we fail to appreciate them properly. We worry too much, and complain too much, and fuss too much over little things. We expect more, regardless of what we have. We have so many things even with little effort on our part, and still we grumble. We complain that "we have no shoes, until we meet a man who has no feet"! Then we sit up and take notice of the many, many things we do have that make life so wonderful.

Have you ever noticed that the people who seem the happiest, are those who have the least to be happy about. They appreciate every little thing they possess. They see beauty in the smallest surroundings. They are just generally blissful, happy people. We could all learn from those dear souls. They are our best teachers.

The simplest fare can sometimes be the best meal you have ever eaten. This recipe is very basic but very satisfying.

Chicken Casserole

2 Cups chopped cooked chicken (or turkey)
1 1/2 Cup finely chopped celery
1/2 Cup chopped nuts (almonds, cashews, or pecans)
1/2 Cup chopped green pepper
1/4 Cup minced onion
1 or 2 teaspoons salt (depending if chicken is seasoned)
1/4 cup fresh lemon juice
3/4 Cup mayonnaise
3/4 Cup shredded cheddar cheese
2 Cups crushed potato chips

Combine all ingredients except cheese and chips. Spread in three quart casserole. Top with cheese and crushed chips. Bake at 350 degrees about 20 minutes until cheese is melted and celery is tender. Makes a great meal for four with a gelatin salad and crusty bread.

Wise was the man who prayed over a bountiful dinner table, "Lord, grant us one more blessing... a thankful heart". Think about it!

Chapter 167 — Early Bird/Night Owl

Are you an early bird or a night owl? Think about it!

When I was a youngster on the farm, we got up EARLY. Early was before the sun came up. We did most of the chores while it was still dark. That way we were ready to do the real work of the day in the cool of the morning. We would go to the garden or the cornfield and gather produce and work under the shade trees preparing the food for being canned before the heat of the day set in. This was before air conditioning, and all we had was a small electric fan, if we were lucky.

That kitchen where we canned was so hot it was like a sauna. We'd die in that heat now, but back then we really did not know anything different and we were used to it. We didn't have an opportunity to run in every little while to cool off in air conditioned comfort... there was none.

Anyway, back to the early bird subject. We either worked early in the morning or late in the evening after the sun had gone behind the horizon, and it began to cool down. Luckily, in the country, one could always find a cool breeze under a shade tree. The winds truly did come sweeping down the plains.

Those hours of work became second nature to us. Grandma got up "with the chickens" even when she was in a nursing home. I asked her one day why she arose so early. Her reply was, "So I can get things done, and go back and take a nice nap." To Grandma that made perfect sense. She simply could not stay under the covers when day was breaking.

Daddy picked up that same habit and if a person had not done what he would call a day's work before 9:00 A.M., he thought they were "burning daylight". He still gets up fairly early and starts stirring things for that spirit of labor before the heat of the day.

I guess it is in our genes somehow, as I have a tendency to get right at work early too. I hit the floor with a plan of action. Lucky for me, Jim has the same inner clock, only he gets up first and reads the paper before I get my eyes open.

It must be difficult for marriage partners who have different time cycles. Noise in the morning must be disturbing to a person sleeping late. Noise in the evening must be just as annoying to a person retiring early. But I guess they work it out to everyone's satisfaction.

Sociologists are discovering that there is a new evergrowing frontier coming into existence. There are the night people and the day people. Both have their own habits and personalities. There is a distinct difference in the way they react to their environment. I guess that is something to be considered when one looks at the future. Each can follow his own tendency and have company.

Whether you chirp in the morning or hoot at night you've got to eat sometime and when you do, what better thing to eat than this casserole. P. S. I could even eat it for breakfast!

Dorotha's Dinner

Put about 2 Tablespoons butter in skillet
Slice one large onion in butter
Cut ends off a medium to large zucchini and slice over onion
Add one can whole tomatos
Add salt and pepper to taste
Add generous sprinkling of garlic salt
Place wieners or cooked link sausages on top

Place lid on tight. Cook over low heat about 20 minutes until vegetables are tender. There probably won't be any left over, but just in case there is, it is delicious heated for another meal or snack in the microwave oven. Note: if sausages are used, you may not wish to use butter.

Early to bed and early to rise makes a man healthy, wealthy and wise. I am not so sure about this, I am still waiting...but I do feel that every day should be productive and make a memory. Think about it!

Are you a fault finder? Think about it!

Haven't you seen people who found everything too hot...or too cold, or too salty...or too bland, or too greasy...or too dry...the list goes on and on.

Don't you really feel sorry for those people? They never seem to be satisfied with what IS. They always want something different.

In life there is little that is perfect. We are usually seeking perfection but seldom does it appear, so we settle for less than perfect. Those who are looking for the perfect man or woman may have to look a long time. They are seldom found. Love them in spite of their differences. Who wants to be married to a robot anyway, or to a "yes person". Jim may not be perfect...but he is perfect for me. That's all that matters. Other married couples feel the same way I am sure.

I never recall that the wonderful teacher in my one room school ever complained about her lot. She never found fault with the system, nor with the extra chores she had to do like building the fires, sweeping the class room, or keeping the water cooler filled. Of course she had help from her students. The older boys brought in the coal. The young students helped dust erasers, etc. In fact everyone thought it was a privilege to help the teacher. No one found fault with the arrangement. Students and parents alike accepted it. Now parent would call it child labor and not allow it. All of us who were raised during the World War II years remember how we had to save and do without certain things to provide for the armed forces. We did not complain and felt it was our patriotic duty. Jim remembers when he was in the Marines and when he went through the chow line took a big gob of butter on his tray. After he finished eating he had a little left so he started to scrape it off his tray to be washed. He was told in no uncertain terms that it was wasting food and to "eat it". He said it was the hardest thing to choke down that pat of butter without anything to go with it. But did he dare find fault? I don't think so! It seems that there was less complaining then than there is now. We were too busy making a living and working to find fault with things.

True appreciation all but eliminates fault finding. We make the best of what we have and what we are. I could complain forever that I am not six feet tall (which I have always wanted to be) but it wouldn't change one thing. I am going to stay being the short, dumpy person that I am. Why complain?

Here is an easy snack that no one would complain about, unless they truly disliked chocolate or butterscotch. I do know one person who is deathly allergic to chocolate. That is not the same thing. Those who can...enjoy!

Touch Downs

3 Cups butterscotch chips
2 Cups chocolate chips
2 Cups miniature marshmallows
1 Cup Rice Krispies
1 Cup chopped pecans

In a large micro-wave safe bowl, combine 2 1/2 Cups butterscotch chips and the chocolate chips. Melt in the micro-wave. Stir until smooth. Add marshmellows, cereal, and pecans. Mix well. Press evenly in a 13 X 9 inch buttered pan. Melt the remaining butterscotch chips with about one teaspoon oil. Stir until smooth and drizzle over the "cake". Cool. Cut in squares. Note: peanut butter chips may be used. If so, use chopped peanuts instead of pecans.

If NO one or NO thing is measuring up to your specifications, better check your yard stick. Think about it!